I0528498

9 781957 109411

איוב

THE
ISRAEL
BIBLE

JOB

EDITED BY

Rabbi Tuly Weisz

ISRAEL
365

The Israel Bible: Job

First Edition, 2021

The Israel Bible was produced by Israel365 in cooperation with Teach for
Israel and is used with permission from Teach for Israel. All rights reserved.
The English translation was adapted by Israel365 from the JPS Tanakh.
Copyright © 1985 by the Jewish Publication Society. All rights reserved.

Cover image used under license from Shutterstock.com

ISBN 978-1-957109-41-1

A CIP catalogue record for this title is available from the British Library

The Israel Bible: Job is a holy book that contains the
name of God and should be treated with respect.

איוב

THE
ISRAEL
BIBLE

JOB

EDITED BY

Rabbi Tuly Weisz

The Israel Bible: Job

First Edition, 2021

The Israel Bible was produced by Israel365 in cooperation with Teach for Israel and is used with permission from Teach for Israel. All rights reserved. The English translation was adapted by Israel365 from the JPS Tanakh. Copyright © 1985 by the Jewish Publication Society. All rights reserved.

Cover image used under license from Shutterstock.com

ISBN 978-1-957109-41-1

A CIP catalogue record for this title is available from the British Library

The Israel Bible: Job is a holy book that contains the name of God and should be treated with respect.

Table of Contents

Introduction

The Hebrew Bible is commonly known as the *Tanakh* which stands for *Torah* (the Five Books of Moses), *Neviim* (the Prophets) and *Ketuvim* (the Writings). The *Tanakh* consists of 24 books that are considered by Jews to be the word of God. While these books have been referred to as the "Old Testament," many Jews reject this label since it implies the replacement of the Hebrew Bible with something newer and prefer the more authentic Jewish name.

The *Tanakh* is not only the most important book known to man, it is God's word that is perfect and absolute. It is therefore a daunting undertaking to publish an edition of the *Tanakh*, and the responsibilities are awesome. There is no room for error or carelessness in dealing with the eternal word of God. Further, upon embarking on such a serious initiative, we ask ourselves if our efforts are gratuitous. Considering the many editions of the Bible in print, is there truly a need for yet another one?

While there are numerous Bibles in circulation today, its most central aspect – the Land of Israel – has often been overlooked. References to Israel appear on nearly every page, and the city of Jerusalem is specifically referred to hundreds of times throughout the Bible. The essential link between Israel and *Torah* is emphasized repeatedly in verses such as, "For instruction (*Torah*) shall come forth from *Tzion*, the word of *Hashem* from *Yerushalayim*" (Micah 4:2).

The miraculous return of the People of Israel to the Land of Israel in our own generation provides the perfect moment for a new volume to fill this void in biblical literature. *The Israel Bible* includes many special features elucidating God's focus on Israel throughout *Tanakh* and there are many additional, multimedia features available on our website **www.theisraelbible.com**.

Ordering and Presentation – In presenting *The Israel Bible*, our goal is to spread awareness of the biblical significance of the Land of Israel as well as the Jewish people's eternal connection to the land, based on the text of the *Tanakh*, the Hebrew Bible. We aim to honor "the God, the People and the Land of Israel" from an Orthodox Jewish perspective. To that end, *The Israel Bible* follows the traditional Jewish ordering of the books and the customary Hebrew division of chapters. Therefore, for example, we count 24 books of *Tanakh* with *Sefer Divrei Hayamim* (Chronicles) appearing last. It is our hope that our rich content will speak to all Jews and non-Jews who appreciate Israel as the God given land of the Jewish people.

English Translation – Throughout history, Jews have studied the Bible in Hebrew, as any form of translation would miss much of the nuance of the original holy tongue in which *Torah* has been transmitted since the days of Moses. However, as many Jews settled in America in the 19th Century, the need for an English translation became necessary. To be sure, there were already English translations prepared over the centuries by Christians, but in the words of the original editors of the Jewish Publication Society (JPS), "The Jew cannot afford to have his Bible translation prepared for him by others. He cannot have it as a gift, even as he cannot borrow his soul from others."

JPS set out in the late 1800s to publish an authoritative English translation "in the spirit of Jewish tradition." It was compiled over decades by some of the leading Jewish scholars of the time. They formed committees and subcommittees to compare existing English versions, considering medieval and modern Jewish commentators. The monumental JPS translation, originally published in 1917, has been updated in recent years, and *The Israel Bible* is proud to utilize the 1984 New Jewish Publication Society (NJPS) version with its modern, clear language, as well as its wide-ranging acceptance as an accurate and high-quality translation. We applied the NJPS translation verbatim, except for a select list of nouns which we replaced with their traditional Hebrew names. This is true even when we found the NJPS translation to be different than the popular translation of a word or phrase and when the NJPS switched the order of the text for the sake of clarity (see, for example, Ezekiel 24:22–24).

Hebrew Transliteration – To give our readers an authentic *Tanakh* experience, every verse that has commentary is transliterated from Hebrew into English. The Hebrew alphabet chart includes our standards for transliteration and pronunciation of Hebrew verses, enabling readers of *The Israel Bible* to decipher key biblical passages in the holy language. Readers can hear the entire Bible read in Hebrew on our website **www.theisraelbible.com**.

There are various standards when it comes to transliterating Hebrew words into English letters. While we have relied primarily on the classical Hebrew transliteration, we have occasionally deviated for the sake of simplicity, clarity and to reflect common usage.

In addition to whole verses, we have also transliterated many proper nouns in the English translation so that our readers can learn the names of key biblical figures and locations in their Hebrew form. As a rule, we chose to transliterate names of people that were central in the establishment and functioning of the nation of Israel, as well as significant places in the Holy Land. Therefore, regarding Adam's sons, for example, only *Shet* (Seth) is transliterated since it was from him that *Noach* (Noah), and ultimately *Avraham* (Abraham), descended. For this reason, there might be verses or sections of *The Israel Bible* that contains multiple names and only some of them are transliterated.

For the same reason, we have transliterated the names of the books of *Tanakh* when referring to them in our introductions and commentary. When referencing a specific chapter or verse, however, we use the English names of the books in our citations for clarity. We also transliterated ideas and concepts that are central to Judaism such as *Shabbat* (Sabbath), the names of the Jewish holidays and the *Beit Hamikdash* (Temple), as well as biblical measurements. Finally, the name of God is transliterated. Out of respect, Orthodox Jews generally refer to the Lord as *Hashem*, which literally means 'the Name.' Referring to God as *Hashem* reminds us that we feel close to Him but also recognize our distance at the same time. To stress this moniker, we transliterated both the Tetragrammaton as well as the name *Elohim* as *Hashem*.

Study Notes – Our unique commentary was compiled by Orthodox Jewish scholars who live in Israel. It is an anthology in the sense that most of the commentary is not original, but draws from traditional teachings of early Jewish Sages and modern rabbinic commentators. We also include quotations from individuals who have played a significant part in the past century of modern Israeli history including Israeli prime ministers, poets and military leaders.

Our commentary can be broken into four categories, three of which are identified by an icon at the beginning of the study note:

 Israel lessons are indicated with an icon bearing the map of Israel and focus on the Land of Israel and the modern State of Israel.

 Jewish lessons are indicated with a *Torah* scroll and teach a concept in Judaism or a classic idea from rabbinic thought.

 Hebrew lessons are represented by an icon bearing the letter *aleph* and focus on the meaning of a Hebrew word or phrase.

All other comments are considered general comments and are not assigned an icon.

Supplemental Material – In addition to our unique translation and original commentary, *The Israel Bible* offers supplementary material to enrich the learning experience of our readers. Before every book of *Tanakh,* we provide an introduction, as well as information, generally in the form of a map, a chart or a list, which is central to the specific book.

Maps – As the purpose of *The Israel Bible* is to highlight the biblical significance of the Land of Israel, significant time was spent researching and preparing maps to bring the physical contours of the holy land to life with great accuracy. However, since there is a lack of information regarding the precise locations of certain ancient cities, some of the places on our maps are approximate or subject to debate. In these cases, we followed the opinion that we are most comfortable with, but acknowledge that there is room for disagreement. We continue to produce new maps, which are available on our website **www.theisraelbible.com/maps**.

Torah **Readings** – The *Torah* is not just a work that is studied privately, it is also read out loud in synagogue. Every *Shabbat* and holiday a portion of the *Torah* is read, as well as a related section from *Neviim,* the prophets, called the *haftarah.* We included the blessings recited before and after the reading of the *Torah,* a list of the weekly *Torah* portions and their corresponding *haftarot,* and a chart of the *Torah* readings for special days with their corresponding *haftarot.* Readers can always find the current week's *Torah* portion by visiting **www.theisraelbible.com/weekly-torah-portion**. In this volume, we indicate where a new *Torah* portion begins by highlighting the Hebrew verse number with a gray box so readers can follow along with the communal *Torah* readings. Furthermore, we have included prayers for the State of Israel and the soldiers of the Israel Defense Forces (IDF) that are generally recited following the *Torah* reading in synagogue. It is our constant prayer that God watch over the State of Israel and the members of the IDF, who defend Israel every hour of every day.

In 1948, the State of Israel was created providing a modern answer to Isaiah's ancient question, "Is a nation born all at once?" (Isaiah 66:8). *The Israel Bible* was first published in the 70th year of God's miraculous restoration of the People of Israel to the Land of Israel. Jewish wisdom teaches that 70 is a significant number: *Moshe* (Moses) translated the *Torah* into 70 languages for all 70 nations of the world. From our very origins, the Jewish people were meant to be a light unto the 70 nations, spreading God's truth to the masses.

In the seven decades since the modern rebirth of the State of Israel, God's plan has been unfolding with unprecedented speed, dramatic highs and heartbreaking lows. Never has Israel been at the forefront of the world's attention as it is in our generation. Efforts to vilify the Jewish State seem to spread every day across the globe. At the same time, so does the growing movement of millions of non-Jewish biblical Zionists who stand with the nation of Israel as an expression of their commitment to God's word. As we seek to understand the clash of these two conflicting worldviews, the need for *The Israel Bible* has never been so important.

Standing on the great shoulders of those who came before us and emanating from the land that has always served as the birthplace for the Bible, we conclude with a heartfelt prayer: May the Almighty bless our efforts in offering this *Tanakh* to influence the hearts, minds and actions of its readers. In this way, it is our hope to spread God's name so that the publication of *The Israel Bible* brings us one step closer to the final redemption of Israel and the entire world.

Rabbi Tuly Weisz
Editor, *The Israel Bible*

Foreword

The mandate to study God's word daily is interestingly not found in the Five Books of Moses (Pentateuch), but rather in the first book of our prophetic writings: "Let not this Book of the Teaching cease from your lips, but recite it day and night, so that you may observe faithfully all that is written in it. Only then will you prosper in your undertakings and only then will you be successful" (Joshua 1:8). Charged with bringing the Israelites into the land covenantally promised to Abraham, Isaac and Jacob, God ensures Joshua of His protection if the nation observes His ways as dictated in the Divine constitution known as the *Torah*.

In Jewish tradition, Joshua (1:8) is directly linked with Deuteronomy (11:14), "You shall gather in your new grain and wine, and oil."[1] Our Sages deduced from this scriptural combination the importance of merging *Torah* study with a profession. Completely dedicating oneself to the study of *Torah* without having the financial means to sustain this lifestyle can lead one to eventually straying from observance of God's will. Poverty and crime can have an intimate relationship.

We must also be careful that our work does not affect our daily study of Scripture. The addiction of becoming a workaholic and not making *Torah* study a priority can also lead one into temptations that can violate our personal relationship with Him as well as our fellow human beings. The goal is to achieve a healthy balance between our study of God's word and our daily work.

The Deuteronomic verse quoted above is part of the second section of the Shema[2] that discusses the concept of reward and punishment. Sanctifying God by fulfilling His commandments results in the Land of Israel practically benefitting from rains that occur in the right season and reaping the abundance from the fields. However, if the nation follows pagan gods and practices, the consequences are devastating – famine and death. The Land of Israel is intrinsically linked with the keeping of the *Torah*. Covenant Land comes with covenant responsibility.

---

1   Talmud Bavli Berachot 35b
2   Consisting of three sections within the Five Books of Moses (Deut. 6:4–8; 11:13–22 and Numbers 15:37–42), the *Shema* is proclamation of accepting God's Kingdom in our lives, loyalty to His commandments and remembering His redemptive act of liberating us from Egypt. Jews recite the *Shema* twice a day as stated in Deut. 6:7.

Born into slavery, Joshua is now leading His people into the Promised Land. More than 500 years separates him from his ancestral forefather Abraham. The historical narratives that took place between Abraham leaving everything behind to follow God in Genesis 12 and the death of Moses in the last chapter of Deuteronomy are filled with intrigue, suspense, joy, sorrow and hope. What began as a family is now a nation actualizing its mission to be a kingdom of priests to the world. However, for the Israelites to succeed in the Land of Israel, they must see the *Torah* as the only compass to direct their lives.

The biblical episodes after our first entry into the land are well known. Our ancestors' triumphs and sins are all on public record. We learned the harsh reality of Leviticus (18:28) "So let not the land spew you out for defiling it as it spewed out the nation that came before you." Twice, we lost the privilege to be stewards of the Land of Israel and to fulfill our nation state mandate to be a light to the world. However, when the annals of history were ready to archive the Jewish people after the Holocaust, God kept His covenantal promise and gathered us from the four corners of the globe to come home. The year 1948 was a game changer. Biblical prophecies were and are being realized. We are now living in the birth pangs of the messianic era.

In our morning prayers, we recite a series of blessings over the *Torah* that include petitioning God to have a sweet tooth for His word, to study it without any ulterior motive and to have Him to teach it to us. They are some congregations that invoke the following liturgical prayer after the completion of these blessings: *May the Torah be my faith and El Shaddai my help. Blessed be the name of His glorious kingdom forever and all time.*

According to Jewish tradition, the neglect of not blessing the *Torah* before engaging in its study was one of the reasons for the destruction of the Temple.[3] This is deduced from the redundancy of words in Jeremiah (9:12) that talks about Israel not following God: "... Because they forsook the teaching I had set before them. They did not obey Me and they did not follow it [did not make a blessing before studying it]." Our inability to properly cherish God's greatest gift to the world, the *Torah*, led to our eventual exile from our land.

On Israel's Independence Day, Jews around the world recite Psalms 113–118 to express our gratitude to God for His Divine hand in helping establish the State of Israel. We have learned from our past and realize the privilege to see firsthand the land, people and *Torah* operating all together in our generation.

---

3   Babylonian Talmud Nedarim 81a

When Rabbi Tuly Weisz approached me about his intent to publish *The Israel Bible* that would highlight commentary about the special relationship between the land and people, I saw this project as another way to publicly demonstrate our appreciation to God for having the State of Israel. In addition, it is another educational tool to ensure biblical literacy. If we are to truly enjoy the Land of Israel, it is incumbent upon us to continually study the *Torah*. Isaiah once prophesied that the Jewish people would return to Zion with songs, "crowned with everlasting joy" (35:10). *The Israel Bible* provides us the lyrical content to express our joy in living in the land that God calls holy.

Rabbi Shlomo Riskin
Chief Rabbi of Efrat
Founder of the Center for Jewish-Christian
Understanding & Cooperation (cjcuc)

Sefer Iyov
The Book of Job

Introduction and commentary by Alexander Jacob Tsykin

Sefer Iyov (Job) is a complex work. It poses the difficult and well-known question of theodicy: Why do bad things happen to good people? *Sefer Iyov* begins with a narrative about an extremely righteous person named *Iyov*, who is to be tormented by *Hashem*. But why is he to be afflicted? What is the reason for his suffering? The answer to these questions remain uncertain.

Chapter one describes a wager God made with the Adversary, known in Hebrew as *Satan* (שטן), a spiritual being who is given the divinely-assigned task of trying to cause people to stumble spiritually. *Hashem* insists that *Iyov* would remain true and loyal even if horribly tormented and knowing that he deserves no punishment. What follows is a description of how all of *Iyov*'s children die, and all of his property is lost. *Iyov* accepts this devastating news with equanimity. The *Satan* then afflicts *Iyov* with a horrible disease, but stops short of taking his life as instructed by *Hashem* (1:12). At this point *Iyov* can no longer cope. He begins to question God's justice, though he never questions God's existence, or even His power.

Iyov's friends come to reassure him, but their way of attempting to comfort him is by insisting that *Hashem*'s justice is absolute, and that he must therefore deserve his terrible suffering. Throughout this surprising remonstration, *Iyov* gets more upset, and continuously protests his innocence of the suggested wrongdoings. Eventually, *Hashem* appears and reprimands *Iyov* for doubting Him, and the friends for sinning against Him, and then *Iyov*'s formerly-happy life is restored.

Throughout the course of the book, *Iyov* is meant to learn humility, and to understand that it is not his place to evaluate or question God. By accepting his suffering, *Iyov* becomes a better person. As the commentary in *The Israel Bible* demonstrates, sometimes it is those who *Hashem* loves most that He causes to suffer, because by doing so, He makes them stronger.

Whether or not we can pinpoint a reason for *Iyov*'s suffering, one thing is clear at the end of the book. We must always remember that there is a divine ruler who controls the world with ultimate wisdom and a perfect sense of justice. Though we may not be able to understand His reasons for running the world as He does, we must put our trust in Him alone, and believe that everything He does is for the best.

There is a debate among the Sages of the Talmud (*Bava Batra* 15a) regarding the period during which *Iyov* lived. A number of opinions are recorded, differing from one another by many generations. There is even one opinion that says he did not live at all, and the story of his suffering is a parable, meant to serve as a model for dealing with suffering and understanding why it occurs. It has also been suggested that the focus of the book is not general, universal human suffering, but the specific suffering of the Jewish people.

Indeed, *Iyov*'s homeland, the land of *Utz*, is understood by many as another name for the Land of Israel. The Jewish people have suffered considerably over the ages. Throughout history, they have lost everything, from their families to their possessions, their homes and even their homeland. They have been afflicted physically, emotionally and spiritually, but like *Iyov*, have been promised that the light of the Jewish nation will never be extinguished. Also like *Iyov*, they have at times remained strong and at times have questioned, but through it all they clung to their belief in the Creator.

Though we might never be able to fully answer the question of why the Children of Israel had to suffer throughout history as much as they did, *Sefer Iyov* reminds us that we must always trust in *Hashem*. We believe that Israel's suffering is ultimately for the good, and we must have the confidence that ultimately, the Nation of Israel will be fully restored to its former glory, safe and secure in *Eretz Yisrael*.

List of Opinions Regarding When *Iyov* (Job) lived

Sefer Iyov does not give much identifying information about its main character. The Talmud (*Bava Batra* 15a–b) offers a number of different suggestions as to when *Iyov* lived, based on various verses in the book:

Opinion attributed to:	Suggestion
Rabbi *Levi* son of *Lachma*	*Iyov* lived in the time of *Moshe*
Rava	*Iyov* lived during the time of the 12 spies
Anonymous opinion	*Iyov* never existed, the story is a parable
Rabbi *Yochanan* and Rabbi *Elazar*	*Iyov* returned with the Jewish exiles from Babylon
Rabbi *Eliezer*	*Iyov* lived at the time of the Judges
Rabbi *Yehoshua* son of *Korcha*	*Iyov* lived at the time of Ahasuerus
Rabbi *Natan*	*Iyov* lived in the days of the kingdom of Sheba
The Sages	*Iyov* lived in the days of the Babylonians under the leadership of Nebuchadnezzar
Some say	*Iyov* lived in the days of *Yaakov* and married *Yaakov's* daughter *Dina*

1 ¹ There was a man in the land of *Utz* named *Iyov*. That man was blameless and upright; he feared *Hashem* and shunned evil.

א אִישׁ הָיָה בְאֶרֶץ־עוּץ אִיּוֹב שְׁמוֹ וְהָיָה הָאִישׁ הַהוּא תָּם וְיָשָׁר וִירֵא אֱלֹהִים וְסָר מֵרָע:

> EESH ha-YAH v'-E-retz UTZ i-YOV sh'-MO v'-ha-YAH ha-EESH
> ha-HU TAM v'-ya-SHAR vee-RAY e-lo-HEEM v'-SAR may-RA

² Seven sons and three daughters were born to him;

ב וַיִּוָּלְדוּ לוֹ שִׁבְעָה בָנִים וְשָׁלוֹשׁ בָּנוֹת:

³ his possessions were seven thousand sheep, three thousand camels, five hundred yoke of oxen and five hundred she-asses, and a very large household. That man was wealthier than anyone in the East.

ג וַיְהִי מִקְנֵהוּ שִׁבְעַת אַלְפֵי־צֹאן וּשְׁלֹשֶׁת אַלְפֵי גְמַלִּים וַחֲמֵשׁ מֵאוֹת צֶמֶד־בָּקָר וַחֲמֵשׁ מֵאוֹת אֲתוֹנוֹת וַעֲבֻדָּה רַבָּה מְאֹד וַיְהִי הָאִישׁ הַהוּא גָּדוֹל מִכָּל־בְּנֵי־קֶדֶם:

⁴ It was the custom of his sons to hold feasts, each on his set day in his own home. They would invite their three sisters to eat and drink with them.

ד וְהָלְכוּ בָנָיו וְעָשׂוּ מִשְׁתֶּה בֵּית אִישׁ יוֹמוֹ וְשָׁלְחוּ וְקָרְאוּ לִשְׁלֹשֶׁת אַחְיֹתֵיהֶם [אַחְיוֹתֵיהֶם] לֶאֱכֹל וְלִשְׁתּוֹת עִמָּהֶם:

⁵ When a round of feast days was over, *Iyov* would send word to them to sanctify themselves, and, rising early in the morning, he would make burnt offerings, one for each of them; for *Iyov* thought, "Perhaps my children have sinned and blasphemed *Hashem* in their thoughts." This is what *Iyov* always used to do.

ה וַיְהִי כִּי הִקִּיפוּ יְמֵי הַמִּשְׁתֶּה וַיִּשְׁלַח אִיּוֹב וַיְקַדְּשֵׁם וְהִשְׁכִּים בַּבֹּקֶר וְהֶעֱלָה עֹלוֹת מִסְפַּר כֻּלָּם כִּי אָמַר אִיּוֹב אוּלַי חָטְאוּ בָנַי וּבֵרְכוּ אֱלֹהִים בִּלְבָבָם כָּכָה יַעֲשֶׂה אִיּוֹב כָּל־הַיָּמִים:

⁶ One day the divine beings presented themselves before *Hashem*, and the Adversary came along with them.

ו וַיְהִי הַיּוֹם וַיָּבֹאוּ בְּנֵי הָאֱלֹהִים לְהִתְיַצֵּב עַל־יְהֹוָה וַיָּבוֹא גַם־הַשָּׂטָן בְּתוֹכָם:

⁷ *Hashem* said to the Adversary, "Where have you been?" The Adversary answered *Hashem*, "I have been roaming all over the earth."

ז וַיֹּאמֶר יְהֹוָה אֶל־הַשָּׂטָן מֵאַיִן תָּבֹא וַיַּעַן הַשָּׂטָן אֶת־יְהֹוָה וַיֹּאמַר מִשּׁוּט בָּאָרֶץ וּמֵהִתְהַלֵּךְ בָּהּ:

⁸ *Hashem* said to the Adversary, "Have you noticed My servant *Iyov*? There is no one like him on earth, a blameless and upright man who fears *Hashem* and shuns evil!"

ח וַיֹּאמֶר יְהֹוָה אֶל־הַשָּׂטָן הֲשַׂמְתָּ לִבְּךָ עַל־עַבְדִּי אִיּוֹב כִּי אֵין כָּמֹהוּ בָּאָרֶץ אִישׁ תָּם וְיָשָׁר יְרֵא אֱלֹהִים וְסָר מֵרָע:

⁹ The Adversary answered *Hashem*, "Does *Iyov* not have good reason to fear *Hashem*?

ט וַיַּעַן הַשָּׂטָן אֶת־יְהֹוָה וַיֹּאמַר הַחִנָּם יָרֵא אִיּוֹב אֱלֹהִים:

A traveler rests under a tree at the Arbel cliff

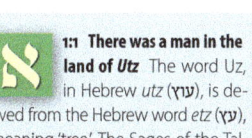 **1:1 There was a man in the land of *Utz*** The word Uz, in Hebrew *utz* (עוּץ), is derived from the Hebrew word *etz* (עֵץ), meaning 'tree.' The Sages of the Talmud (*Bava Batra* 15a) teach that phrase "land of *Utz*" refers to *Eretz Yisrael*, called *Utz* in honor of *Iyov*, who protected the people of his generation with his steadfast righteousness. Just as a tree provides shade and protection from the sun, *Iyov's* merit protected the inhabitants of the land. Similarly, before *Moshe* sent spies into *Eretz Yisrael*, he asked them to check whether or not there were any trees in the land (Numbers 13:20). The medieval commentator *Rashi* explains that *Moshe* was really asking, "Does the Land of Israel have a worthy man living in it, who will protect the inhabitants with his merit?"

עוּץ

¹⁰ Why, it is You who have fenced him round, him and his household and all that he has. You have blessed his efforts so that his possessions spread out in the land.

¹¹ But lay Your hand upon all that he has and he will surely blaspheme You to Your face."

¹² *Hashem* replied to the Adversary, "See, all that he has is in your power; only do not lay a hand on him." The Adversary departed from the presence of *Hashem*.

¹³ One day, as his sons and daughters were eating and drinking wine in the house of their eldest brother,

¹⁴ a messenger came to *Iyov* and said, "The oxen were plowing and the she-asses were grazing alongside them

¹⁵ when Sabeans attacked them and carried them off, and put the boys to the sword; I alone have escaped to tell you."

¹⁶ This one was still speaking when another came and said, "*Hashem*'s fire fell from heaven, took hold of the sheep and the boys, and burned them up; I alone have escaped to tell you."

¹⁷ This one was still speaking when another came and said, "A Chaldean formation of three columns made a raid on the camels and carried them off and put the boys to the sword; I alone have escaped to tell you."

¹⁸ This one was still speaking when another came and said, "Your sons and daughters were eating and drinking wine in the house of their eldest brother

¹⁹ when suddenly a mighty wind came from the wilderness. It struck the four corners of the house so that it collapsed upon the young people and they died; I alone have escaped to tell you."

²⁰ Then *Iyov* arose, tore his robe, cut off his hair, and threw himself on the ground and worshiped.

²¹ He said, "Naked came I out of my mother's womb, and naked shall I return there; *Hashem* has given, and *Hashem* has taken away; blessed be the name of *Hashem*."

²² For all that, *Iyov* did not sin nor did he cast reproach on *Hashem*.

י הֲלֹא־אַתָּ [אַתָּה] שַׂ֩כְתָּ֩ בַעֲד֨וֹ וּבְעַד־
בֵּית֜וֹ וּבְעַ֧ד כׇּל־אֲשֶׁר־ל֛וֹ מִסָּבִ֖יב מַעֲשֵׂ֥ה
יָדָ֣יו בֵּרַ֑כְתָּ וּמִקְנֵ֖הוּ פָּרַ֥ץ בָּאָֽרֶץ׃

יא וְאוּלָ֗ם שְֽׁלַֽח־נָ֣א יָֽדְךָ֔ וְגַ֖ע בְּכׇל־אֲשֶׁר־ל֑וֹ
אִם־לֹ֥א עַל־פָּנֶ֖יךָ יְבָרְכֶֽךָּ׃

יב וַיֹּ֨אמֶר יְהֹוָ֜ה אֶל־הַשָּׂטָ֗ן הִנֵּ֤ה כׇל־אֲשֶׁר־
לוֹ֙ בְּיָדֶ֔ךָ רַ֣ק אֵלָ֔יו אַל־תִּשְׁלַ֖ח יָדֶ֑ךָ וַיֵּצֵא֙
הַשָּׂטָ֔ן מֵעִ֖ם פְּנֵ֥י יְהֹוָֽה׃

יג וַיְהִ֖י הַיּ֑וֹם וּבָנָ֨יו וּבְנֹתָ֤יו אֹֽכְלִים֙ וְשֹׁתִ֣ים
יַ֔יִן בְּבֵ֖ית אֲחִיהֶ֥ם הַבְּכֽוֹר׃

יד וּמַלְאָ֛ךְ בָּ֥א אֶל־אִיּ֖וֹב וַיֹּאמַ֑ר הַבָּקָר֙ הָי֣וּ
חֹֽרְשׁ֔וֹת וְהָאֲתֹנ֖וֹת רֹע֥וֹת עַל־יְדֵיהֶֽם׃

טו וַתִּפֹּ֤ל שְׁבָא֙ וַתִּקָּחֵ֔ם וְאֶת־הַנְּעָרִ֖ים הִכּ֣וּ
לְפִי־חָ֑רֶב וָֽאִמָּ֨לְטָ֧ה רַק־אֲנִ֛י לְבַדִּ֖י לְהַגִּ֥יד
לָֽךְ׃

טז ע֣וֹד ׀ זֶ֣ה מְדַבֵּ֗ר וְזֶ֤ה בָּא֙ וַיֹּאמַ֔ר אֵ֣שׁ
אֱלֹהִ֗ים נָֽפְלָה֙ מִן־הַשָּׁמַ֔יִם וַתִּבְעַ֥ר בַּצֹּ֛אן
וּבַנְּעָרִ֖ים וַתֹּאכְלֵ֑ם וָאִמָּ֨לְטָ֧ה רַק־אֲנִ֛י
לְבַדִּ֖י לְהַגִּ֥יד לָֽךְ׃

יז ע֣וֹד ׀ זֶ֣ה מְדַבֵּ֗ר וְזֶה֮ בָּ֣א וַיֹּאמַר֒ כַּשְׂדִּ֞ים
שָׂ֣מוּ ׀ שְׁלֹשָׁ֣ה רָאשִׁ֗ים וַֽיִּפְשְׁט֤וּ עַל־
הַגְּמַלִּים֙ וַיִּקָּח֔וּם וְאֶת־הַנְּעָרִ֖ים הִכּ֣וּ
לְפִי־חָ֑רֶב וָאִמָּ֨לְטָ֧ה רַק־אֲנִ֛י לְבַדִּ֖י לְהַגִּ֥יד
לָֽךְ׃

יח עַ֚ד זֶ֣ה מְדַבֵּ֔ר וְזֶ֖ה בָּ֣א וַיֹּאמַ֑ר בָּנֶ֨יךָ
וּבְנוֹתֶ֤יךָ אֹֽכְלִים֙ וְשֹׁתִ֣ים יַ֔יִן בְּבֵ֖ית
אֲחִיהֶ֥ם הַבְּכֽוֹר׃

יט וְהִנֵּה֩ ר֨וּחַ גְּדוֹלָ֜ה בָּ֣אָה ׀ מֵעֵ֣בֶר הַמִּדְבָּ֗ר
וַיִּגַּע֙ בְּאַרְבַּע֙ פִּנּ֣וֹת הַבַּ֔יִת וַיִּפֹּ֥ל עַל־
הַנְּעָרִ֖ים וַיָּמ֑וּתוּ וָאִמָּ֨לְטָ֧ה רַק־אֲנִ֛י לְבַדִּ֖י
לְהַגִּ֥יד לָֽךְ׃

כ וַיָּ֤קׇם אִיּוֹב֙ וַיִּקְרַ֣ע אֶת־מְעִל֔וֹ וַיָּ֖גׇז אֶת־
רֹאשׁ֑וֹ וַיִּפֹּ֥ל אַ֖רְצָה וַיִּשְׁתָּֽחוּ׃

כא וַיֹּ֩אמֶר֩ עָרֹ֨ם יָצָ֜תִי [יָצָ֗אתִי] מִבֶּ֣טֶן אִמִּ֗י
וְעָרֹם֙ אָשׁ֣וּב שָׁ֔מָּה יְהֹוָ֣ה נָתַ֔ן וַיהֹוָ֖ה
לָקָ֑ח יְהִ֛י שֵׁ֥ם יְהֹוָ֖ה מְבֹרָֽךְ׃

כב בְּכׇל־זֹ֖את לֹא־חָטָ֣א אִיּ֑וֹב וְלֹא־נָתַ֥ן
תִּפְלָ֖ה לֵאלֹהִֽים׃

2 ¹ One day the divine beings presented themselves before *Hashem*. The Adversary came along with them to present himself before *Hashem*.

ב א וַיְהִי הַיּוֹם וַיָּבֹאוּ בְּנֵי הָאֱלֹהִים לְהִתְיַצֵּב עַל־יְהֹוָה וַיָּבוֹא גַם־הַשָּׂטָן בְּתֹכָם לְהִתְיַצֵּב עַל־יְהֹוָה:

² *Hashem* said to the Adversary, "Where have you been?" The Adversary answered *Hashem*, "I have been roaming all over the earth."

ב וַיֹּאמֶר יְהֹוָה אֶל־הַשָּׂטָן אֵי מִזֶּה תָּבֹא וַיַּעַן הַשָּׂטָן אֶת־יְהֹוָה וַיֹּאמַר מִשֻּׁט בָּאָרֶץ וּמֵהִתְהַלֵּךְ בָּהּ:

³ *Hashem* said to the Adversary, "Have you noticed My servant *Iyov*? There is no one like him on earth, a blameless and upright man who fears *Hashem* and shuns evil. He still keeps his integrity; so you have incited Me against him to destroy him for no good reason."

ג וַיֹּאמֶר יְהֹוָה אֶל־הַשָּׂטָן הֲשַׂמְתָּ לִבְּךָ אֶל־עַבְדִּי אִיּוֹב כִּי אֵין כָּמֹהוּ בָּאָרֶץ אִישׁ תָּם וְיָשָׁר יְרֵא אֱלֹהִים וְסָר מֵרָע וְעֹדֶנּוּ מַחֲזִיק בְּתֻמָּתוֹ וַתְּסִיתֵנִי בוֹ לְבַלְּעוֹ חִנָּם:

⁴ The Adversary answered *Hashem*, "Skin for skin – all that a man has he will give up for his life.

ד וַיַּעַן הַשָּׂטָן אֶת־יְהֹוָה וַיֹּאמַר עוֹר בְּעַד־עוֹר וְכֹל אֲשֶׁר לָאִישׁ יִתֵּן בְּעַד נַפְשׁוֹ:

⁵ But lay a hand on his bones and his flesh, and he will surely blaspheme You to Your face."

ה אוּלָם שְׁלַח־נָא יָדְךָ וְגַע אֶל־עַצְמוֹ וְאֶל־בְּשָׂרוֹ אִם־לֹא אֶל־פָּנֶיךָ יְבָרְכֶךָּ:

⁶ So *Hashem* said to the Adversary, "See, he is in your power; only spare his life."

ו וַיֹּאמֶר יְהֹוָה אֶל־הַשָּׂטָן הִנּוֹ בְיָדֶךָ אַךְ אֶת־נַפְשׁוֹ שְׁמֹר:

⁷ The Adversary departed from the presence of *Hashem* and inflicted a severe inflammation on *Iyov* from the sole of his foot to the crown of his head.

ז וַיֵּצֵא הַשָּׂטָן מֵאֵת פְּנֵי יְהֹוָה וַיַּךְ אֶת־אִיּוֹב בִּשְׁחִין רָע מִכַּף רַגְלוֹ עַד [וְעַד] קָדְקֳדוֹ:

va-yay-TZAY ha-sa-TAN may-AYT p'-NAY a-do-NAI va-YAKH et i-YOV bish-KHEEN RA mi-KAF rag-LO v'-AD kod-ko-DO

⁸ He took a potsherd to scratch himself as he sat in ashes.

ח וַיִּקַּח־לוֹ חֶרֶשׂ לְהִתְגָּרֵד בּוֹ וְהוּא יֹשֵׁב בְּתוֹךְ־הָאֵפֶר:

⁹ His wife said to him, "You still keep your integrity! Blaspheme *Hashem* and die!"

ט וַתֹּאמֶר לוֹ אִשְׁתּוֹ עֹדְךָ מַחֲזִיק בְּתֻמָּתֶךָ בָּרֵךְ אֱלֹהִים וָמֻת:

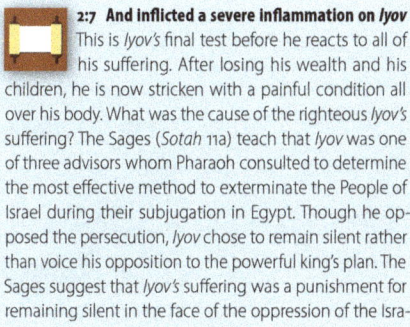

2:7 And inflicted a severe inflammation on *Iyov* This is *Iyov*'s final test before he reacts to all of his suffering. After losing his wealth and his children, he is now stricken with a painful condition all over his body. What was the cause of the righteous *Iyov*'s suffering? The Sages (*Sotah* 11a) teach that *Iyov* was one of three advisors whom Pharaoh consulted to determine the most effective method to exterminate the People of Israel during their subjugation in Egypt. Though he opposed the persecution, *Iyov* chose to remain silent rather than voice his opposition to the powerful king's plan. The Sages suggest that *Iyov*'s suffering was a punishment for remaining silent in the face of the oppression of the Isra-elites. Because *Iyov* remained silent against the suffering of others, he was afflicted to the point where he cried out due to his own anguish.

Rabbi Tuly Weisz helping Israeli vicitms of arson

Today, the People of Israel are still faced with many threats and experience many tragedies. We must learn from *Iyov*'s mistake to never remain silent, even if we don't feel personally threatened or afflicted. Rather, we must feel the pain of others as our own.

3

10 But he said to her, "You talk as any shameless woman might talk! Should we accept only good from *Hashem* and not accept evil?" For all that, *Iyov* said nothing sinful.

וַיֹּאמֶר אֵלֶיהָ כְּדַבֵּר אַחַת הַנְּבָלוֹת תְּדַבֵּרִי גַּם אֶת־הַטּוֹב נְקַבֵּל מֵאֵת הָאֱלֹהִים וְאֶת־הָרָע לֹא נְקַבֵּל בְּכָל־זֹאת לֹא־חָטָא אִיּוֹב בִּשְׂפָתָיו:

11 When *Iyov*'s three friends heard about all these calamities that had befallen him, each came from his home – Eliphaz the Temanite, Bildad the Shuhite, and Zophar the Naamathite. They met together to go and console and comfort him.

וַיִּשְׁמְעוּ שְׁלֹשֶׁת רֵעֵי אִיּוֹב אֵת כָּל־הָרָעָה הַזֹּאת הַבָּאָה עָלָיו וַיָּבֹאוּ אִישׁ מִמְּקֹמוֹ אֱלִיפַז הַתֵּימָנִי וּבִלְדַּד הַשּׁוּחִי וְצוֹפַר הַנַּעֲמָתִי וַיִּוָּעֲדוּ יַחְדָּו לָבוֹא לָנוּד־לוֹ וּלְנַחֲמוֹ:

12 When they saw him from a distance, they could not recognize him, and they broke into loud weeping; each one tore his robe and threw dust into the air onto his head.

וַיִּשְׂאוּ אֶת־עֵינֵיהֶם מֵרָחוֹק וְלֹא הִכִּירֻהוּ וַיִּשְׂאוּ קוֹלָם וַיִּבְכּוּ וַיִּקְרְעוּ אִישׁ מְעִלוֹ וַיִּזְרְקוּ עָפָר עַל־רָאשֵׁיהֶם הַשָּׁמָיְמָה:

13 They sat with him on the ground seven days and seven nights. None spoke a word to him for they saw how very great was his suffering.

וַיֵּשְׁבוּ אִתּוֹ לָאָרֶץ שִׁבְעַת יָמִים וְשִׁבְעַת לֵילוֹת וְאֵין־דֹּבֵר אֵלָיו דָּבָר כִּי רָאוּ כִּי־גָדַל הַכְּאֵב מְאֹד:

3 1 Afterward, *Iyov* began to speak and cursed the day of his birth.

ג א אַחֲרֵי־כֵן פָּתַח אִיּוֹב אֶת־פִּיהוּ וַיְקַלֵּל אֶת־יוֹמוֹ:

a-kha-ray KHAYN pa-TAKH i-YOV et PEE-hu vai-ka-LAYL et yo-MO

2 *Iyov* spoke up and said:

ב וַיַּעַן אִיּוֹב וַיֹּאמַר:

3 Perish the day on which I was born, And the night it was announced, "A male has been conceived!"

ג יֹאבַד יוֹם אִוָּלֶד בּוֹ וְהַלַּיְלָה אָמַר הֹרָה גָבֶר:

4 May that day be darkness; May *Hashem* above have no concern for it; May light not shine on it;

ד הַיּוֹם הַהוּא יְהִי חֹשֶׁךְ אַל־יִדְרְשֵׁהוּ אֱלוֹהַּ מִמָּעַל וְאַל־תּוֹפַע עָלָיו נְהָרָה:

5 May darkness and deep gloom reclaim it; May a pall lie over it; May what blackens the day terrify it.

ה יִגְאָלֻהוּ חֹשֶׁךְ וְצַלְמָוֶת תִּשְׁכָּן־עָלָיו עֲנָנָה יְבַעֲתֻהוּ כִּמְרִירֵי יוֹם:

6 May obscurity carry off that night; May it not be counted among the days of the year; May it not appear in any of its months;

ו הַלַּיְלָה הַהוּא יִקָּחֵהוּ אֹפֶל אַל־יִחַדְּ בִּימֵי שָׁנָה בְּמִסְפַּר יְרָחִים אַל־יָבֹא:

7 May that night be desolate; May no sound of joy be heard in it;

ז הִנֵּה הַלַּיְלָה הַהוּא יְהִי גַלְמוּד אַל־תָּבֹא רְנָנָה בוֹ:

8 May those who cast spells upon the day damn it, Those prepared to disable Leviathan;

ח יִקְּבֻהוּ אֹרְרֵי־יוֹם הָעֲתִידִים עֹרֵר לִוְיָתָן:

3:1 Cursed the day of his birth The righteous *Iyov*'s initial reaction to the suffering that befell him was not to blaspheme God, but rather, to curse his own birth. Why be born, he calls out painfully, if one's labor on this earth is pointless? With his reaction, *Iyov* gives us a model for coping with trials and tribulations. While we may express our personal pain, we should not vent our frustration on our Creator.

A young man prays to God at the Western Wall

Job

4

9 May its twilight stars remain dark; May it hope for light and have none; May it not see the glimmerings of the dawn –

ט יֶחְשְׁכוּ כּוֹכְבֵי נִשְׁפּוֹ יְקַו־לְאוֹר וָאַיִן וְאַל־יִרְאֶה בְּעַפְעַפֵּי־שָׁחַר:

10 Because it did not block my mother's womb, And hide trouble from my eyes.

י כִּי לֹא סָגַר דַּלְתֵי בִטְנִי וַיַּסְתֵּר עָמָל מֵעֵינָי:

11 Why did I not die at birth, Expire as I came forth from the womb?

יא לָמָּה לֹּא מֵרֶחֶם אָמוּת מִבֶּטֶן יָצָאתִי וְאֶגְוָע:

12 Why were there knees to receive me, Or breasts for me to suck?

יב מַדּוּעַ קִדְּמוּנִי בִרְכָּיִם וּמַה־שָּׁדַיִם כִּי אִינָק:

13 For now would I be lying in repose, asleep and at rest,

יג כִּי־עַתָּה שָׁכַבְתִּי וְאֶשְׁקוֹט יָשַׁנְתִּי אָז יָנוּחַ לִי:

14 With the world's kings and counselors who rebuild ruins for themselves,

יד עִם־מְלָכִים וְיֹעֲצֵי אָרֶץ הַבֹּנִים חֳרָבוֹת לָמוֹ:

15 Or with nobles who possess gold and who fill their houses with silver.

טו אוֹ עִם־שָׂרִים זָהָב לָהֶם הַמְמַלְאִים בָּתֵּיהֶם כָּסֶף:

16 Or why was I not like a buried stillbirth, Like babies who never saw the light?

טז אוֹ כְנֵפֶל טָמוּן לֹא אֶהְיֶה כְּעֹלְלִים לֹא־רָאוּ אוֹר:

17 There the wicked cease from troubling; There rest those whose strength is spent.

יז שָׁם רְשָׁעִים חָדְלוּ רֹגֶז וְשָׁם יָנוּחוּ יְגִיעֵי כֹחַ:

18 Prisoners are wholly at ease; They do not hear the taskmaster's voice.

יח יַחַד אֲסִירִים שַׁאֲנָנוּ לֹא שָׁמְעוּ קוֹל נֹגֵשׂ:

19 Small and great alike are there, And the slave is free of his master.

יט קָטֹן וְגָדוֹל שָׁם הוּא וְעֶבֶד חָפְשִׁי מֵאֲדֹנָיו:

20 Why does He give light to the sufferer And life to the bitter in spirit;

כ לָמָּה יִתֵּן לְעָמֵל אוֹר וְחַיִּים לְמָרֵי נָפֶשׁ:

21 To those who wait for death but it does not come, Who search for it more than for treasure,

כא הַמְחַכִּים לַמָּוֶת וְאֵינֶנּוּ וַיַּחְפְּרֻהוּ מִמַּטְמוֹנִים:

22 Who rejoice to exultation, And are glad to reach the grave;

כב הַשְּׂמֵחִים אֱלֵי־גִיל יָשִׂישׂוּ כִּי יִמְצְאוּ־קָבֶר:

23 To the man who has lost his way, Whom *Hashem* has hedged about?

כג לְגֶבֶר אֲשֶׁר־דַּרְכּוֹ נִסְתָּרָה וַיָּסֶךְ אֱלוֹהַּ בַּעֲדוֹ:

24 My groaning serves as my bread; My roaring pours forth as water.

כד כִּי־לִפְנֵי לַחְמִי אַנְחָתִי תָבֹא וַיִּתְּכוּ כַמַּיִם שַׁאֲגֹתָי:

25 For what I feared has overtaken me; What I dreaded has come upon me.

כה כִּי פַחַד פָּחַדְתִּי וַיֶּאֱתָיֵנִי וַאֲשֶׁר יָגֹרְתִּי יָבֹא לִי:

26 I had no repose, no quiet, no rest, And trouble came.

כו לֹא שָׁלַוְתִּי וְלֹא שָׁקַטְתִּי וְלֹא־נָחְתִּי וַיָּבֹא רֹגֶז:

4 1 Then Eliphaz the Temanite said in reply:

ד א וַיַּעַן אֱלִיפַז הַתֵּימָנִי וַיֹּאמַר:

va-YA-an e-lee-FAZ ha-tay-ma-NEE va-yo-MAR

2 If one ventures a word with you, will it be too much? But who can hold back his words?

ב הֲנִסָּה דָבָר אֵלֶיךָ תִּלְאֶה וַעְצֹר בְּמִלִּין מִי יוּכָל:

3 See, you have encouraged many; You have strengthened failing hands.

ג הִנֵּה יִסַּרְתָּ רַבִּים וְיָדַיִם רָפוֹת תְּחַזֵּק:

4 Your words have kept him who stumbled from falling; You have braced knees that gave way.

ד כּוֹשֵׁל יְקִימוּן מִלֶּיךָ וּבִרְכַּיִם כֹּרְעוֹת תְּאַמֵּץ:

5 But now that it overtakes you, it is too much; It reaches you, and you are unnerved.

ה כִּי עַתָּה תָּבוֹא אֵלֶיךָ וַתֵּלֶא תִּגַּע עָדֶיךָ וַתִּבָּהֵל:

6 Is not your piety your confidence, Your integrity your hope?

ו הֲלֹא יִרְאָתְךָ כִּסְלָתֶךָ תִּקְוָתְךָ וְתֹם דְּרָכֶיךָ:

7 Think now, what innocent man ever perished? Where have the upright been destroyed?

ז זְכָר־נָא מִי הוּא נָקִי אָבָד וְאֵיפֹה יְשָׁרִים נִכְחָדוּ:

8 As I have seen, those who plow evil And sow mischief reap them.

ח כַּאֲשֶׁר רָאִיתִי חֹרְשֵׁי אָוֶן וְזֹרְעֵי עָמָל יִקְצְרֻהוּ:

9 They perish by a blast from *Hashem*, Are gone at the breath of His nostrils.

ט מִנִּשְׁמַת אֱלוֹהַ יֹאבֵדוּ וּמֵרוּחַ אַפּוֹ יִכְלוּ:

10 The lion may roar, the cub may howl, But the teeth of the king of beasts are broken.

י שַׁאֲגַת אַרְיֵה וְקוֹל שָׁחַל וְשִׁנֵּי כְפִירִים נִתָּעוּ:

11 The lion perishes for lack of prey, And its whelps are scattered.

יא לַיִשׁ אֹבֵד מִבְּלִי־טָרֶף וּבְנֵי לָבִיא יִתְפָּרָדוּ:

12 A word came to me in stealth; My ear caught a whisper of it.

יב וְאֵלַי דָּבָר יְגֻנָּב וַתִּקַּח אָזְנִי שֵׁמֶץ מֶנְהוּ:

13 In thought-filled visions of the night, When deep sleep falls on men,

יג בִּשְׂעִפִּים מֵחֶזְיוֹנוֹת לָיְלָה בִּנְפֹל תַּרְדֵּמָה עַל־אֲנָשִׁים:

14 Fear and trembling came upon me, Causing all my bones to quake with fright.

יד פַּחַד קְרָאַנִי וּרְעָדָה וְרֹב עַצְמוֹתַי הִפְחִיד:

15 A wind passed by me, Making the hair of my flesh bristle.

טו וְרוּחַ עַל־פָּנַי יַחֲלֹף תְּסַמֵּר שַׂעֲרַת בְּשָׂרִי:

4:1 Then Eliphaz the Temanite said in reply Eliphaz the Temanite is the first of *Iyov's* friends to respond to his suffering. He asserts that *Hashem* would not punish those who are free of sin, as *Iyov* seems to believe; since all people sin, *Iyov* must not be an exception. He urges *Iyov* to confess his secret sins in order to alleviate his suffering. Though he means well, Eliphaz's view of divine justice is criticized by God Himself at the end of the book (42:7). Eliphaz is called a Temanite, presumably because he is from the city called Teman, which belonged to the descendants of Esau, the Edomites, and is mentioned in *Sefer Ovadya* (1:9). Eliphaz was also the name of Esau's firstborn son (Genesis 36:4). Many therefore assume that Eliphaz is an Edomite, and in *Sefer Iyov* represents Edomite wisdom, which was well-known in biblical times (see Jeremiah 49:7).

Salt formations in the Dead Sea with the Edom Mountains in the background

16 It halted; its appearance was strange to me; A form loomed before my eyes; I heard a murmur, a voice,

טז יַעֲמֹד וְלֹא־אַכִּיר מַרְאֵהוּ תְּמוּנָה לְנֶגֶד עֵינָי דְּמָמָה וָקוֹל אֶשְׁמָע:

17 "Can mortals be acquitted by *Hashem*? Can man be cleared by his Maker?

יז הַאֱנוֹשׁ מֵאֱלוֹהַּ יִצְדָּק אִם מֵעֹשֵׂהוּ יִטְהַר־גָּבֶר:

18 If He cannot trust His own servants, And casts reproach on His angels,

יח הֵן בַּעֲבָדָיו לֹא יַאֲמִין וּבְמַלְאָכָיו יָשִׂים תָּהֳלָה:

19 How much less those who dwell in houses of clay, Whose origin is dust, Who are crushed like the moth,

יט אַף שֹׁכְנֵי בָתֵּי־חֹמֶר אֲשֶׁר־בֶּעָפָר יְסוֹדָם יְדַכְּאוּם לִפְנֵי־עָשׁ:

20 Shattered between daybreak and evening, Perishing forever, unnoticed.

כ מִבֹּקֶר לָעֶרֶב יֻכַּתּוּ מִבְּלִי מֵשִׂים לָנֶצַח יֹאבֵדוּ:

21 Their cord is pulled up And they die, and not with wisdom."

כא הֲלֹא־נִסַּע יִתְרָם בָּם יָמוּתוּ וְלֹא בְחָכְמָה:

5 ¹ Call now! Will anyone answer you? To whom among the holy beings will you turn?

ה א קְרָא־נָא הֲיֵשׁ עוֹנֶךָּ וְאֶל־מִי מִקְּדֹשִׁים תִּפְנֶה:

² Vexation kills the fool; Passion slays the simpleton.

ב כִּי־לֶאֱוִיל יַהֲרָג־כָּעַשׂ וּפֹתֶה תָּמִית קִנְאָה:

³ I myself saw a fool who had struck roots; Impulsively, I cursed his home:

ג אֲנִי־רָאִיתִי אֱוִיל מַשְׁרִישׁ וָאֶקּוֹב נָוֵהוּ פִּתְאֹם:

⁴ May his children be far from success; May they be oppressed in the gate with none to deliver them;

ד יִרְחֲקוּ בָנָיו מִיֶּשַׁע וְיִדַּכְּאוּ בַשַּׁעַר וְאֵין מַצִּיל:

⁵ May the hungry devour his harvest, Carrying it off in baskets; May the thirsty swallow their wealth.

ה אֲשֶׁר קְצִירוֹ רָעֵב יֹאכֵל וְאֶל־מִצִּנִּים יִקָּחֵהוּ וְשָׁאַף צַמִּים חֵילָם:

⁶ Evil does not grow out of the soil, Nor does mischief spring from the ground;

ו כִּי לֹא־יֵצֵא מֵעָפָר אָוֶן וּמֵאֲדָמָה לֹא־יִצְמַח עָמָל:

KEE lo yay-TZAY may-a-FAR A-ven u-may-a-da-MAH lo yitz-MAKH a-MAL

⁷ For man is born to [do] mischief, Just as sparks fly upward.

ז כִּי־אָדָם לְעָמָל יוּלָּד וּבְנֵי־רֶשֶׁף יַגְבִּיהוּ עוּף:

⁸ But I would resort to *Hashem*; I would lay my case before *Hashem*,

ח אוּלָם אֲנִי אֶדְרֹשׁ אֶל־אֵל וְאֶל־אֱלֹהִים אָשִׂים דִּבְרָתִי:

⁹ Who performs great deeds which cannot be fathomed, Wondrous things without number;

ט עֹשֶׂה גְדֹלוֹת וְאֵין חֵקֶר נִפְלָאוֹת עַד־אֵין מִסְפָּר:

A view of the "earth" near the Sea of Galilee through a rocky window

אדם
אדמה

5:6 Nor does mischief spring from the ground Eliphaz says that suffering does not spring forth out of the ground, but rather comes as a result of a person's sins. Since no one is free of sin, every person is born to tribulations (verse 7). Even *Iyov's* location in the Land of Israel cannot free him from the taint of sin. Eliphaz reminds *Iyov* that suffering is part of the human condition, intrinsic in being an *adam* (אדם), 'a person,' and not something which comes on its own out of the *adama* (אדמה), 'earth.' Only those who disconnect from their humanity, therefore, can escape affliction.

7

¹⁰ Who gives rain to the earth, And sends water over the fields;

¹¹ Who raises the lowly up high, So that the dejected are secure in victory;

¹² Who thwarts the designs of the crafty, So that their hands cannot gain success;

¹³ Who traps the clever in their own wiles; The plans of the crafty go awry.

¹⁴ By day they encounter darkness, At noon they grope as in the night.

¹⁵ But He saves the needy from the sword of their mouth, From the clutches of the strong.

¹⁶ So there is hope for the wretched; The mouth of wrongdoing is stopped.

¹⁷ See how happy is the man whom *Hashem* reproves; Do not reject the discipline of the Almighty.

¹⁸ He injures, but He binds up; He wounds, but His hands heal.

¹⁹ He will deliver you from six troubles; In seven no harm will reach you:

²⁰ In famine He will redeem you from death, In war, from the sword.

²¹ You will be sheltered from the scourging tongue; You will have no fear when violence comes.

²² You will laugh at violence and starvation, And have no fear of wild beasts.

²³ For you will have a pact with the rocks in the field, And the beasts of the field will be your allies.

²⁴ You will know that all is well in your tent; When you visit your wife you will never fail.

²⁵ You will see that your offspring are many, Your descendants like the grass of the earth.

²⁶ You will come to the grave in ripe old age, As shocks of grain are taken away in their season.

²⁷ See, we have inquired into this and it is so; Hear it and accept it.

6 ¹ Then *Iyov* said in reply:

² If my anguish were weighed, My full calamity laid on the scales,

י הַנֹּתֵן מָטָר עַל־פְּנֵי־אָרֶץ וְשֹׁלֵחַ מַיִם עַל־פְּנֵי חוּצֽוֹת׃

יא לָשׂוּם שְׁפָלִים לְמָרוֹם וְקֹדְרִים שָׂגְבוּ יֶֽשַׁע׃

יב מֵפֵר מַחְשְׁבוֹת עֲרוּמִים וְלֹא־תַעֲשֶׂינָה יְדֵיהֶם תּוּשִׁיָּֽה׃

יג לֹכֵד חֲכָמִים בְּעָרְמָם וַעֲצַת נִפְתָּלִים נִמְהָֽרָה׃

יד יוֹמָם יְפַגְּשׁוּ־חֹשֶׁךְ וְכַלַּיְלָה יְמַשְׁשׁוּ בַֽצׇּהֳרָֽיִם׃

טו וַיֹּשַׁע מֵחֶרֶב מִפִּיהֶם וּמִיַּד חָזָק אֶבְיֽוֹן׃

טז וַתְּהִי לַדַּל תִּקְוָה וְעֹלָתָה קָפְצָה פִּֽיהָ׃

יז הִנֵּה אַשְׁרֵי אֱנוֹשׁ יוֹכִחֶנּוּ אֱלוֹהַּ וּמוּסַר שַׁדַּי אַל־תִּמְאָֽס׃

יח כִּי הוּא יַכְאִיב וְיֶחְבָּשׁ יִמְחַץ וידו [וְיָדָיו] תִּרְפֶּֽינָה׃

יט בְּשֵׁשׁ צָרוֹת יַצִּילֶךָּ וּבְשֶׁבַע לֹא־יִגַּע בְּךָ רָֽע׃

כ בְּרָעָב פָּֽדְךָ מִמָּוֶת וּבְמִלְחָמָה מִידֵי חָֽרֶב׃

כא בְּשׁוֹט לָשׁוֹן תֵּחָבֵא וְלֹא־תִירָא מִשֹּׁד כִּי יָבֽוֹא׃

כב לְשֹׁד וּלְכָפָן תִּשְׂחָק וּֽמֵחַיַּת הָאָרֶץ אַל־תִּירָֽא׃

כג כִּי עִם־אַבְנֵי הַשָּׂדֶה בְרִיתֶךָ וְחַיַּת הַשָּׂדֶה הׇשְׁלְמָה־לָֽךְ׃

כד וְיָדַעְתָּ כִּי־שָׁלוֹם אׇהֳלֶךָ וּפָקַדְתָּ נָוְךָ וְלֹא תֶחֱטָֽא׃

כה וְֽיָדַעְתָּ כִּי־רַב זַרְעֶךָ וְצֶאֱצָאֶיךָ כְּעֵשֶׂב הָאָֽרֶץ׃

כו תָּבוֹא בְכֶלַח אֱלֵי־קָבֶר כַּעֲלוֹת גָּדִישׁ בְּעִתּֽוֹ׃

כז הִנֵּה־זֹאת חֲקַרְנוּהָ כֶּן־הִיא שְׁמָעֶנָּה וְאַתָּה דַֽע־לָֽךְ׃

א וַיַּעַן אִיּוֹב וַיֹּאמַֽר׃

ב לוּ שָׁקוֹל יִשָּׁקֵל כַּעְשִׂי והיתי [וְהַוָּתִי] בְּֽמֹאזְנַיִם יִשְׂאוּ־יָֽחַד׃

³ It would be heavier than the sand of the sea; That is why I spoke recklessly.

ג כִּי־עַתָּה מֵחוֹל יַמִּים יִכְבָּד עַל־כֵּן דְּבָרַי לָעוּ:

⁴ For the arrows of the Almighty are in me; My spirit absorbs their poison; *Hashem*'s terrors are arrayed against me.

ד כִּי חִצֵּי שַׁדַּי עִמָּדִי אֲשֶׁר חֲמָתָם שֹׁתָה רוּחִי בִּעוּתֵי אֱלוֹהַּ יַעַרְכוּנִי:

⁵ Does a wild ass bray when he has grass? Does a bull bellow over his fodder?

ה הֲיִנְהַק־פֶּרֶא עֲלֵי־דֶשֶׁא אִם יִגְעֶה־שּׁוֹר עַל־בְּלִילוֹ:

⁶ Can what is tasteless be eaten without salt? Does mallow juice have any flavor?

ו הֲיֵאָכֵל תָּפֵל מִבְּלִי־מֶלַח אִם־יֶשׁ־טַעַם בְּרִיר חַלָּמוּת:

⁷ I refuse to touch them; They are like food when I am sick.

ז מֵאֲנָה לִנְגּוֹעַ נַפְשִׁי הֵמָּה כִּדְוֵי לַחְמִי:

⁸ Would that my request were granted, That *Hashem* gave me what I wished for;

ח מִי־יִתֵּן תָּבוֹא שֶׁאֱלָתִי וְתִקְוָתִי יִתֵּן אֱלוֹהַּ:

⁹ Would that *Hashem* consented to crush me, Loosed His hand and cut me off.

ט וְיֹאֵל אֱלוֹהַּ וִידַכְּאֵנִי יַתֵּר יָדוֹ וִיבַצְּעֵנִי:

¹⁰ Then this would be my consolation, As I writhed in unsparing pains: That I did not suppress my words against the Holy One.

י וּתְהִי עוֹד נֶחָמָתִי וַאֲסַלְּדָה בְחִילָה לֹא יַחְמוֹל כִּי־לֹא כִחַדְתִּי אִמְרֵי קָדוֹשׁ:

¹¹ What strength have I, that I should endure? How long have I to live, that I should be patient?

יא מַה־כֹּחִי כִי־אֲיַחֵל וּמַה־קִּצִּי כִּי־אַאֲרִיךְ נַפְשִׁי:

¹² Is my strength the strength of rock? Is my flesh bronze?

יב אִם־כֹּחַ אֲבָנִים כֹּחִי אִם־בְּשָׂרִי נָחוּשׁ:

¹³ Truly, I cannot help myself; I have been deprived of resourcefulness.

יג הַאִם אֵין עֶזְרָתִי בִי וְתֻשִׁיָּה נִדְּחָה מִמֶּנִּי:

¹⁴ A friend owes loyalty to one who fails, Though he forsakes the fear of the Almighty;

יד לַמָּס מֵרֵעֵהוּ חָסֶד וְיִרְאַת שַׁדַּי יַעֲזוֹב:

¹⁵ My comrades are fickle, like a wadi, Like a bed on which streams once ran.

טו אַחַי בָּגְדוּ כְמוֹ־נָחַל כַּאֲפִיק נְחָלִים יַעֲבֹרוּ:

¹⁶ They are dark with ice; Snow obscures them;

טז הַקֹּדְרִים מִנִּי־קָרַח עָלֵימוֹ יִתְעַלֶּם־שָׁלֶג:

¹⁷ But when they thaw, they vanish; In the heat, they disappear where they are.

יז בְּעֵת יְזֹרְבוּ נִצְמָתוּ בְּחֻמּוֹ נִדְעֲכוּ מִמְּקוֹמָם:

¹⁸ Their course twists and turns; They run into the desert and perish.

יח יִלָּפְתוּ אָרְחוֹת דַּרְכָּם יַעֲלוּ בַתֹּהוּ וְיֹאבֵדוּ:

¹⁹ Caravans from Tema look to them; Processions from Sheba count on them.

יט הִבִּיטוּ אָרְחוֹת תֵּמָא הֲלִיכֹת שְׁבָא קִוּוּ־לָמוֹ:

²⁰ They are disappointed in their hopes; When they reach the place, they stand aghast.

כ בֹּשׁוּ כִּי־בָטָח בָּאוּ עָדֶיהָ וַיֶּחְפָּרוּ:

²¹ So you are as nothing: At the sight of misfortune, you take fright.

כא כִּי־עַתָּה הֱיִיתֶם לֹא [לוֹ] תִּרְאוּ חֲתַת וַתִּירָאוּ:

²² Did I say to you, "I need your gift; Pay a bribe for me out of your wealth;

כג הֲכִי־אָמַרְתִּי הָבוּ לִי וּמִכֹּחֲכֶם שִׁחֲדוּ בַעֲדִי:

²³ Deliver me from the clutches of my enemy; Redeem me from violent men"?

כג וּמַלְּטוּנִי מִיַּד־צָר וּמִיַּד עָרִיצִים תִּפְדּוּנִי:

²⁴ Teach me; I shall be silent; Tell me where I am wrong.

כד הוֹרוּנִי וַאֲנִי אַחֲרִישׁ וּמַה־שָּׁגִיתִי הָבִינוּ לִי:

²⁵ How trenchant honest words are; But what sort of reproof comes from you?

כה מַה־נִּמְרְצוּ אִמְרֵי־יֹשֶׁר וּמַה־יּוֹכִיחַ הוֹכֵחַ מִכֶּם:

²⁶ Do you devise words of reproof, But count a hopeless man's words as wind?

כו הַלְהוֹכַח מִלִּים תַּחְשֹׁבוּ וּלְרוּחַ אִמְרֵי נֹאָשׁ:

²⁷ You would even cast lots over an orphan, Or barter away your friend.

כז אַף־עַל־יָתוֹם תַּפִּילוּ וְתִכְרוּ עַל־רֵיעֲכֶם:

af al ya-TOM ta-PEE-lu v'-tikh-RU al ray-a-KHEM

²⁸ Now be so good as to face me; I will not lie to your face.

כח וְעַתָּה הוֹאִילוּ פְנוּ־בִי וְעַל־פְּנֵיכֶם אִם־אֲכַזֵּב:

²⁹ Relent! Let there not be injustice; Relent! I am still in the right.

כט שֻׁבוּ־נָא אַל־תְּהִי עַוְלָה וְשֻׁבִי [וְשֻׁבוּ] עוֹד צִדְקִי־בָהּ:

³⁰ Is injustice on my tongue? Can my palate not discern evil?

ל הֲיֵשׁ־בִּלְשׁוֹנִי עַוְלָה אִם־חִכִּי לֹא־יָבִין הַוּוֹת:

7¹ Truly man has a term of service on earth; His days are like those of a hireling –

ז א הֲלֹא־צָבָא לֶאֱנוֹשׁ על־[עֲלֵי־] אָרֶץ וְכִימֵי שָׂכִיר יָמָיו:

² Like a slave who longs for [evening's] shadows, Like a hireling who waits for his wage.

ב כְּעֶבֶד יִשְׁאַף־צֵל וּכְשָׂכִיר יְקַוֶּה פָעֳלוֹ:

³ So have I been allotted months of futility; Nights of misery have been apportioned to me.

ג כֵּן הָנְחַלְתִּי לִי יַרְחֵי־שָׁוְא וְלֵילוֹת עָמָל מִנּוּ־לִי:

⁴ When I lie down, I think, "When shall I rise?" Night drags on, And I am sated with tossings till morning twilight.

ד אִם־שָׁכַבְתִּי וְאָמַרְתִּי מָתַי אָקוּם וּמִדַּד־עָרֶב וְשָׂבַעְתִּי נְדֻדִים עֲדֵי־נָשֶׁף:

⁵ My flesh is covered with maggots and clods of earth; My skin is broken and festering.

ה לָבַשׁ בְּשָׂרִי רִמָּה וגיש [וְגוּשׁ] עָפָר עוֹרִי רָגַע וַיִּמָּאֵס:

⁶ My days fly faster than a weaver's shuttle, And come to their end without hope.

ו יָמַי קַלּוּ מִנִּי־אָרֶג וַיִּכְלוּ בְּאֶפֶס תִּקְוָה:

6:27 You would even cast lots over an orphan In *Sefer Yeshayahu*, the impending destruction of the Land of Israel and exile of its people is attributed to the corruption of the residents of *Yerushalayim. Yeshayahu* illustrates this corruption with examples, such as failing to pursue justice for orphans (Isaiah 1:23). Similarly, *Iyov* warns his fellows that while they might view themselves as righteous, it is for their kindness to the needy, such as himself, that they will be rewarded, and for its lack that they will be punished.

Israel365 provides clothing for Ukranian Jewish orphans in Israel

⁷ Consider that my life is but wind; I shall never see happiness again.

ז זְכֹר כִּי־רוּחַ חַיָּי לֹא־תָשׁוּב עֵינִי לִרְאוֹת טוֹב:

⁸ The eye that gazes on me will not see me; Your eye will seek me, but I shall be gone.

ח לֹא־תְשׁוּרֵנִי עֵין רֹאִי עֵינֶיךָ בִּי וְאֵינֶנִּי:

⁹ As a cloud fades away, So whoever goes down to Sheol does not come up;

ט כָּלָה עָנָן וַיֵּלַךְ כֵּן יוֹרֵד שְׁאוֹל לֹא יַעֲלֶה:

¹⁰ He returns no more to his home; His place does not know him.

י לֹא־יָשׁוּב עוֹד לְבֵיתוֹ וְלֹא־יַכִּירֶנּוּ עוֹד מְקֹמוֹ:

¹¹ On my part, I will not speak with restraint; I will give voice to the anguish of my spirit; I will complain in the bitterness of my soul.

יא גַּם־אֲנִי לֹא אֶחֱשָׂךְ פִּי אֲדַבְּרָה בְּצַר רוּחִי אָשִׂיחָה בְּמַר נַפְשִׁי:

¹² Am I the sea or the Dragon, That You have set a watch over me?

יב הֲיָם־אָנִי אִם־תַּנִּין כִּי־תָשִׂים עָלַי מִשְׁמָר:

¹³ When I think, "My bed will comfort me, My couch will share my sorrow,"

יג כִּי־אָמַרְתִּי תְּנַחֲמֵנִי עַרְשִׂי יִשָּׂא בְשִׂיחִי מִשְׁכָּבִי:

¹⁴ You frighten me with dreams, And terrify me with visions,

יד וְחִתַּתַּנִי בַחֲלֹמוֹת וּמֵחֶזְיֹנוֹת תְּבַעֲתַנִּי:

¹⁵ Till I prefer strangulation, Death, to my wasted frame.

טו וַתִּבְחַר מַחֲנָק נַפְשִׁי מָוֶת מֵעַצְמוֹתָי:

¹⁶ I am sick of it. I shall not live forever; Let me be, for my days are a breath.

טז מָאַסְתִּי לֹא־לְעֹלָם אֶחְיֶה חֲדַל מִמֶּנִּי כִּי־הֶבֶל יָמָי:

¹⁷ What is man, that You make much of him, That You fix Your attention upon him?

יז מָה־אֱנוֹשׁ כִּי תְגַדְּלֶנּוּ וְכִי־תָשִׁית אֵלָיו לִבֶּךָ:

mah e-NOSH KEE t'-ga-d'-LE-nu v'-KHEE ta-SHEET ay-LAV li-BE-kha

¹⁸ You inspect him every morning, Examine him every minute.

יח וַתִּפְקְדֶנּוּ לִבְקָרִים לִרְגָעִים תִּבְחָנֶנּוּ:

¹⁹ Will You not look away from me for a while, Let me be, till I swallow my spittle?

יט כַּמָּה לֹא־תִשְׁעֶה מִמֶּנִּי לֹא־תַרְפֵּנִי עַד־בִּלְעִי רֻקִּי:

²⁰ If I have sinned, what have I done to You, Watcher of men? Why make of me Your target, And a burden to myself?

כ חָטָאתִי מָה אֶפְעַל לָךְ נֹצֵר הָאָדָם לָמָה שַׂמְתַּנִי לְמִפְגָּע לָךְ וָאֶהְיֶה עָלַי לְמַשָּׂא:

A man admires the sunrise at Ramon Crater in the Negev

7:17 What is man, that You make much of him In his despair, *Iyov* doubts the very worth of humanity. He declares that because man is insignificant, he is unworthy of *Hashem*'s attention and should be free from punishment and suffering. These words parallel the famous words of the psalmist: "What is man, that You have been mindful of him, mortal man that You have taken note of him?" However, the psalmist's conclusion is very different from *Iyov*'s: "That You have made him little less than divine, and adorned him with glory and majesty" (Psalms 8:5–6). While *Iyov* bemoans the esteem given by God to man, the psalmist praises *Hashem* for granting man the capacity for greatness, though in reality he is undeserving.

²¹ Why do You not pardon my transgression And forgive my iniquity? For soon I shall lie down in the dust; When You seek me, I shall be gone.

כא וּמֶה לֹא־תִשָּׂא פִשְׁעִי וְתַעֲבִיר אֶת־עֲוֹנִי כִּי־עַתָּה לֶעָפָר אֶשְׁכָּב וְשִׁחֲרְתַּנִי וְאֵינֶנִּי:

8 ¹ Bildad the Shuhite said in reply:

ח א וַיַּעַן בִּלְדַּד הַשּׁוּחִי וַיֹּאמַר:

² How long will you speak such things? Your utterances are a mighty wind!

ב עַד־אָן תְּמַלֶּל־אֵלֶּה וְרוּחַ כַּבִּיר אִמְרֵי־פִיךָ:

³ Will *Hashem* pervert the right? Will the Almighty pervert justice?

ג הַאֵל יְעַוֵּת מִשְׁפָּט וְאִם־שַׁדַּי יְעַוֵּת־צֶדֶק:

⁴ If your sons sinned against Him, He dispatched them for their transgression.

ד אִם־בָּנֶיךָ חָטְאוּ־לוֹ וַיְשַׁלְּחֵם בְּיַד־פִּשְׁעָם:

⁵ But if you seek *Hashem* And supplicate the Almighty,

ה אִם־אַתָּה תְּשַׁחֵר אֶל־אֵל וְאֶל־שַׁדַּי תִּתְחַנָּן:

⁶ If you are blameless and upright, He will protect you, And grant well-being to your righteous home.

ו אִם־זַךְ וְיָשָׁר אָתָּה כִּי־עַתָּה יָעִיר עָלֶיךָ וְשִׁלַּם נְוַת צִדְקֶךָ:

⁷ Though your beginning be small, In the end you will grow very great.

ז וְהָיָה רֵאשִׁיתְךָ מִצְעָר וְאַחֲרִיתְךָ יִשְׂגֶּה מְאֹד:

⁸ Ask the generation past, Study what their fathers have searched out –

ח כִּי־שְׁאַל־נָא לְדֹר רִישׁוֹן וְכוֹנֵן לְחֵקֶר אֲבוֹתָם:

⁹ For we are of yesterday and know nothing; Our days on earth are a shadow –

ט כִּי־תְמוֹל אֲנַחְנוּ וְלֹא נֵדָע כִּי צֵל יָמֵינוּ עֲלֵי־אָרֶץ:

¹⁰ Surely they will teach you and tell you, Speaking out of their understanding.

י הֲלֹא־הֵם יוֹרוּךָ יֹאמְרוּ לָךְ וּמִלִּבָּם יוֹצִאוּ מִלִּים:

¹¹ Can papyrus thrive without marsh? Can rushes grow without water?

יא הֲיִגְאֶה־גֹּמֶא בְּלֹא בִצָּה יִשְׂגֶּה־אָחוּ בְלִי־מָיִם:

¹² While still tender, not yet plucked, They would wither before any other grass.

יב עֹדֶנּוּ בְאִבּוֹ לֹא יִקָּטֵף וְלִפְנֵי כָל־חָצִיר יִיבָשׁ:

¹³ Such is the fate of all who forget *Hashem*; The hope of the impious man comes to naught –

יג כֵּן אָרְחוֹת כָּל־שֹׁכְחֵי אֵל וְתִקְוַת חָנֵף תֹּאבֵד:

¹⁴ Whose confidence is a thread of gossamer, Whose trust is a spider's web.

יד אֲשֶׁר־יָקוֹט כִּסְלוֹ וּבֵית עַכָּבִישׁ מִבְטַחוֹ:

¹⁵ He leans on his house – it will not stand; He seizes hold of it, but it will not hold.

טו יִשָּׁעֵן עַל־בֵּיתוֹ וְלֹא יַעֲמֹד יַחֲזִיק בּוֹ וְלֹא יָקוּם:

¹⁶ He stays fresh even in the sun; His shoots spring up in his garden;

טז רָטֹב הוּא לִפְנֵי־שָׁמֶשׁ וְעַל גַּנָּתוֹ יֹנַקְתּוֹ תֵצֵא:

¹⁷ His roots are twined around a heap, They take hold of a house of stones.

יז עַל־גַּל שָׁרָשָׁיו יְסֻבָּכוּ בֵּית אֲבָנִים יֶחֱזֶה:

¹⁸ When he is uprooted from his place, It denies him, [saying,] "I never saw you."

יח אִם־יְבַלְּעֶנּוּ מִמְּקֹמוֹ וְכִחֶשׁ בּוֹ לֹא רְאִיתִיךָ:

¹⁹ Such is his happy lot; And from the earth others will grow.

הֶן־הוּא מְשׂוֹשׂ דַּרְכּוֹ וּמֵעָפָר אַחֵר יִצְמָחוּ: יט

²⁰ Surely *Hashem* does not despise the blameless; He gives no support to evildoers.

הֶן־אֵל לֹא יִמְאַס־תָּם וְלֹא־יַחֲזִיק בְּיַד־מְרֵעִים: כ

²¹ He will yet fill your mouth with laughter, And your lips with shouts of joy.

עַד־יְמַלֶּה שְׂחוֹק פִּיךָ וּשְׂפָתֶיךָ תְרוּעָה: כא

ad y'-ma-LAY s'-KHOK PEE-kha us-fa-TE-kha t'-ru-AH

²² Your enemies will be clothed in disgrace; The tent of the wicked will vanish.

שֹׂנְאֶיךָ יִלְבְּשׁוּ־בֹשֶׁת וְאֹהֶל רְשָׁעִים אֵינֶנּוּ: כב

9¹ *Iyov* said in reply:

וַיַּעַן אִיּוֹב וַיֹּאמַר: ט א

² Indeed I know that it is so: Man cannot win a suit against *Hashem*.

אָמְנָם יָדַעְתִּי כִי־כֵן וּמַה־יִּצְדַּק אֱנוֹשׁ עִם־אֵל: ב

³ If he insisted on a trial with Him, He would not answer one charge in a thousand.

אִם־יַחְפֹּץ לָרִיב עִמּוֹ לֹא־יַעֲנֶנּוּ אַחַת מִנִּי־אָלֶף: ג

⁴ Wise of heart and mighty in power – Who ever challenged Him and came out whole? –

חֲכַם לֵבָב וְאַמִּיץ כֹּחַ מִי־הִקְשָׁה אֵלָיו וַיִּשְׁלָם: ד

kha-KHAM lay-VAV v'-a-MEETZ KO-akh mee hik-SHAH ay-LAV va-yish-LAM

⁵ Him who moves mountains without their knowing it, Who overturns them in His anger;

הַמַּעְתִּיק הָרִים וְלֹא יָדָעוּ אֲשֶׁר הֲפָכָם בְּאַפּוֹ: ה

⁶ Who shakes the earth from its place, Till its pillars quake;

הַמַּרְגִּיז אֶרֶץ מִמְּקוֹמָהּ וְעַמּוּדֶיהָ יִתְפַלָּצוּן: ו

⁷ Who commands the sun not to shine; Who seals up the stars;

הָאֹמֵר לַחֶרֶס וְלֹא יִזְרָח וּבְעַד כּוֹכָבִים יַחְתֹּם: ז

A young boy laughs as he waves his flags in honor of Israel's Independence Day

8:21 He will yet fill your mouth with laughter *Bildad* attempts to comfort *Iyov* by telling him that if he is as righteous as he claims to be, his suffering will not last long. When the suffering ends, he will feel so happy that his mouth will be filled with laughter. These words are reminiscent of the description, found in *Sefer Tehillim* (126:2), of the return of the exiled Jews to the Land of Israel: "Our mouths shall be filled with laughter." It is often said that what causes someone to laugh is an unexpected ending. While he is in the midst of his suffering, it is almost impossible for *Iyov* to imagine relief from his misery. Similarly, the Jewish people in exile could not always envision an actual redemption. When it comes, therefore, it not only causes feelings of happiness and joy, but laughter as well.

9:4 Wise of heart and mighty in power The words in this verse, translated as "wise of heart," are understood by the Sages to mean "wise about hearts," or "wise about innermost thoughts." This means that *Hashem* knows what is in people's hearts, and judges them accordingly. While man has the capacity to judge his fellow only by what is obvious to the human eye, *Hashem* knows what is really in a person's heart. *Iyov*'s friends understand this in a negative sense; while *Iyov* seems righteous externally, he must have committed sins in secret. However, the opposite is also true. Someone might seem evil on the outside, but might have good intentions in his heart. It is man's challenge to behave as God does, and instead of making assumptions solely on the basis of external appearances, to understand that there is more in a person's heart that might not be apparent from the outside. We are therefore called upon to judge others favorably by always giving them the benefit of the doubt.

⁸ Who by Himself spread out the heavens, And trod on the back of the sea;

ח נֹטֶ֣ה שָׁמַ֣יִם לְבַדּ֑וֹ וְ֝דוֹרֵ֗ךְ עַל־בָּ֥מֳתֵי יָֽם׃

⁹ Who made the Bear and Orion, Pleiades, and the chambers of the south wind;

ט עֹֽשֶׂה־עָ֭שׁ כְּסִ֥יל וְכִימָ֗ה וְחַדְרֵ֥י תֵמָֽן׃

¹⁰ Who performs great deeds which cannot be fathomed, And wondrous things without number.

י עֹשֶׂ֣ה גְ֭דֹלוֹת עַד־אֵ֣ין חֵ֑קֶר וְנִפְלָא֗וֹת עַד־אֵ֥ין מִסְפָּֽר׃

¹¹ He passes me by – I do not see Him; He goes by me, but I do not perceive Him.

יא הֵ֤ן יַעֲבֹ֣ר עָ֭לַי וְלֹ֣א אֶרְאֶ֑ה וְ֝יַחֲלֹ֗ף וְלֹֽא־אָבִ֥ין לֽוֹ׃

¹² He snatches away – who can stop Him? Who can say to Him, "What are You doing?"

יב הֵ֣ן יַ֭חְתֹּף מִ֣י יְשִׁיבֶ֑נּוּ מִֽי־יֹאמַ֥ר אֵ֝לָ֗יו מַֽה־תַּעֲשֶֽׂה׃

¹³ *Hashem* does not restrain His anger; Under Him Rahab's helpers sink down.

יג אֱ֭לוֹהַּ לֹא־יָשִׁ֣יב אַפּ֑וֹ תחתו [תַּֽחְתָּ֥יו] שָׁ֝חֲח֗וּ עֹ֣זְרֵי רָֽהַב׃

¹⁴ How then can I answer Him, Or choose my arguments against Him?

יד אַ֭ף כִּֽי־אָנֹכִ֣י אֶעֱנֶ֑נּוּ אֶבְחֲרָ֖ה דְבָרַ֣י עִמּֽוֹ׃

¹⁵ Though I were in the right, I could not speak out, But I would plead for mercy with my judge.

טו אֲשֶׁ֣ר אִם־צָ֭דַקְתִּי לֹ֣א אֶעֱנֶ֑ה לִ֝מְשֹׁפְטִ֗י אֶתְחַנָּֽן׃

¹⁶ If I summoned Him and He responded, I do not believe He would lend me His ear.

טז אִם־קָרָ֥אתִי וַֽיַּעֲנֵ֑נִי לֹֽא־אַ֝אֲמִ֗ין כִּֽי־יַאֲזִ֥ין קוֹלִֽי׃

¹⁷ For He crushes me for a hair; He wounds me much for no cause.

יז אֲשֶׁר־בִּשְׂעָרָ֥ה יְשׁוּפֵ֑נִי וְהִרְבָּ֖ה פְצָעַ֣י חִנָּֽם׃

¹⁸ He does not let me catch my breath, But sates me with bitterness.

יח לֹֽא־יִ֖תְּנֵנִי הָשֵׁ֣ב רוּחִ֑י כִּ֥י יַ֝שְׂבִּעַ֗נִי מַמְּרֹרִֽים׃

¹⁹ If a trial of strength – He is the strong one; If a trial in court – who will summon Him for me?

יט אִם־לְכֹ֣חַ אַמִּ֣יץ הִנֵּ֑ה וְאִם־לְ֝מִשְׁפָּ֗ט מִ֣י יוֹעִידֵֽנִי׃

²⁰ Though I were innocent, My mouth would condemn me; Though I were blameless, He would prove me crooked.

כ אִם־אֶ֭צְדָּק פִּ֣י יַרְשִׁיעֵ֑נִי תָּֽם־אָ֝֗נִי וַֽיַּעְקְשֵֽׁנִי׃

²¹ I am blameless – I am distraught; I am sick of life.

כא תָּֽם־אָ֗נִי לֹֽא־אֵדַ֥ע נַפְשִׁ֗י אֶמְאַ֥ס חַיָּֽי׃

²² It is all one; therefore I say, "He destroys the blameless and the guilty."

כב אַחַ֗ת הִ֥יא עַל־כֵּ֥ן אָמַ֑רְתִּי תָּ֥ם וְ֝רָשָׁ֗ע ה֣וּא מְכַלֶּֽה׃

²³ When suddenly a scourge brings death, He mocks as the innocent fail.

כג אִם־שׁ֭וֹט יָמִ֣ית פִּתְאֹ֑ם לְמַסַּ֖ת נְקִיִּ֣ם יִלְעָֽג׃

²⁴ The earth is handed over to the wicked one; He covers the eyes of its judges. If it is not He, then who?

כד אֶ֤רֶץ ׀ נִתְּנָ֬ה בְֽיַד־רָשָׁ֗ע פְּנֵֽי־שֹׁפְטֶ֥יהָ יְכַסֶּ֑ה אִם־לֹ֖א אֵפ֣וֹא מִי־הֽוּא׃

²⁵ My days fly swifter than a runner; They flee without seeing happiness;

כה וְיָמַ֣י קַ֭לּוּ מִנִּי־רָ֑ץ בָּֽ֝רְח֗וּ לֹא־רָא֥וּ טוֹבָֽה׃

²⁶ They pass like reed-boats, Like an eagle swooping onto its prey.

כו חָ֭לְפוּ עִם־אֳנִיּ֣וֹת אֵבֶ֑ה כְּ֝נֶ֗שֶׁר יָט֥וּשׂ עֲלֵי־אֹֽכֶל׃

27 If I say, "I will forget my complaint; Abandon my sorrow and be diverted,"

כז אִם־אָמְרִי אֶשְׁכְּחָה שִׂיחִי אֶעֶזְבָה פָנַי וְאַבְלִיגָה:

28 I remain in dread of all my suffering; I know that You will not acquit me.

כח יָגֹרְתִּי כָל־עַצְּבֹתָי יָדַעְתִּי כִּי־לֹא תְנַקֵּנִי:

29 It will be I who am in the wrong; Why then should I waste effort?

כט אָנֹכִי אֶרְשָׁע לָמָּה־זֶּה הֶבֶל אִיגָע:

30 If I washed with soap, Cleansed my hands with lye,

ל אִם־הִתְרָחַצְתִּי במו־[בְמֵי־] שָׁלֶג וַהֲזִכּוֹתִי בְּבֹר כַּפָּי:

31 You would dip me in muck Till my clothes would abhor me.

לא אָז בַּשַּׁחַת תִּטְבְּלֵנִי וְתִעֲבוּנִי שַׂלְמוֹתָי:

32 He is not a man, like me, that I can answer Him, That we can go to law together.

לב כִּי־לֹא־אִישׁ כָּמֹנִי אֶעֱנֶנּוּ נָבוֹא יַחְדָּו בַּמִּשְׁפָּט:

33 No arbiter is between us To lay his hand on us both.

לג לֹא יֵשׁ־בֵּינֵינוּ מוֹכִיחַ יָשֵׁת יָדוֹ עַל־שְׁנֵינוּ:

34 If He would only take His rod away from me And not let His terror frighten me,

לד יָסֵר מֵעָלַי שִׁבְטוֹ וְאֵמָתוֹ אַל־תְּבַעֲתַנִּי:

35 Then I would speak out without fear of Him; For I know myself not to be so.

לה אֲדַבְּרָה וְלֹא אִירָאֶנּוּ כִּי לֹא־כֵן אָנֹכִי עִמָּדִי:

10 1 I am disgusted with life; I will give rein to my complaint, Speak in the bitterness of my soul.

י א נָקְטָה נַפְשִׁי בְּחַיָּי אֶעֶזְבָה עָלַי שִׂיחִי אֲדַבְּרָה בְּמַר נַפְשִׁי:

2 I say to *Hashem*, "Do not condemn me; Let me know what You charge me with.

ב אֹמַר אֶל־אֱלוֹהַּ אַל־תַּרְשִׁיעֵנִי הוֹדִיעֵנִי עַל מַה־תְּרִיבֵנִי:

3 Does it benefit You to defraud, To despise the toil of Your hands, While smiling on the counsel of the wicked?

ג הֲטוֹב לְךָ כִּי־תַעֲשֹׁק כִּי־תִמְאַס יְגִיעַ כַּפֶּיךָ וְעַל־עֲצַת רְשָׁעִים הוֹפָעְתָּ:

4 Do You have the eyes of flesh? Is Your vision that of mere men?

ד הַעֵינֵי בָשָׂר לָךְ אִם־כִּרְאוֹת אֱנוֹשׁ תִּרְאֶה:

5 Are Your days the days of a mortal, Are Your years the years of a man,

ה הֲכִימֵי אֱנוֹשׁ יָמֶיךָ אִם־שְׁנוֹתֶיךָ כִּימֵי גָבֶר:

6 That You seek my iniquity And search out my sin?

ו כִּי־תְבַקֵּשׁ לַעֲוֹנִי וּלְחַטָּאתִי תִדְרוֹשׁ:

7 You know that I am not guilty, And that there is none to deliver from Your hand.

ז עַל־דַּעְתְּךָ כִּי־לֹא אֶרְשָׁע וְאֵין מִיָּדְךָ מַצִּיל:

8 "Your hands shaped and fashioned me, Then destroyed every part of me.

ח יָדֶיךָ עִצְּבוּנִי וַיַּעֲשׂוּנִי יַחַד סָבִיב וַתְּבַלְּעֵנִי:

9 Consider that You fashioned me like clay; Will You then turn me back into dust?

ט זְכָר־נָא כִּי־כַחֹמֶר עֲשִׂיתָנִי וְאֶל־עָפָר תְּשִׁיבֵנִי:

10 You poured me out like milk, Congealed me like cheese;

י הֲלֹא כֶחָלָב תַּתִּיכֵנִי וְכַגְּבִנָּה תַּקְפִּיאֵנִי:

¹¹ You clothed me with skin and flesh And wove me of bones and sinews;

יא עוֹר וּבָשָׂר תַּלְבִּישֵׁנִי וּבַעֲצָמוֹת וְגִידִים תְּסֹכְכֵנִי:

¹² You bestowed on me life and care; Your providence watched over my spirit.

יב חַיִּים וָחֶסֶד עָשִׂיתָ עִמָּדִי וּפְקֻדָּתְךָ שָׁמְרָה רוּחִי:

¹³ Yet these things You hid in Your heart; I know that You had this in mind:

יג וְאֵלֶּה צָפַנְתָּ בִלְבָבֶךָ יָדַעְתִּי כִּי־זֹאת עִמָּךְ:

¹⁴ To watch me when I sinned And not clear me of my iniquity;

יד אִם־חָטָאתִי וּשְׁמַרְתָּנִי וּמֵעֲוֺנִי לֹא תְנַקֵּנִי:

¹⁵ Should I be guilty – the worse for me! And even when innocent, I cannot lift my head; So sated am I with shame, And drenched in my misery.

טו אִם־רָשַׁעְתִּי אַלְלַי לִי וְצָדַקְתִּי לֹא־אֶשָּׂא רֹאשִׁי שְׂבַע קָלוֹן וּרְאֵה עָנְיִי:

¹⁶ It is something to be proud of to hunt me like a lion, To show Yourself wondrous through me time and again!

טז וְיִגְאֶה כַּשַּׁחַל תְּצוּדֵנִי וְתָשֹׁב תִּתְפַּלָּא־בִי:

¹⁷ You keep sending fresh witnesses against me, Letting Your vexation with me grow. I serve my term and am my own replacement.

יז תְּחַדֵּשׁ עֵדֶיךָ נֶגְדִּי וְתֶרֶב כַּעַשְׂךָ עִמָּדִי חֲלִיפוֹת וְצָבָא עִמִּי:

¹⁸ "Why did You let me come out of the womb? Better had I expired before any eye saw me,

יח וְלָמָּה מֵרֶחֶם הֹצֵאתָנִי אֶגְוַע וְעַיִן לֹא־תִרְאֵנִי:

v'-LA-mah may-RE-khem ho-tzay-TA-nee eg-VA v'-A-yin lo tir-AY-nee

¹⁹ Had I been as though I never was, Had I been carried from the womb to the grave.

יט כַּאֲשֶׁר לֹא־הָיִיתִי אֶהְיֶה מִבֶּטֶן לַקֶּבֶר אוּבָל:

²⁰ My days are few, so desist! Leave me alone, let me be diverted a while

כ הֲלֹא־מְעַט יָמַי יֶחְדָּל [וַחֲדָל] יָשִׁית [וְשִׁית] מִמֶּנִּי וְאַבְלִיגָה מְּעָט:

²¹ Before I depart – never to return – For the land of deepest gloom;

כא בְּטֶרֶם אֵלֵךְ וְלֹא אָשׁוּב אֶל־אֶרֶץ חֹשֶׁךְ וְצַלְמָוֶת:

²² A land whose light is darkness, All gloom and disarray, Whose light is like darkness."

כב אֶרֶץ עֵיפָתָה כְּמוֹ אֹפֶל צַלְמָוֶת וְלֹא סְדָרִים וַתֹּפַע כְּמוֹ־אֹפֶל:

11 ¹ Then Zophar the Naamathite said in reply:

יא א וַיַּעַן צֹפַר הַנַּעֲמָתִי וַיֹּאמַר:

² Is a multitude of words unanswerable? Must a loquacious person be right?

ב הֲרֹב דְּבָרִים לֹא יֵעָנֶה וְאִם־אִישׁ שְׂפָתַיִם יִצְדָּק:

³ Your prattle may silence men; You may mock without being rebuked,

ג בַּדֶּיךָ מְתִים יַחֲרִישׁוּ וַתִּלְעַג וְאֵין מַכְלִם:

Mother and son at sunset on the Tel Aviv coast

10:18 Why did You let me come out of the womb? The Hebrew word for 'womb,' *rekhem* (רחם), shares a root with the word for 'compassion,' which is *rakhamim* (רחמים). While at first glance the connection between these two words may be unclear, upon further thought it becomes obvious. A mother has a natural love and compassion for her offspring, the fruit of her womb. *Iyov* wishes he had never been taken out of the womb, because he feels bereft not only of *Hashem*'s justice, but also of His compassion and mercy.

רחם
רחמים

4 And say, "My doctrine is pure, And I have been innocent in Your sight."

ד וַתֹּאמֶר זַךְ לִקְחִי וּבַר הָיִיתִי בְעֵינֶיךָ:

5 But would that *Hashem* might speak, And talk to you Himself.

ה וְאוּלָם מִי־יִתֵּן אֱלוֹהַּ דַּבֵּר וְיִפְתַּח שְׂפָתָיו עִמָּךְ:

6 He would tell you the secrets of wisdom, For there are many sides to sagacity; And know that *Hashem* has overlooked for you some of your iniquity.

ו וְיַגֶּד־לְךָ תַּעֲלֻמוֹת חָכְמָה כִּי־כִפְלַיִם לְתוּשִׁיָּה וְדַע כִּי־יַשֶּׁה לְךָ אֱלוֹהַּ מֵעֲוֺנֶךָ:

7 Would you discover the mystery of *Hashem*? Would you discover the limit of the Almighty?

ז הַחֵקֶר אֱלוֹהַּ תִּמְצָא אִם עַד־תַּכְלִית שַׁדַּי תִּמְצָא:

ha-KHAY-ker e-LO-ha tim-TZA IM ad takh-LEET sha-DAI tim-TZA

8 Higher than heaven – what can you do? Deeper than Sheol – what can you know?

ח גׇּבְהֵי שָׁמַיִם מַה־תִּפְעָל עֲמֻקָּה מִשְּׁאוֹל מַה־תֵּדָע:

9 Its measure is longer than the earth And broader than the sea.

ט אֲרֻכָּה מֵאֶרֶץ מִדָּהּ וּרְחָבָה מִנִּי־יָם:

10 Should He pass by, or confine, Or call an assembly, who can stop Him?

י אִם־יַחֲלֹף וְיַסְגִּיר וְיַקְהִיל וּמִי יְשִׁיבֶנּוּ:

11 For He knows deceitful men; When He sees iniquity, does He not discern it?

יא כִּי־הוּא יָדַע מְתֵי־שָׁוְא וַיַּרְא־אָוֶן וְלֹא יִתְבּוֹנָן:

12 A hollow man will get understanding, When a wild ass is born a man.

יב וְאִישׁ נָבוּב יִלָּבֵב וְעַיִר פֶּרֶא אָדָם יִוָּלֵד:

13 But if you direct your mind, And spread forth your hands toward Him –

יג אִם־אַתָּה הֲכִינוֹתָ לִבֶּךָ וּפָרַשְׂתָּ אֵלָיו כַּפֶּךָ:

14 If there is iniquity with you, remove it, And do not let injustice reside in your tent –

יד אִם־אָוֶן בְּיָדְךָ הַרְחִיקֵהוּ וְאַל־תַּשְׁכֵּן בְּאֹהָלֶיךָ עַוְלָה:

15 Then, free of blemish, you will hold your head high, And, when in straits, be unafraid.

טו כִּי־אָז תִּשָּׂא פָנֶיךָ מִמּוּם וְהָיִיתָ מֻצָק וְלֹא תִירָא:

16 You will then put your misery out of mind, Consider it as water that has flowed past.

טז כִּי־אַתָּה עָמָל תִּשְׁכָּח כְּמַיִם עָבְרוּ תִזְכֹּר:

Job

11:7 Would you discover the mystery of *Hashem*? Zophar questions *Iyov's* insistence that he is innocent, suggesting that *Iyov* is perhaps not as pure as he thinks he is, since man cannot comprehend *Hashem's* mind nor his desires of us. Even *Moshe*, the greatest prophet of all time, was denied his request to fully comprehend the ways of *Hashem*. After the sin of the golden calf, *Moshe* prays for the people and seeks closeness to God. Sensing that this was a time of mercy, he pleads with *Hashem* to let him understand His ways, and requests of Him: "Let me behold Your presence" (Exodus 33:18). God's response, however, is, "You cannot see My face, for man may not see Me and live" (ibid. verse 20). The Sages understand this request to see God's face as a metaphor for *Moshe's* plea to understand *Hashem*. In fact, the Sages of the Talmud (*Berachot* 7a) suggest that *Moshe* was specifically seeking the answer to the question of theodicy, wondering why bad things happen to good people and vice versa. This is indeed the question that bothers *Iyov* throughout his book, and continues to trouble us for eternity. However, as *Moshe* is told, we cannot comprehend the ways of God and might never understand the answer to this question as long as we are living.

Man lifting up his hands to Heaven in prayer

¹⁷ Life will be brighter than noon; You will shine, you will be like the morning.

יז וּמִצָּהֳרַיִם יָקוּם חָלֶד תָּעֻפָה כַּבֹּקֶר תִּהְיֶה:

¹⁸ **You will be secure, for there is hope, And, entrenched, you will rest secure;**

יח וּבָטַחְתָּ כִּי־יֵשׁ תִּקְוָה וְחָפַרְתָּ לָבֶטַח תִּשְׁכָּב:

u-va-takh-TA kee YAYSH tik-VAH v'-kha-far-TA la-VE-takh tish-KAV

¹⁹ You will lie down undisturbed; The great will court your favor.

יט וְרָבַצְתָּ וְאֵין מַחֲרִיד וְחִלּוּ פָנֶיךָ רַבִּים:

²⁰ But the eyes of the wicked pine away; Escape is cut off from them; They have only their last breath to look forward to.

כ וְעֵינֵי רְשָׁעִים תִּכְלֶינָה וּמָנוֹס אָבַד מִנְהֶם וְתִקְוָתָם מַפַּח־נָפֶשׁ:

12 ¹ Then *Iyov* said in reply:

יב א וַיַּעַן אִיּוֹב וַיֹּאמַר:

² Indeed, you are the [voice of] the people, And wisdom will die with you.

ב אָמְנָם כִּי אַתֶּם־עָם וְעִמָּכֶם תָּמוּת חָכְמָה:

³ But I, like you, have a mind, And am not less than you. Who does not know such things?

ג גַּם־לִי לֵבָב כְּמוֹכֶם לֹא־נֹפֵל אָנֹכִי מִכֶּם וְאֶת־מִי־אֵין כְּמוֹ־אֵלֶּה:

⁴ I have become a laughingstock to my friend – "One who calls to *Hashem* and is answered, Blamelessly innocent" – a laughingstock.

ד שְׂחֹק לְרֵעֵהוּ אֶהְיֶה קֹרֵא לֶאֱלוֹהַּ וַיַּעֲנֵהוּ שְׂחוֹק צַדִּיק תָּמִים:

⁵ In the thought of the complacent there is contempt for calamity; It is ready for those whose foot slips.

ה לַפִּיד בּוּז לְעַשְׁתּוּת שַׁאֲנָן נָכוֹן לְמוֹעֲדֵי רָגֶל:

⁶ Robbers live untroubled in their tents, And those who provoke *Hashem* are secure, Those whom *Hashem's* hands have produced.

ו יִשְׁלָיוּ אֹהָלִים לְשֹׁדְדִים וּבַטֻּחוֹת לְמַרְגִּיזֵי אֵל לַאֲשֶׁר הֵבִיא אֱלוֹהַּ בְּיָדוֹ:

yish-LA-yu o-ha-LEEM l'-sho-d'-DEEM u-va-tu-KHOT l'-mar-GEE-zay AYL la-a-SHER hay-VEE e-LO-ha b'-ya-DO

11:18 You will be secure, for there is hope In Jewish culture, hope is considered one of the most potent tools at humanity's disposal for fulfilling its mission of perfecting the world. Asher Ginsberg, better known by his pen-name, *Achad Ha'am* (literally, "One of the People"), was the 19th–20th century founder of the movement known as "Cultural Zionism." He envisioned the upcoming state as a Jewish spiritual center; not merely a State of Jews, but a Jewish State. On this topic, he writes: "The national self of a nation is the link between its past and future. Memories on the one hand, and hope on the other. Our prophets, and later our sages, implanted in the Jew hope in the future, and to the Jew this was not a fantastic hope, but a reality. And this was the best spiritual food to sustain our life. Without this hope, the Torah alone could not have preserved us." With these beautiful words, *Achad Ha'am* illustrates how hope and *Torah* are inherently, and eternally, intertwined.

12:6 Robbers live untroubled in their tents *Iyov* protests his friends' assertion that *Hashem* does not punish those who do not deserve to be punish. He boldly states what most people know inherently: The righteous do indeed suffer, and evil people are rewarded. Furthermore, says *Iyov*, even the animals are aware of this reality (verse 7). The desire to understand God as just has blinded *Iyov's* friends to the truth which is obvious to everyone else. However, as King *Shlomo* reassures us in *Mishlei* (28:8), the wicked who prosper in this world, those who get rich by inappropriate means, are merely accumulating wealth for the benefit of the righteous, as *Hashem* will ultimately ensure that it arrives in their possession.

Achad Ha'am
(1856–1927)

7 But ask the beasts, and they will teach you; The birds of the sky, they will tell you,

ז וְאוּלָם שְׁאַל־נָא בְהֵמוֹת וְתֹרֶךָ וְעוֹף הַשָּׁמַיִם וְיַגֶּד־לָךְ:

8 Or speak to the earth, it will teach you; The fish of the sea, they will inform you.

ח אוֹ שִׂיחַ לָאָרֶץ וְתֹרֶךָ וִיסַפְּרוּ לְךָ דְּגֵי הַיָּם:

9 Who among all these does not know That the hand of *Hashem* has done this?

ט מִי לֹא־יָדַע בְּכָל־אֵלֶּה כִּי יַד־יְהוָה עָשְׂתָה זֹּאת:

10 In His hand is every living soul And the breath of all mankind.

י אֲשֶׁר בְּיָדוֹ נֶפֶשׁ כָּל־חָי וְרוּחַ כָּל־בְּשַׂר־אִישׁ:

11 Truly, the ear tests arguments As the palate tastes foods.

יא הֲלֹא־אֹזֶן מִלִּין תִּבְחָן וְחֵךְ אֹכֶל יִטְעַם־לוֹ:

12 Is wisdom in the aged And understanding in the long-lived?

יב בִּישִׁישִׁים חָכְמָה וְאֹרֶךְ יָמִים תְּבוּנָה:

13 With Him are wisdom and courage; His are counsel and understanding.

יג עִמּוֹ חָכְמָה וּגְבוּרָה לוֹ עֵצָה וּתְבוּנָה:

14 Whatever He tears down cannot be rebuilt; Whomever He imprisons cannot be set free.

יד הֵן יַהֲרוֹס וְלֹא יִבָּנֶה יִסְגֹּר עַל־אִישׁ וְלֹא יִפָּתֵחַ:

15 When He holds back the waters, they dry up; When He lets them loose, they tear up the land.

טו הֵן יַעְצֹר בַּמַּיִם וְיִבָשׁוּ וִישַׁלְּחֵם וְיַהַפְכוּ אָרֶץ:

16 With Him are strength and resourcefulness; Erring and causing to err are from Him.

טז עִמּוֹ עֹז וְתוּשִׁיָּה לוֹ שֹׁגֵג וּמַשְׁגֶּה:

17 He makes counselors go about naked And causes judges to go mad.

יז מוֹלִיךְ יוֹעֲצִים שׁוֹלָל וְשֹׁפְטִים יְהוֹלֵל:

18 He undoes the belts of kings, And fastens loincloths on them.

יח מוּסַר מְלָכִים פִּתֵּחַ וַיֶּאְסֹר אֵזוֹר בְּמָתְנֵיהֶם:

19 He makes *Kohanim* go about naked, And leads temple-servants astray.

יט מוֹלִיךְ כֹּהֲנִים שׁוֹלָל וְאֵתָנִים יְסַלֵּף:

20 He deprives trusty men of speech, And takes away the reason of elders.

כ מֵסִיר שָׂפָה לְנֶאֱמָנִים וְטַעַם זְקֵנִים יִקָּח:

21 He pours disgrace upon great men, And loosens the belt of the mighty.

כא שׁוֹפֵךְ בּוּז עַל־נְדִיבִים וּמְזִיחַ אֲפִיקִים רִפָּה:

22 He draws mysteries out of the darkness, And brings obscurities to light.

כב מְגַלֶּה עֲמֻקוֹת מִנִּי־חֹשֶׁךְ וַיֹּצֵא לָאוֹר צַלְמָוֶת:

m'-ga-LEH a-mu-KOT mi-nee KHO-shekh va-yo-TZAY la-OR tzal-MA-vet

---

גלות

12:22 He draws mysteries out of the darkness The Hebrew words for "He draws mysteries" are *m'galeh amukot* (מגלה עמוקות). The word *m'galeh* comes from the root *legalot* (לגלות), which means to reveal or discover. The same Hebrew letters are also found in the word *galut* (גלות), meaning exile or expulsion. This similarity is no mere play on words. Rather, according to Rabbi David Stavsky, a profound lesson emerges from the connection between these two words.

"Nothing is more difficult for a human being than to be exiled from his native land, yet nothing can be more rewarding than discovering a way out of exile." In the connection between the Hebrew

Light shines through a darkened sky at the Red Sea in Eilat

²³ He exalts nations, then destroys them; He expands nations, then leads them away.

כג מַשְׂגִּיא לַגּוֹיִם וַיְאַבְּדֵם שֹׁטֵחַ לַגּוֹיִם וַיַּנְחֵֽם:

²⁴ He deranges the leaders of the people, And makes them wander in a trackless waste.

כד מֵסִיר לֵב רָאשֵׁי עַם־הָאָרֶץ וַיַּתְעֵם בְּתֹהוּ לֹא־דָֽרֶךְ:

²⁵ They grope without light in the darkness; He makes them wander as if drunk.

כה יְמַשְׁשׁוּ־חֹשֶׁךְ וְלֹא־אוֹר וַיַּתְעֵם כַּשִּׁכּֽוֹר:

13 ¹ My eye has seen all this; My ear has heard and understood it.

יג א הֶן־כֹּל רָאֲתָה עֵינִי שָׁמְעָה אָזְנִי וַתָּבֶן לָֽהּ:

² What you know, I know also; I am not less than you.

ב כְּדַעְתְּכֶם יָדַעְתִּי גַם־אָנִי לֹא־נֹפֵל אָנֹכִי מִכֶּֽם:

³ Indeed, I would speak to the Almighty; I insist on arguing with *Hashem*.

ג אוּלָם אֲנִי אֶל־שַׁדַּי אֲדַבֵּר וְהוֹכֵחַ אֶל־אֵל אֶחְפָּֽץ:

⁴ But you invent lies; All of you are quacks.

ד וְֽאוּלָם אַתֶּם טֹפְלֵי־שָׁקֶר רֹפְאֵי אֱלִל כֻּלְּכֶֽם:

⁵ If you would only keep quiet It would be considered wisdom on your part.

ה מִי־יִתֵּן הַחֲרֵשׁ תַּחֲרִישׁוּן וּתְהִי לָכֶם לְחָכְמָֽה:

⁶ Hear now my arguments, Listen to my pleading.

ו שִׁמְעוּ־נָא תוֹכַחְתִּי וְרִבוֹת שְׂפָתַי הַקְשִֽׁיבוּ:

⁷ Will you speak unjustly on *Hashem*'s behalf? Will you speak deceitfully for Him?

ז הַלְאֵל תְּדַבְּרוּ עַוְלָה וְלוֹ תְּדַבְּרוּ רְמִיָּֽה:

⁸ Will you be partial toward Him? Will you plead *Hashem*'s cause?

ח הֲפָנָיו תִּשָּׂאוּן אִם־לָאֵל תְּרִיבֽוּן:

⁹ Will it go well when He examines you? Will you fool Him as one fools men?

ט הֲטוֹב כִּי־יַחְקֹר אֶתְכֶם אִם־כְּהָתֵל בֶּאֱנוֹשׁ תְּהָתֵלּוּ בֽוֹ:

¹⁰ He will surely reprove you If in your heart you are partial toward Him.

י הוֹכֵחַ יוֹכִיחַ אֶתְכֶם אִם־בַּסֵּתֶר פָּנִים תִּשָּׂאֽוּן:

¹¹ His threat will terrify you, And His fear will seize you.

יא הֲלֹא שְׂאֵתוֹ תְּבַעֵת אֶתְכֶם וּפַחְדּוֹ יִפֹּל עֲלֵיכֶֽם:

¹² Your briefs are empty platitudes; Your responses are unsubstantial.

יב זִכְרֹנֵיכֶם מִשְׁלֵי־אֵפֶר לְגַבֵּי־חֹמֶר גַּבֵּיכֶֽם:

¹³ Keep quiet; I will have my say, Come what may upon me.

יג הַחֲרִישׁוּ מִמֶּנִּי וַאֲדַבְּרָה־אָנִי וְיַעֲבֹר עָלַי מָֽה:

¹⁴ How long! I will take my flesh in my teeth; I will take my life in my hands.

יד עַל־מָה אֶשָּׂא בְשָׂרִי בְשִׁנָּי וְנַפְשִׁי אָשִׂים בְּכַפִּֽי:

¹⁵ He may well slay me; I may have no hope; Yet I will argue my case before Him.

טו הֵן יִקְטְלֵנִי לֹא [לוֹ] אֲיַחֵל אַךְ־דְּרָכַי אֶל־פָּנָיו אוֹכִֽיחַ:

words for exile and discovery, we see the great aspiration of the Jewish people to end their exile through the dis-covery of, and return to, their native homeland.

16 In this too is my salvation: That no impious man can come into His presence.

גַּם־הוּא־לִי לִישׁוּעָה כִּי־לֹא לְפָנָיו חָנֵף יָבוֹא:

gam hu LEE lee-shu-AH kee LO l'-fa-NAV kha-NAYF ya-VO

17 Listen closely to my words; Give ear to my discourse.

שִׁמְעוּ שָׁמוֹעַ מִלָּתִי וְאַחֲוָתִי בְּאָזְנֵיכֶם:

18 See now, I have prepared a case; I know that I will win it.

הִנֵּה־נָא עָרַכְתִּי מִשְׁפָּט יָדַעְתִּי כִּי־אֲנִי אֶצְדָּק:

19 For who is it that would challenge me? I should then keep silent and expire.

מִי־הוּא יָרִיב עִמָּדִי כִּי־עַתָּה אַחֲרִישׁ וְאֶגְוָע:

20 But two things do not do to me, So that I need not hide from You:

אַךְ־שְׁתַּיִם אַל־תַּעַשׂ עִמָּדִי אָז מִפָּנֶיךָ לֹא אֶסָּתֵר:

21 Remove Your hand from me, And let not Your terror frighten me.

כַּפְּךָ מֵעָלַי הַרְחַק וְאֵמָתְךָ אַל־תְּבַעֲתַנִּי:

22 Then summon me and I will respond, Or I will speak and You reply to me.

וּקְרָא וְאָנֹכִי אֶעֱנֶה אוֹ־אֲדַבֵּר וַהֲשִׁיבֵנִי:

23 How many are my iniquities and sins? Advise me of my transgression and sin.

כַּמָּה לִי עֲוֹנוֹת וְחַטָּאוֹת פִּשְׁעִי וְחַטָּאתִי הֹדִיעֵנִי:

24 Why do You hide Your face, And treat me like an enemy?

לָמָּה־פָנֶיךָ תַסְתִּיר וְתַחְשְׁבֵנִי לְאוֹיֵב לָךְ:

25 Will You harass a driven leaf, Will You pursue dried-up straw,

הֶעָלֶה נִדָּף תַּעֲרוֹץ וְאֶת־קַשׁ יָבֵשׁ תִּרְדֹּף:

26 That You decree for me bitter things And make me answer for the iniquities of my youth,

כִּי־תִכְתֹּב עָלַי מְרֹרוֹת וְתוֹרִישֵׁנִי עֲוֹנוֹת נְעוּרָי:

27 That You put my feet in the stocks And watch all my ways, Hemming in my footsteps?

וְתָשֵׂם בַּסַּד רַגְלַי וְתִשְׁמוֹר כָּל־אָרְחוֹתָי עַל־שָׁרְשֵׁי רַגְלַי תִּתְחַקֶּה:

28 Man wastes away like a rotten thing, Like a garment eaten by moths.

וְהוּא כְּרָקָב יִבְלֶה כְּבֶגֶד אֲכָלוֹ עָשׁ:

14 1 Man born of woman is short-lived and sated with trouble.

יד א אָדָם יְלוּד אִשָּׁה קְצַר יָמִים וּשְׂבַע־רֹגֶז:

2 He blossoms like a flower and withers; He vanishes like a shadow and does not endure.

ב כְּצִיץ יָצָא וַיִּמָּל וַיִּבְרַח כַּצֵּל וְלֹא יַעֲמוֹד:

Rabbi Joseph
B. Soloveitchik
(1903–1993)

13:16 That no impious man can come into His presence *Iyov* rebukes those who come to comfort him by telling them that although he challenges *Hashem*'s justice and they do not, he is still more righteous than they are. He, at least, approaches God honestly, not hypocritically. Rabbi Joseph B. Soloveitchik explains that it was the prophet *Yirmiyahu* who set the precedent for challenging *Hashem* in difficult times.

In *Megillat Eicha*, instead of merely accepting what has happened, *Yirmiyahu* demands of God an explanation for the ruin of *Yerushalayim* and the devastation of the Land of Israel. While it is permissible to question *Hashem*, this must be coupled with the firm belief that although we might not understand His ways, they are ultimately for the good.

Job

³ Do You fix Your gaze on such a one? Will You go to law with me?

ג אַף־עַל־זֶה פָּקַחְתָּ עֵינֶךָ וְאֹתִי תָבִיא בְמִשְׁפָּט עִמָּךְ:

⁴ Who can produce a clean thing out of an unclean one? No one!

ד מִי־יִתֵּן טָהוֹר מִטָּמֵא לֹא אֶחָד:

⁵ His days are determined; You know the number of his months; You have set him limits that he cannot pass.

ה אִם חֲרוּצִים יָמָיו מִסְפַּר־חֳדָשָׁיו אִתָּךְ חֻקּוֹ [חֻקָּיו] עָשִׂיתָ וְלֹא יַעֲבוֹר:

⁶ Turn away from him, that he may be at ease Until, like a hireling, he finishes out his day.

ו שְׁעֵה מֵעָלָיו וְיֶחְדָּל עַד־יִרְצֶה כְּשָׂכִיר יוֹמוֹ:

⁷ There is hope for a tree; If it is cut down it will renew itself; Its shoots will not cease.

ז כִּי יֵשׁ לָעֵץ תִּקְוָה אִם־יִכָּרֵת וְעוֹד יַחֲלִיף וְיֹנַקְתּוֹ לֹא תֶחְדָּל:

KEE YAYSH la-AYTZ tik-VAH im yi-ka-RAYT v'-OD
ya-kha-LEEF v'-yo-nak-TO LO tekh-DAL

⁸ If its roots are old in the earth, And its stump dies in the ground,

ח אִם־יַזְקִין בָּאָרֶץ שָׁרְשׁוֹ וּבֶעָפָר יָמוּת גִּזְעוֹ:

⁹ At the scent of water it will bud And produce branches like a sapling.

ט מֵרֵיחַ מַיִם יַפְרִחַ וְעָשָׂה קָצִיר כְּמוֹ־נָטַע:

¹⁰ But mortals languish and die; Man expires; where is he?

י וְגֶבֶר יָמוּת וַיֶּחֱלָשׁ וַיִּגְוַע אָדָם וְאַיּוֹ:

¹¹ The waters of the sea fail, And the river dries up and is parched.

יא אָזְלוּ־מַיִם מִנִּי־יָם וְנָהָר יֶחֱרַב וְיָבֵשׁ:

¹² So man lies down never to rise; He will awake only when the heavens are no more, Only then be aroused from his sleep.

יב וְאִישׁ שָׁכַב וְלֹא־יָקוּם עַד־בִּלְתִּי שָׁמַיִם לֹא יָקִיצוּ וְלֹא־יֵעֹרוּ מִשְּׁנָתָם:

¹³ O that You would hide me in Sheol, Conceal me until Your anger passes, Set me a fixed time to attend to me.

יג מִי יִתֵּן בִּשְׁאוֹל תַּצְפִּנֵנִי תַּסְתִּירֵנִי עַד־שׁוּב אַפֶּךָ תָּשִׁית לִי חֹק וְתִזְכְּרֵנִי:

¹⁴ If a man dies, can he live again? All the time of my service I wait Until my replacement comes.

יד אִם־יָמוּת גֶּבֶר הֲיִחְיֶה כָּל־יְמֵי צְבָאִי אֲיַחֵל עַד־בּוֹא חֲלִיפָתִי:

¹⁵ You would call and I would answer You; You would set Your heart on Your handiwork.

טו תִּקְרָא וְאָנֹכִי אֶעֱנֶךָּ לְמַעֲשֵׂה יָדֶיךָ תִכְסֹף:

¹⁶ Then You would not count my steps, Or keep watch over my sin.

טז כִּי־עַתָּה צְעָדַי תִּסְפּוֹר לֹא־תִשְׁמוֹר עַל־חַטָּאתִי:

14:7 There is hope for a tree *Iyov* contrasts the passing of man to the death of a tree. Once a man has departed from this world, he cannot be brought back to life. A tree, on the other hand, though seemingly lifeless, can be revived. Similarly, *Yeshayahu* writes (6:13) that though a tree appears dead after it sheds its leaves, the trunk remains, and from there, the tree will flower again in the spring. *Yeshayahu* compares the Children of Israel to a tree. Though at times it appears that they have been annihilated and will cease to exist, a holy remnant always remains, from which they will grow anew and flourish.

An old olive tree in *Yerushalayim*

¹⁷ My transgression would be sealed up in a pouch; You would coat over my iniquity.

חָתֻם בִּצְרוֹר פִּשְׁעִי וַתִּטְפֹּל עַל־עֲוֺנִי:

¹⁸ Mountains collapse and crumble; Rocks are dislodged from their place.

וְאוּלָם הַר־נוֹפֵל יִבּוֹל וְצוּר יֶעְתַּק מִמְּקֹמוֹ:

¹⁹ Water wears away stone; Torrents wash away earth; So you destroy man's hope,

אֲבָנִים שָׁחֲקוּ מַיִם תִּשְׁטֹף־סְפִיחֶיהָ עֲפַר־אָרֶץ וְתִקְוַת אֱנוֹשׁ הֶאֱבַדְתָּ:

²⁰ You overpower him forever and he perishes; You alter his visage and dispatch him.

תִּתְקְפֵהוּ לָנֶצַח וַיַּהֲלֹךְ מְשַׁנֶּה פָנָיו וַתְּשַׁלְּחֵהוּ:

²¹ His sons attain honor and he does not know it; They are humbled and he is not aware of it.

יִכְבְּדוּ בָנָיו וְלֹא יֵדָע וְיִצְעֲרוּ וְלֹא־יָבִין לָמוֹ:

²² He feels only the pain of his flesh, And his spirit mourns in him.

אַךְ־בְּשָׂרוֹ עָלָיו יִכְאָב וְנַפְשׁוֹ עָלָיו תֶּאֱבָל:

15 ¹ Eliphaz the Temanite said in reply:

וַיַּעַן אֱלִיפַז הַתֵּימָנִי וַיֹּאמַר: א **טו**

² Does a wise man answer with windy opinions, And fill his belly with the east wind?

הֶחָכָם יַעֲנֶה דַעַת־רוּחַ וִימַלֵּא קָדִים בִּטְנוֹ:

³ Should he argue with useless talk, With words that are of no worth?

הוֹכֵחַ בְּדָבָר לֹא יִסְכּוֹן וּמִלִּים לֹא־יוֹעִיל בָּם:

⁴ You subvert piety And restrain prayer to *Hashem*.

אַף־אַתָּה תָּפֵר יִרְאָה וְתִגְרַע שִׂיחָה לִפְנֵי־אֵל:

af a-TAH ta-FAYR yir-AH v'-tig-RA see-KHAH lif-nay AYL

⁵ Your sinfulness dictates your speech, So you choose crafty language.

כִּי יְאַלֵּף עֲוֺנְךָ פִּיךָ וְתִבְחַר לְשׁוֹן עֲרוּמִים:

⁶ Your own mouth condemns you – not I; Your lips testify against you.

יַרְשִׁיעֲךָ פִיךָ וְלֹא־אָנִי וּשְׂפָתֶיךָ יַעֲנוּ־בָךְ:

⁷ Were you the first man born? Were you created before the hills?

הֲרִאישׁוֹן אָדָם תִּוָּלֵד וְלִפְנֵי גְבָעוֹת חוֹלָלְתָּ:

⁸ Have you listened in on the council of *Hashem*? Have you sole possession of wisdom?

הַבְסוֹד אֱלוֹהַּ תִּשְׁמָע וְתִגְרַע אֵלֶיךָ חָכְמָה:

⁹ What do you know that we do not know, Or understand that we do not?

מַה־יָּדַעְתָּ וְלֹא נֵדָע תָּבִין וְלֹא־עִמָּנוּ הוּא:

¹⁰ Among us are gray-haired old men, Older by far than your father.

גַּם־שָׂב גַּם־יָשִׁישׁ בָּנוּ כַּבִּיר מֵאָבִיךָ יָמִים:

  15:4 You subvert piety *Yirah* (יראה), translated here as 'piety,' literally means 'fear' or 'awe.' Eliphaz tells *Iyov* that he has dispensed with fear of *Hashem*, and, in so doing, has also abandoned wisdom, as implied in verse 2. The link between these two concepts can be seen in *Sefer Mishlei* (1:7): "The fear of *Hashem* is the beginning of knowledge." Without awe of God, knowledge is empty and can be twisted for any number of negative purposes. However, knowledge rooted in fear of *Hashem* leads to scrupulous attention to His word, for which one is rewarded in both this world and the world to come.

A father teaching his son the prayers at the Western Wall

¹¹ Are *Hashem*'s consolations not enough for you, And His gentle words to you?

¹² How your heart has carried you away, How your eyes have failed you,

¹³ That you could vent your anger on *Hashem*, And let such words out of your mouth!

¹⁴ What is man that he can be cleared of guilt, One born of woman, that he be in the right?

¹⁵ He puts no trust in His holy ones; The heavens are not guiltless in His sight;

¹⁶ What then of one loathsome and foul, Man, who drinks wrongdoing like water!

¹⁷ I will hold forth; listen to me; What I have seen, I will declare –

¹⁸ That which wise men have transmitted from their fathers, And have not withheld,

¹⁹ To whom alone the land was given, No stranger passing among them:

²⁰ The wicked man writhes in torment all his days; Few years are reserved for the ruthless.

²¹ Frightening sounds fill his ears; When he is at ease a robber falls upon him.

²² He is never sure he will come back from the dark; A sword stares him in the face.

²³ He wanders about for bread – where is it? He knows that the day of darkness has been readied for him.

²⁴ Troubles terrify him, anxiety overpowers him, Like a king expecting a siege.

²⁵ For he has raised his arm against *Hashem* And played the hero against the Almighty.

²⁶ He runs at Him defiantly With his thickly bossed shield.

²⁷ His face is covered with fat And his loins with blubber.

²⁸ He dwells in cities doomed to ruin, In houses that shall not be lived in, That are destined to become heaps of rubble.

²⁹ He will not be rich; His wealth will not endure; His produce shall not bend to the earth.

יא הַמְעַט מִמְּךָ תַּנְחֻמוֹת אֵל וְדָבָר לָאַט עִמָּךְ:

יב מַה־יִּקָּחֲךָ לִבֶּךָ וּמַה־יִּרְזְמוּן עֵינֶיךָ:

יג כִּי־תָשִׁיב אֶל־אֵל רוּחֶךָ וְהֹצֵאתָ מִפִּיךָ מִלִּין:

יד מָה־אֱנוֹשׁ כִּי־יִזְכֶּה וְכִי־יִצְדַּק יְלוּד אִשָּׁה:

טו הֵן בקדשו [בִּקְדֹשָׁיו] לֹא יַאֲמִין וְשָׁמַיִם לֹא־זַכּוּ בְעֵינָיו:

טז אַף כִּי־נִתְעָב וְנֶאֱלָח אִישׁ־שֹׁתֶה כַמַּיִם עַוְלָה:

יז אֲחַוְךָ שְׁמַע־לִי וְזֶה־חָזִיתִי וַאֲסַפֵּרָה:

יח אֲשֶׁר־חֲכָמִים יַגִּידוּ וְלֹא כִחֲדוּ מֵאֲבוֹתָם:

יט לָהֶם לְבַדָּם נִתְּנָה הָאָרֶץ וְלֹא־עָבַר זָר בְּתוֹכָם:

כ כָּל־יְמֵי רָשָׁע הוּא מִתְחוֹלֵל וּמִסְפַּר שָׁנִים נִצְפְּנוּ לֶעָרִיץ:

כא קוֹל־פְּחָדִים בְּאָזְנָיו בַּשָּׁלוֹם שׁוֹדֵד יְבוֹאֶנּוּ:

כב לֹא־יַאֲמִין שׁוּב מִנִּי־חֹשֶׁךְ וצפו [וְצָפוּי] הוּא אֱלֵי־חָרֶב:

כג נֹדֵד הוּא לַלֶּחֶם אַיֵּה יָדַע כִּי־נָכוֹן בְּיָדוֹ יוֹם־חֹשֶׁךְ:

כד יְבַעֲתֻהוּ צַר וּמְצוּקָה תִּתְקְפֵהוּ כְּמֶלֶךְ עָתִיד לַכִּידוֹר:

כה כִּי־נָטָה אֶל־אֵל יָדוֹ וְאֶל־שַׁדַּי יִתְגַּבָּר:

כו יָרוּץ אֵלָיו בְּצַוָּאר בַּעֲבִי גַּבֵּי מָגִנָּיו:

כז כִּי־כִסָּה פָנָיו בְּחֶלְבּוֹ וַיַּעַשׂ פִּימָה עֲלֵי־כָסֶל:

כח וַיִּשְׁכּוֹן עָרִים נִכְחָדוֹת בָּתִּים לֹא־יֵשְׁבוּ לָמוֹ אֲשֶׁר הִתְעַתְּדוּ לְגַלִּים:

כט לֹא־יֶעְשַׁר וְלֹא־יָקוּם חֵילוֹ וְלֹא־יִטֶּה לָאָרֶץ מִנְלָם:

30 He will never get away from the darkness; Flames will sear his shoots; He will pass away by the breath of His mouth.

ל לֹא־יָסוּר מִנִּי־חֹשֶׁךְ יֹנַקְתּוֹ תְּיַבֵּשׁ שַׁלְהָבֶת וְיָסוּר בְּרוּחַ פִּיו:

31 He will not be trusted; He will be misled by falsehood, And falsehood will be his recompense.

לא אַל־יַאֲמֵן בשו [בַּשָּׁיו] נִתְעָה כִּי־שָׁוְא תִּהְיֶה תְמוּרָתוֹ:

32 He will wither before his time, His boughs never having flourished.

לב בְּלֹא־יוֹמוֹ תִּמָּלֵא וְכִפָּתוֹ לֹא רַעֲנָנָה:

33 He will drop his unripe grapes like a vine; He will shed his blossoms like an olive tree.

לג יַחְמֹס כַּגֶּפֶן בִּסְרוֹ וְיַשְׁלֵךְ כַּזַּיִת נִצָּתוֹ:

34 For the company of the impious is desolate; Fire consumes the tents of the briber;

לד כִּי־עֲדַת חָנֵף גַּלְמוּד וְאֵשׁ אָכְלָה אָהֳלֵי־שֹׁחַד:

35 For they have conceived mischief, given birth to evil, And their womb has produced deceit.

לה הָרֹה עָמָל וְיָלֹד אָוֶן וּבִטְנָם תָּכִין מִרְמָה:

16 ¹ *Iyov* said in reply:

טז א וַיַּעַן אִיּוֹב וַיֹּאמַר:

2 I have often heard such things; You are all mischievous comforters.

ב שָׁמַעְתִּי כְאֵלֶּה רַבּוֹת מְנַחֲמֵי עָמָל כֻּלְּכֶם:

3 Have windy words no limit? What afflicts you that you speak on?

ג הֲקֵץ לְדִבְרֵי־רוּחַ אוֹ מַה־יַּמְרִיצְךָ כִּי תַעֲנֶה:

4 I would also talk like you If you were in my place; I would barrage you with words, I would wag my head over you.

ד גַּם אָנֹכִי כָּכֶם אֲדַבֵּרָה לוּ־יֵשׁ נַפְשְׁכֶם תַּחַת נַפְשִׁי אַחְבִּירָה עֲלֵיכֶם בְּמִלִּים וְאָנִיעָה עֲלֵיכֶם בְּמוֹ רֹאשִׁי:

5 I would encourage you with words, My moving lips would bring relief.

ה אֲאַמִּצְכֶם בְּמוֹ־פִי וְנִיד שְׂפָתַי יַחְשֹׂךְ:

6 If I speak, my pain will not be relieved, And if I do not – what have I lost?

ו אִם־אֲדַבְּרָה לֹא־יֵחָשֵׂךְ כְּאֵבִי וְאַחְדְּלָה מַה־מִנִּי יַהֲלֹךְ:

7 Now He has truly worn me out; You have destroyed my whole community.

ז אַךְ־עַתָּה הֶלְאָנִי הֲשִׁמּוֹתָ כָּל־עֲדָתִי:

8 You have shriveled me; My gauntness serves as a witness, And testifies against me.

ח וַתִּקְמְטֵנִי לְעֵד הָיָה וַיָּקָם בִּי כַחֲשִׁי בְּפָנַי יַעֲנֶה:

9 In His anger He tears and persecutes me; He gnashes His teeth at me; My foe stabs me with his eyes.

ט אַפּוֹ טָרַף וַיִּשְׂטְמֵנִי חָרַק עָלַי בְּשִׁנָּיו צָרִי יִלְטוֹשׁ עֵינָיו לִי:

10 They open wide their mouths at me; Reviling me, they strike my cheeks; They inflame themselves against me.

י פָּעֲרוּ עָלַי בְּפִיהֶם בְּחֶרְפָּה הִכּוּ לְחָיָי יַחַד עָלַי יִתְמַלָּאוּן:

11 *Hashem* hands me over to an evil man, Thrusts me into the clutches of the wicked.

יא יַסְגִּירֵנִי אֵל אֶל עֲוִיל וְעַל־יְדֵי רְשָׁעִים יִרְטֵנִי:

12 I had been untroubled, and He broke me in pieces; He took me by the scruff and shattered me; He set me up as His target;

יב שָׁלֵו הָיִיתִי וַיְפַרְפְּרֵנִי וְאָחַז בְּעָרְפִּי וַיְפַצְפְּצֵנִי וַיְקִימֵנִי לוֹ לְמַטָּרָה:

13 His bowmen surrounded me; He pierced my kidneys; He showed no mercy; He spilled my bile onto the ground.

יג יָסֹבּוּ עָלַי ׀ רַבָּיו יְפַלַּח כִּלְיוֹתַי וְלֹא יַחְמוֹל יִשְׁפֹּךְ לָאָרֶץ מְרֵרָתִי:

14 He breached me, breach after breach; He rushed at me like a warrior.

יד יִפְרְצֵנִי פֶרֶץ עַל־פְּנֵי־פָרֶץ יָרֻץ עָלַי כְּגִבּוֹר:

15 I sewed sackcloth over my skin; I buried my glory in the dust.

טו שַׂק תָּפַרְתִּי עֲלֵי גִלְדִּי וְעֹלַלְתִּי בֶעָפָר קַרְנִי:

16 My face is red with weeping; Darkness covers my eyes

טז פָּנַי חֳמַרְמְרָה [חֳמַרְמְרוּ] מִנִּי־בֶכִי וְעַל עַפְעַפַּי צַלְמָוֶת:

17 For no injustice on my part And for the purity of my prayer!

יז עַל לֹא־חָמָס בְּכַפָּי וּתְפִלָּתִי זַכָּה:

18 Earth, do not cover my blood; Let there be no resting place for my outcry!

יח אֶרֶץ אַל־תְּכַסִּי דָמִי וְאַל־יְהִי מָקוֹם לְזַעֲקָתִי:

E-retz al t'-kha-SEE da-MEE v'-AL y'-HEE ma-KOM l'-za-a-ka-TEE

19 Surely now my witness is in heaven; He who can testify for me is on high.

יט גַּם־עַתָּה הִנֵּה־בַשָּׁמַיִם עֵדִי וְשָׂהֲדִי בַּמְּרוֹמִים:

20 O my advocates, my fellows, Before *Hashem* my eyes shed tears;

כ מְלִיצַי רֵעָי אֶל־אֱלוֹהַּ דָּלְפָה עֵינִי:

21 Let Him arbitrate between a man and *Hashem* As between a man and his fellow.

כא וְיוֹכַח לְגֶבֶר עִם־אֱלוֹהַּ וּבֶן־אָדָם לְרֵעֵהוּ:

22 For a few more years will pass, And I shall go the way of no return.

כב כִּי־שְׁנוֹת מִסְפָּר יֶאֱתָיוּ וְאֹרַח לֹא־אָשׁוּב אֶהֱלֹךְ:

17 1 My spirit is crushed, my days run out; The graveyard waits for me.

יז א רוּחִי חֻבָּלָה יָמַי נִזְעָכוּ קְבָרִים לִי:

2 Surely mocking men keep me company, And with their provocations I close my eyes.

ב אִם־לֹא הֲתֻלִים עִמָּדִי וּבְהַמְּרוֹתָם תָּלַן עֵינִי:

3 Come now, stand surety for me! Who will give his hand on my behalf?

ג שִׂימָה־נָּא עָרְבֵנִי עִמָּךְ מִי הוּא לְיָדִי יִתָּקֵעַ:

4 You have hidden understanding from their minds; Therefore You must not exalt [them].

ד כִּי־לִבָּם צָפַנְתָּ מִּשָּׂכֶל עַל־כֵּן לֹא תְרֹמֵם:

16:18 Earth, do not cover my blood By asking the earth not to cover up his blood, *Iyov* invokes the murder of Abel by Cain in response to which the ground "opened its mouth to receive… [Abel's] blood" (Genesis 4:11). The commentators wonder what argument led to the first murder in history, in which a person killed his own brother. According to Rabbi Yehuda Halevi, they were fighting over the Land of Israel. In his words, "They desired to know which of them would be *Adam*'s successor, and heir to his essence and intrinsic perfection, to inherit the land, and to stand in connection with the divine influence, while the other would be a nonentity." From the beginning of time, *Eretz Yisrael* has been the object of desire and the source of conflict among those who wish to inherit it. However, *Hashem* states explicitly in the Bible that He gave it to *Avraham* to pass on to the Children of Israel as their eternal inheritance (see, e.g., Genesis 13:15).

Child planting an Israeli flag on the beach in Haifa

⁵ He informs on his friends for a share [of their property], And his children's eyes pine away.	ה לְחֵלֶק יַגִּיד רֵעִים וְעֵינֵי בָנָיו תִּכְלֶנָה:
⁶ He made me a byword among people; I have become like Tophet of old.	ו וְהִצִּגַנִי לִמְשֹׁל עַמִּים וְתֹפֶת לְפָנִים אֶהְיֶה:
⁷ My eyes fail from vexation; All shapes seem to me like shadows.	ז וַתֵּכַהּ מִכַּעַשׂ עֵינִי וִיצֻרַי כַּצֵּל כֻּלָּם:
⁸ The upright are amazed at this; The pure are aroused against the impious.	ח יָשֹׁמּוּ יְשָׁרִים עַל־זֹאת וְנָקִי עַל־חָנֵף יִתְעֹרָר:
⁹ The righteous man holds to his way; He whose hands are clean grows stronger.	ט וְיֹאחֵז צַדִּיק דַּרְכּוֹ וּטֳהָר־יָדַיִם יֹסִיף אֹמֶץ:
¹⁰ But all of you, come back now; I shall not find a wise man among you.	י וְאוּלָם כֻּלָּם תָּשֻׁבוּ וּבֹאוּ נָא וְלֹא־אֶמְצָא בָכֶם חָכָם:
¹¹ My days are done, my tendons severed, The strings of my heart. *ya-MAI a-v'-RU zi-mo-TAI ni-t'-KU mo-ra-SHAY l'-va-VEE*	יא יָמַי עָבְרוּ זִמֹּתַי נִתְּקוּ מוֹרָשֵׁי לְבָבִי:
¹² They say that night is day, That light is here – in the face of darkness.	יב לַיְלָה לְיוֹם יָשִׂימוּ אוֹר קָרוֹב מִפְּנֵי־חֹשֶׁךְ:
¹³ If I must look forward to Sheol as my home, And make my bed in the dark place,	יג אִם־אֲקַוֶּה שְׁאוֹל בֵּיתִי בַּחֹשֶׁךְ רִפַּדְתִּי יְצוּעָי:
¹⁴ Say to the Pit, "You are my father," To the maggots, "Mother," "Sister" –	יד לַשַּׁחַת קָרָאתִי אָבִי אַתָּה אִמִּי וַאֲחֹתִי לָרִמָּה:
¹⁵ Where, then, is my hope? Who can see hope for me?	טו וְאַיֵּה אֵפוֹ תִקְוָתִי וְתִקְוָתִי מִי יְשׁוּרֶנָּה:
¹⁶ Will it descend to Sheol? Shall we go down together to the dust?	טז בַּדֵּי שְׁאֹל תֵּרַדְנָה אִם־יַחַד עַל־עָפָר נָחַת:
18 ¹ Then Bildad the Shuhite said in reply:	יח א וַיַּעַן בִּלְדַּד הַשֻּׁחִי וַיֹּאמַר:
² How long? Put an end to talk! Consider, and then we shall speak.	ב עַד־אָנָה תְּשִׂימוּן קִנְצֵי לְמִלִּין תָּבִינוּ וְאַחַר נְדַבֵּר:

Rabbi Abraham
Isaac Kook
(1865–1935)

17:11 My tendons severed *Iyov* begins to feel distanced from God, and to believe that he can no longer communicate meaningfully with Him. *Iyov* can no longer beg *Hashem* to give him succor and end his suffering, and therefore feels he is close to death. Similarly, the Sages (*Berachot* 32b) state that from the time of the destruction of the *Beit Hamikdash*, an iron wall separates mankind from their Father in Heaven. Rabbi Abraham Isaac Kook explains the symbolism of this image: Iron is symbolic of death and destruction, as it is a material used to make instruments of war and execution. Conversely, the goal of the *Beit Hamikdash* was to prolong life and to promote peace in the world. With the destruction of the Temple, its influence in the world was replaced by the influence of iron. Rabbi Kook concludes that only when justice and integrity will be restored will the iron wall come down, and then the *Beit Hamikdash* will resume its place as the center of prayer and inspiration for the entire world.

³ Why are we thought of as brutes, Regarded by you as stupid?

ג מַדּוּעַ נֶחְשַׁבְנוּ כַבְּהֵמָה נִטְמִינוּ בְּעֵינֵיכֶם:

⁴ You who tear yourself to pieces in anger – Will earth's order be disrupted for your sake? Will rocks be dislodged from their place?

ד טֹרֵף נַפְשׁוֹ בְּאַפּוֹ הֲלְמַעַנְךָ תֵּעָזַב אָרֶץ וְיֶעְתַּק־צוּר מִמְּקֹמוֹ:

⁵ Indeed, the light of the wicked fails; The flame of his fire does not shine.

ה גַּם אוֹר רְשָׁעִים יִדְעָךְ וְלֹא־יִגַּהּ שְׁבִיב אִשּׁוֹ:

⁶ The light in his tent darkens; His lamp fails him.

ו אוֹר חָשַׁךְ בְּאָהֳלוֹ וְנֵרוֹ עָלָיו יִדְעָךְ:

⁷ His iniquitous strides are hobbled; His schemes overthrow him.

ז יֵצְרוּ צַעֲדֵי אוֹנוֹ וְתַשְׁלִיכֵהוּ עֲצָתוֹ:

⁸ He is led by his feet into the net; He walks onto the toils.

ח כִּי־שֻׁלַּח בְּרֶשֶׁת בְּרַגְלָיו וְעַל־שְׂבָכָה יִתְהַלָּךְ:

⁹ The trap seizes his heel; The noose tightens on him.

ט יֹאחֵז בְּעָקֵב פָּח יַחֲזֵק עָלָיו צַמִּים:

¹⁰ The rope for him lies hidden on the ground; His snare, on the path.

י טָמוּן בָּאָרֶץ חַבְלוֹ וּמַלְכֻּדְתּוֹ עֲלֵי נָתִיב:

¹¹ Terrors assault him on all sides And send his feet flying.

יא סָבִיב בִּעֲתֻהוּ בַלָּהוֹת וֶהֱפִיצֻהוּ לְרַגְלָיו:

¹² His progeny hunger; Disaster awaits his wife.

יב יְהִי־רָעֵב אֹנוֹ וְאֵיד נָכוֹן לְצַלְעוֹ:

¹³ The tendons under his skin are consumed; Death's first-born consumes his tendons.

יג יֹאכַל בַּדֵּי עוֹרוֹ יֹאכַל בַּדָּיו בְּכוֹר מָוֶת:

¹⁴ He is torn from the safety of his tent; Terror marches him to the king.

יד יִנָּתֵק מֵאָהֳלוֹ מִבְטַחוֹ וְתַצְעִדֵהוּ לְמֶלֶךְ בַּלָּהוֹת:

¹⁵ It lodges in his desolate tent; Sulfur is strewn upon his home.

טו תִּשְׁכּוֹן בְּאָהֳלוֹ מִבְּלִי־לוֹ יְזֹרֶה עַל־נָוֵהוּ גָפְרִית:

¹⁶ His roots below dry up, And above, his branches wither.

טז מִתַּחַת שָׁרָשָׁיו יִבָשׁוּ וּמִמַּעַל יִמַּל קְצִירוֹ:

¹⁷ All mention of him vanishes from the earth; He has no name abroad.

יז זִכְרוֹ־אָבַד מִנִּי־אָרֶץ וְלֹא־שֵׁם לוֹ עַל־פְּנֵי־חוּץ:

¹⁸ He is thrust from light to darkness, Driven from the world.

יח יֶהְדְּפֻהוּ מֵאוֹר אֶל־חֹשֶׁךְ וּמִתֵּבֵל יְנִדֻּהוּ:

¹⁹ He has no seed or breed among his people, No survivor where he once lived.

יט לֹא נִין לוֹ וְלֹא־נֶכֶד בְּעַמּוֹ וְאֵין שָׂרִיד בִּמְגוּרָיו:

²⁰ Generations to come will be appalled at his fate, As the previous ones are seized with horror.

כ עַל־יוֹמוֹ נָשַׁמּוּ אַחֲרֹנִים וְקַדְמֹנִים אָחֲזוּ שָׂעַר:

al YO-mo na-SHA-mu a-kha-ro-NEEM v'-kad-mo-NEEM A-kha-zu SA-ar

---

18:20 Generations to come will be appalled at his fate In this chapter, *Bildad* describes the pain and misery that he believes *Iyov* must endure because he has sinned. He assumes that since *Iyov* is suffering, he must be evil, and will therefore meet the fate of an evildoer, especially since he refuses to acknowledge his sins and repent. *Bildad* declares that the devastation will be so overwhelming that "Generations to come will be appalled at his fate." The idea

²¹ "These were the haunts of the wicked; Here was the place of him who knew not *Hashem*."

כא אַךְ־אֵלֶּה מִשְׁכְּנוֹת עַוָּל וְזֶה מְקוֹם לֹא־יָדַע־אֵל:

19 ¹ *Iyov* said in reply:

יט א וַיַּעַן אִיּוֹב וַיֹּאמַר:

² How long will you grieve my spirit, And crush me with words?

ב עַד־אָנָה תּוֹגְיוּן נַפְשִׁי וּתְדַכְּאוּנַנִי בְמִלִּים:

³ Time and again you humiliate me, And are not ashamed to abuse me.

ג זֶה עֶשֶׂר פְּעָמִים תַּכְלִימוּנִי לֹא־תֵבֹשׁוּ תַּהְכְּרוּ־לִי:

⁴ If indeed I have erred, My error remains with me.

ד וְאַף־אָמְנָם שָׁגִיתִי אִתִּי תָּלִין מְשׁוּגָתִי:

⁵ Though you are overbearing toward me, Reproaching me with my disgrace,

ה אִם־אָמְנָם עָלַי תַּגְדִּילוּ וְתוֹכִיחוּ עָלַי חֶרְפָּתִי:

⁶ Yet know that *Hashem* has wronged me; He has thrown up siege works around me.

ו דְּעוּ־אֵפוֹ כִּי־אֱלוֹהַּ עִוְּתָנִי וּמְצוּדוֹ עָלַי הִקִּיף:

⁷ I cry, "Violence!" but am not answered; I shout, but can get no justice.

ז הֵן אֶצְעַק חָמָס וְלֹא אֵעָנֶה אֲשַׁוַּע וְאֵין מִשְׁפָּט:

HAYN etz-AK kha-MAS v'-LO ay-a-NEH a-sha-VA v'-AYN mish-PAT

⁸ He has barred my way; I cannot pass; He has laid darkness upon my path.

ח אָרְחִי גָדַר וְלֹא אֶעֱבוֹר וְעַל נְתִיבוֹתַי חֹשֶׁךְ יָשִׂים:

⁹ He has stripped me of my glory, Removed the crown from my head.

ט כְּבוֹדִי מֵעָלַי הִפְשִׁיט וַיָּסַר עֲטֶרֶת רֹאשִׁי:

¹⁰ He tears down every part of me; I perish; He uproots my hope like a tree.

י יִתְּצֵנִי סָבִיב וָאֵלַךְ וַיַּסַּע כָּעֵץ תִּקְוָתִי:

¹¹ He kindles His anger against me; He regards me as one of His foes.

יא וַיַּחַר עָלַי אַפּוֹ וַיַּחְשְׁבֵנִי לוֹ כְצָרָיו:

¹² His troops advance together; They build their road toward me And encamp around my tent.

יב יַחַד יָבֹאוּ גְדוּדָיו וַיָּסֹלּוּ עָלַי דַּרְכָּם וַיַּחֲנוּ סָבִיב לְאָהֳלִי:

of future generations being astonished implies complete ruin and devastation. Similarly, in response to the sins of the People of Israel, the *Torah* writes: "The children who succeed you, and foreigners who come from distant lands" will all be surprised by the complete ruin of the Land of Israel after its destruction (Deuteronomy 29:21). This, too, was caused by a lack of diligence in performing God's commands, and its reversal requires complete adherence to the word of *Hashem*.

חמס

Renewal of the land: Mezar waterfall in the Golan Heights

19:7 I cry, "Violence!" The word *chamas* (חמס), 'violence,' appears a number of times in the Bible. It is used as a general term for violence, and in particular is also used as a term for robbery. The Bible tells us that it was *chamas* that almost led to the destruction of the city of Nineveh in the time of *Yona* (Jonah 3:8), and that *Hashem* brought the flood in the time of *Noach* because of *chamas* (Genesis 6:11). In fact, it was the *chamas* of the generation of the flood that sealed their fate, even though they were also guilty of sexual immorality and idolatry. Rabbi Samson Raphael Hirsch explains that this is because *chamas* refers to petty injustice and underhanded dealings which are not punishable in court. This is even worse than overt sin and immorality, as it corrodes the entire social framework of society.

¹³ He alienated my kin from me; My acquaintances disown me.

¹⁴ My relatives are gone; My friends have forgotten me.

¹⁵ My dependents and maidservants regard me as a stranger; I am an outsider to them.

¹⁶ I summon my servant but he does not respond; I must myself entreat him.

¹⁷ My odor is repulsive to my wife; I am loathsome to my children.

¹⁸ Even youngsters disdain me; When I rise, they speak against me.

¹⁹ All my bosom friends detest me; Those I love have turned against me.

²⁰ My bones stick to my skin and flesh; I escape with the skin of my teeth.

²¹ Pity me, pity me! You are my friends; For the hand of *Hashem* has struck me!

²² Why do you pursue me like *Hashem*, Maligning me insatiably?

²³ O that my words were written down; Would they were inscribed in a record,

²⁴ Incised on a rock forever With iron stylus and lead!

²⁵ But I know that my Vindicator lives; In the end He will testify on earth –

²⁶ This, after my skin will have been peeled off. But I would behold *Hashem* while still in my flesh,

²⁷ I myself, not another, would behold Him; Would see with my own eyes: My heart pines within me.

²⁸ You say, "How do we persecute him? The root of the matter is in him."

²⁹ Be in fear of the sword, For [your] fury is iniquity worthy of the sword; Know there is a judgment!

20 ¹ Zophar the Naamathite said in reply:

² In truth, my thoughts urge me to answer (It is because of my feelings

³ When I hear reproof that insults me); A spirit out of my understanding makes me reply:

יג אֶחַי מֵעָלַי הִרְחִיק וְיֹדְעַי אַךְ־זָרוּ מִמֶּנִּי:

יד חָדְלוּ קְרוֹבָי וּמְיֻדָּעַי שְׁכֵחוּנִי:

טו גָּרֵי בֵיתִי וְאַמְהֹתַי לְזָר תַּחְשְׁבֻנִי נׇכְרִי הָיִיתִי בְעֵינֵיהֶם:

טז לְעַבְדִּי קָרָאתִי וְלֹא יַעֲנֶה בְּמוֹ־פִי אֶתְחַנֶּן־לוֹ:

יז רוּחִי זָרָה לְאִשְׁתִּי וְחַנֹּתִי לִבְנֵי בִטְנִי:

יח גַּם־עֲוִילִים מָאֲסוּ בִי אָקוּמָה וַיְדַבְּרוּ־בִי:

יט תִּעֲבוּנִי כׇּל־מְתֵי סוֹדִי וְזֶה־אָהַבְתִּי נֶהְפְּכוּ־בִי:

כ בְּעוֹרִי וּבִבְשָׂרִי דָּבְקָה עַצְמִי וָאֶתְמַלְּטָה בְּעוֹר שִׁנָּי:

כא חָנֻּנִי חָנֻּנִי אַתֶּם רֵעָי כִּי יַד־אֱלוֹהַּ נָגְעָה בִּי:

כב לָמָּה תִּרְדְּפֻנִי כְמוֹ־אֵל וּמִבְּשָׂרִי לֹא תִשְׂבָּעוּ:

כג מִי־יִתֵּן אֵפוֹ וְיִכָּתְבוּן מִלָּי מִי־יִתֵּן בַּסֵּפֶר וְיֻחָקוּ:

כד בְּעֵט־בַּרְזֶל וְעֹפָרֶת לָעַד בַּצּוּר יֵחָצְבוּן:

כה וַאֲנִי יָדַעְתִּי גֹּאֲלִי חָי וְאַחֲרוֹן עַל־עָפָר יָקוּם:

כו וְאַחַר עוֹרִי נִקְּפוּ־זֹאת וּמִבְּשָׂרִי אֶחֱזֶה אֱלוֹהַּ:

כז אֲשֶׁר אֲנִי אֶחֱזֶה־לִּי וְעֵינַי רָאוּ וְלֹא־זָר כָּלוּ כִלְיֹתַי בְּחֵקִי:

כח כִּי תֹאמְרוּ מַה־נִּרְדׇּף־לוֹ וְשֹׁרֶשׁ דָּבָר נִמְצָא־בִי:

כט גּוּרוּ לָכֶם מִפְּנֵי־חֶרֶב כִּי־חֵמָה עֲוֺנוֹת חָרֶב לְמַעַן תֵּדְעוּן שַׁדִּין [שַׁדּוּן]:

כ א וַיַּעַן צֹפַר הַנַּעֲמָתִי וַיֹּאמַר:

ב לָכֵן שְׂעִפַּי יְשִׁיבוּנִי וּבַעֲבוּר חוּשִׁי בִי:

ג מוּסַר כְּלִמָּתִי אֶשְׁמָע וְרוּחַ מִבִּינָתִי יַעֲנֵנִי:

⁴ Do you not know this, that from time immemorial, Since man was set on earth,

ד הֲזֹאת יָדַעְתָּ מִנִּי־עַד מִנִּי שִׂים אָדָם עֲלֵי־אָרֶץ:

⁵ The joy of the wicked has been brief, The happiness of the impious, fleeting?

ה כִּי רִנְנַת רְשָׁעִים מִקָּרוֹב וְשִׂמְחַת חָנֵף עֲדֵי־רָגַע:

⁶ Though he grows as high as the sky, His head reaching the clouds,

ו אִם־יַעֲלֶה לַשָּׁמַיִם שִׂיאוֹ וְרֹאשׁוֹ לָעָב יַגִּיעַ:

⁷ He perishes forever, like his dung; Those who saw him will say, "Where is he?"

ז כְּגֶלֲלוֹ לָנֶצַח יֹאבֵד רֹאָיו יֹאמְרוּ אַיּוֹ:

⁸ He flies away like a dream and cannot be found; He is banished like a night vision.

ח כַּחֲלוֹם יָעוּף וְלֹא יִמְצָאוּהוּ וְיֻדַּד כְּחֶזְיוֹן לָיְלָה:

⁹ Eyes that glimpsed him do so no more; They cannot see him in his place any longer.

ט עַיִן שְׁזָפַתּוּ וְלֹא תוֹסִיף וְלֹא־עוֹד תְּשׁוּרֶנּוּ מְקוֹמוֹ:

¹⁰ His sons ingratiate themselves with the poor; His own hands must give back his wealth.

י בָּנָיו יְרַצּוּ דַלִּים וְיָדָיו תָּשֵׁבְנָה אוֹנוֹ:

¹¹ His bones, still full of vigor, Lie down in the dust with him.

יא עַצְמוֹתָיו מָלְאוּ עלומו [עֲלוּמָיו] וְעִמּוֹ עַל־עָפָר תִּשְׁכָּב:

¹² Though evil is sweet to his taste, And he conceals it under his tongue;

יב אִם־תַּמְתִּיק בְּפִיו רָעָה יַכְחִידֶנָּה תַּחַת לְשׁוֹנוֹ:

¹³ Though he saves it, does not let it go, Holds it inside his mouth,

יג יַחְמֹל עָלֶיהָ וְלֹא יַעַזְבֶנָּה וְיִמְנָעֶנָּה בְּתוֹךְ חִכּוֹ:

¹⁴ His food in his bowels turns Into asps' venom within him.

יד לַחְמוֹ בְּמֵעָיו נֶהְפָּךְ מְרוֹרַת פְּתָנִים בְּקִרְבּוֹ:

¹⁵ The riches he swallows he vomits; *Hashem* empties it out of his stomach.

טו חַיִל בָּלַע וַיְקִאֶנּוּ מִבִּטְנוֹ יוֹרִשֶׁנּוּ אֵל:

¹⁶ He sucks the poison of asps; The tongue of the viper kills him.

טז רֹאשׁ־פְּתָנִים יִינָק תַּהַרְגֵהוּ לְשׁוֹן אֶפְעֶה:

¹⁷ Let him not enjoy the streams, The rivers of honey, the brooks of cream.

יז אַל־יֵרֶא בִפְלַגּוֹת נַהֲרֵי נַחֲלֵי דְּבַשׁ וְחֶמְאָה:

¹⁸ He will give back the goods unswallowed; The value of the riches, undigested.

יח מֵשִׁיב יָגָע וְלֹא יִבְלָע כְּחֵיל תְּמוּרָתוֹ וְלֹא יַעֲלֹס:

¹⁹ Because he crushed and tortured the poor, He will not build up the house he took by force.

יט כִּי־רִצַּץ עָזַב דַּלִּים בַּיִת גָּזַל וְלֹא יִבְנֵהוּ:

²⁰ He will not see his children tranquil; He will not preserve one of his dear ones.

כ כִּי לֹא־יָדַע שָׁלֵו בְּבִטְנוֹ בַּחֲמוּדוֹ לֹא יְמַלֵּט:

²¹ With no survivor to enjoy it, His fortune will not prosper.

כא אֵין־שָׂרִיד לְאָכְלוֹ עַל־כֵּן לֹא־יָחִיל טוּבוֹ:

²² When he has all he wants, trouble will come; Misfortunes of all kinds will batter him.

כב בִּמְלֹאות שִׂפְקוֹ יֵצֶר לוֹ כָּל־יַד עָמֵל תְּבוֹאֶנּוּ:

23 Let that fill his belly; Let Him loose His burning anger at him, And rain down His weapons upon him.

כג יְהִי לְמַלֵּא בִטְנוֹ יְשַׁלַּח־בּוֹ חֲרוֹן אַפּוֹ וְיַמְטֵר עָלֵימוֹ בִּלְחוּמוֹ:

24 Fleeing from iron arrows, He is shot through from a bow of bronze.

כד יִבְרַח מִנֵּשֶׁק בַּרְזֶל תַּחְלְפֵהוּ קֶשֶׁת נְחוּשָׁה:

25 Brandished and run through his body, The blade, through his gall, Strikes terror into him.

כה שָׁלַף וַיֵּצֵא מִגֵּוָה וּבָרָק מִמְּרֹרָתוֹ יַהֲלֹךְ עָלָיו אֵמִים:

26 Utter darkness waits for his treasured ones; A fire fanned by no man will consume him; Who survives in his tent will be crushed.

כו כָּל־חֹשֶׁךְ טָמוּן לִצְפּוּנָיו תְּאָכְלֵהוּ אֵשׁ לֹא־נֻפָּח יֵרַע שָׂרִיד בְּאָהֳלוֹ:

kol KHO-shekh ta-MUN litz-pu-NAV t'-a-kh'-LAY-hu
AYSH lo nu-PAKH yay-RA sa-REED b'-a-ho-LO

27 Heaven will expose his iniquity; Earth will rise up against him.

כז יְגַלּוּ שָׁמַיִם עֲוֹנוֹ וְאֶרֶץ מִתְקוֹמָמָה לוֹ:

28 His household will be cast forth by a flood, Spilled out on the day of His wrath.

כח יִגֶל יְבוּל בֵּיתוֹ נִגָּרוֹת בְּיוֹם אַפּוֹ:

29 This is the wicked man's portion from *Hashem*, The lot *Hashem* has ordained for him.

כט זֶה חֵלֶק־אָדָם רָשָׁע מֵאֱלֹהִים וְנַחֲלַת אִמְרוֹ מֵאֵל:

21 1 *Iyov* said in reply:

כא א וַיַּעַן אִיּוֹב וַיֹּאמַר:

2 Listen well to what I say, And let that be your consolation.

ב שִׁמְעוּ שָׁמוֹעַ מִלָּתִי וּתְהִי־זֹאת תַּנְחוּמֹתֵיכֶם:

3 Bear with me while I speak, And after I have spoken, you may mock.

ג שָׂאוּנִי וְאָנֹכִי אֲדַבֵּר וְאַחַר דַּבְּרִי תַלְעִיג:

4 Is my complaint directed toward a man? Why should I not lose my patience?

ד הֶאָנֹכִי לְאָדָם שִׂיחִי וְאִם־מַדּוּעַ לֹא־תִקְצַר רוּחִי:

5 Look at me and be appalled, And clap your hand to your mouth.

ה פְּנוּ־אֵלַי וְהָשַׁמּוּ וְשִׂימוּ יָד עַל־פֶּה:

6 When I think of it I am terrified; My body is seized with shuddering.

ו וְאִם־זָכַרְתִּי וְנִבְהָלְתִּי וְאָחַז בְּשָׂרִי פַּלָּצוּת:

20:26 Who survives in his tent will be crushed Zophar asserts that anyone associated with an evil person will be punished as a result of that association. Why is it so important to avoid associating with evildoers? Associating with a sinner can cause a desecration of God's name, since righteous people are thought to be less virtuous due to these inappropriate associations. Furthermore, a righteous person must avoid being influenced by evildoers, lest they lead him to sin. This idea is applied by *Rashi* (Numbers 3:29) to explain why the tribe of *Reuven* joined the rebellion of *Korach*, who was from the *Kehat* family of the tribe of *Levi*. "Since the tribe of *Reuven* was settled in the south when they camped, thus being neighbors of *Kehat* and his children who were also camped in the south, they joined with *Korach* in his rebellion. Woe to the wicked, and woe to his neighbor!"

A tent on the shore of the Sea of Galilee

⁷ Why do the wicked live on, Prosper and grow wealthy?

מַדּוּעַ רְשָׁעִים יִחְיוּ עָתְקוּ גַּם־גָּבְרוּ חָיִל: ז

ma-DU-a r'-sha-EEM yikh-YU a-t'-KU gam ga-v'-RU KHA-yil

⁸ Their children are with them always, And they see their children's children.

זַרְעָם נָכוֹן לִפְנֵיהֶם עִמָּם וְצֶאֱצָאֵיהֶם לְעֵינֵיהֶם: ח

⁹ Their homes are secure, without fear; They do not feel the rod of *Hashem*.

בָּתֵּיהֶם שָׁלוֹם מִפָּחַד וְלֹא שֵׁבֶט אֱלוֹהַּ עֲלֵיהֶם: ט

¹⁰ Their bull breeds and does not fail; Their cow calves and never miscarries;

שׁוֹרוֹ עִבַּר וְלֹא יַגְעִל תְּפַלֵּט פָּרָתוֹ וְלֹא תְשַׁכֵּל: י

¹¹ They let their infants run loose like sheep, And their children skip about.

יְשַׁלְּחוּ כַצֹּאן עֲוִילֵיהֶם וְיַלְדֵיהֶם יְרַקֵּדוּן: יא

¹² They sing to the music of timbrel and lute, And revel to the tune of the pipe;

יִשְׂאוּ כְּתֹף וְכִנּוֹר וְיִשְׂמְחוּ לְקוֹל עוּגָב: יב

¹³ They spend their days in happiness, And go down to Sheol in peace.

יבלו [יְכַלּוּ] בַטּוֹב יְמֵיהֶם וּבְרֶגַע שְׁאוֹל יֵחָתּוּ: יג

¹⁴ They say to *Hashem*, "Leave us alone, We do not want to learn Your ways;

וַיֹּאמְרוּ לָאֵל סוּר מִמֶּנּוּ וְדַעַת דְּרָכֶיךָ לֹא חָפָצְנוּ: יד

¹⁵ What is *Shaddai* that we should serve Him? What will we gain by praying to Him?"

מַה־שַׁדַּי כִּי־נַעַבְדֶנּוּ וּמַה־נּוֹעִיל כִּי נִפְגַּע־בּוֹ: טו

¹⁶ Their happiness is not their own doing. (The thoughts of the wicked are beyond me!)

הֵן לֹא בְיָדָם טוּבָם עֲצַת רְשָׁעִים רָחֲקָה מֶנִּי: טז

¹⁷ How seldom does the lamp of the wicked fail, Does the calamity they deserve befall them, Does He apportion [their] lot in anger!

כַּמָּה נֵר־רְשָׁעִים יִדְעָךְ וְיָבֹא עָלֵימוֹ אֵידָם חֲבָלִים יְחַלֵּק בְּאַפּוֹ: יז

¹⁸ Let them become like straw in the wind, Like chaff carried off by a storm.

יִהְיוּ כְּתֶבֶן לִפְנֵי־רוּחַ וּכְמֹץ גְּנָבַתּוּ סוּפָה: יח

¹⁹ [You say,] "*Hashem* is reserving his punishment for his sons"; Let it be paid back to him that he may feel it,

אֱלוֹהַּ יִצְפֹּן־לְבָנָיו אוֹנוֹ יְשַׁלֵּם אֵלָיו וְיֵדָע: יט

²⁰ Let his eyes see his ruin, And let him drink the wrath of *Shaddai*!

יראו עינו [עֵינָיו] כִּידוֹ וּמֵחֲמַת שַׁדַּי יִשְׁתֶּה: כ

²¹ For what does he care about the fate of his family, When his number of months runs out?

כִּי מַה־חֶפְצוֹ בְּבֵיתוֹ אַחֲרָיו וּמִסְפַּר חֳדָשָׁיו חֻצָּצוּ: כא

The Western Wall in *Yerushalayim*

21:7 Why do the wicked live on This question that *Iyov* asks is the crux of the entire book: Why do the righteous suffer while the wicked go unpunished? Though *Iyov* is troubled by this because of his personal experiences, he does not abandon his faith in God. If he did, the question would lose its meaning, for the seeming randomness of good and bad fortunes presents a difficulty only if one supposes that the world is ruled by a benevolent God. *Iyov* teaches that while it is acceptable to ask the questions, they must come from a place of faith in *Hashem* and His integrity, rather than denial and doubt.

Job

²² Can *Hashem* be instructed in knowledge, He who judges from such heights?

כב הַלְאֵל יְלַמֶּד־דָּעַת וְהוּא רָמִים יִשְׁפּוֹט:

²³ One man dies in robust health, All tranquil and untroubled;

כג זֶה יָמוּת בְּעֶצֶם תֻּמּוֹ כֻּלּוֹ שַׁלְאֲנַן וְשָׁלֵיו:

²⁴ His pails are full of milk; The marrow of his bones is juicy.

כד עֲטִינָיו מָלְאוּ חָלָב וּמֹחַ עַצְמוֹתָיו יְשֻׁקֶּה:

²⁵ Another dies embittered, Never having tasted happiness.

כה וְזֶה יָמוּת בְּנֶפֶשׁ מָרָה וְלֹא־אָכַל בַּטּוֹבָה:

²⁶ They both lie in the dust And are covered with worms.

כו יַחַד עַל־עָפָר יִשְׁכָּבוּ וְרִמָּה תְּכַסֶּה עֲלֵיהֶם:

²⁷ Oh, I know your thoughts, And the tactics you will devise against me.

כז הֵן יָדַעְתִּי מַחְשְׁבוֹתֵיכֶם וּמְזִמּוֹת עָלַי תַּחְמֹסוּ:

²⁸ You will say, "Where is the house of the great man – And where the tent in which the wicked dwelled?"

כח כִּי תֹאמְרוּ אַיֵּה בֵית־נָדִיב וְאַיֵּה אֹהֶל מִשְׁכְּנוֹת רְשָׁעִים:

²⁹ You must have consulted the wayfarers; You cannot deny their evidence.

כט הֲלֹא שְׁאֶלְתֶּם עוֹבְרֵי דָרֶךְ וְאֹתֹתָם לֹא תְנַכֵּרוּ:

³⁰ For the evil man is spared on the day of calamity, On the day when wrath is led forth.

ל כִּי לְיוֹם אֵיד יֵחָשֶׂךְ רָע לְיוֹם עֲבָרוֹת יוּבָלוּ:

³¹ Who will upbraid him to his face? Who will requite him for what he has done?

לא מִי־יַגִּיד עַל־פָּנָיו דַּרְכּוֹ וְהוּא־עָשָׂה מִי יְשַׁלֶּם־לוֹ:

³² He is brought to the grave, While a watch is kept at his tomb.

לב וְהוּא לִקְבָרוֹת יוּבָל וְעַל־גָּדִישׁ יִשְׁקוֹד:

³³ The clods of the wadi are sweet to him, Everyone follows behind him, Innumerable are those who precede him.

לג מָתְקוּ־לוֹ רִגְבֵי נָחַל וְאַחֲרָיו כָּל־אָדָם יִמְשׁוֹךְ וּלְפָנָיו אֵין מִסְפָּר:

³⁴ Why then do you offer me empty consolation? Of your replies only the perfidy remains.

לד וְאֵיךְ תְּנַחֲמוּנִי הָבֶל וּתְשׁוּבֹתֵיכֶם נִשְׁאַר־מָעַל:

22 ¹ Eliphaz the Temanite said in reply:

כב א וַיַּעַן אֱלִיפַז הַתֵּמָנִי וַיֹּאמַר:

² Can a man be of use to *Hashem*, A wise man benefit Him?

ב הַלְאֵל יִסְכָּן־גָּבֶר כִּי־יִסְכֹּן עָלֵימוֹ מַשְׂכִּיל:

³ Does *Shaddai* gain if you are righteous? Does He profit if your conduct is blameless?

ג הַחֵפֶץ לְשַׁדַּי כִּי תִצְדָּק וְאִם־בֶּצַע כִּי־תַתֵּם דְּרָכֶיךָ:

ha-KHAY-fetz l'-sha-DAI KEE titz-DAK v'-im BE-tza kee ta-TAYM d'-ra-KHE-kha

22:3 Does *Shaddai* gain if you are righteous? Eliphaz states that *Hashem* does not desire piety, but rather good deeds. This is reminiscent of the first chapter of *Sefer Yeshayahu*. In *Sefer Yeshayahu*, God is angry at the inhabitants of *Yerushalayim* because they are engaged in unacceptable behavior towards their fellow men, such as murder, even as they continue to worship *Hashem* through prayer and sacrifice (Isaiah 1:11,15). *Yeshayahu* declares: "Alas, she has become a harlot, the faithful city that was filled with justice, where

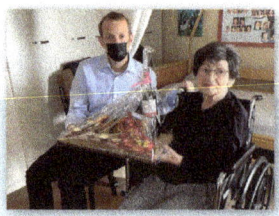
Rabbi Tuly Weisz delivering Purim baskets to Holocaust survivors

⁴ Is it because of your piety that He arraigns you, And enters into judgment with you?

ד הֲמִיִּרְאָתְךָ יֹכִיחֶךָ יָבוֹא עִמְּךָ בַּמִּשְׁפָּט:

⁵ You know that your wickedness is great, And that your iniquities have no limit.

ה הֲלֹא רָעָתְךָ רַבָּה וְאֵין־קֵץ לַעֲוֺנֹתֶיךָ:

⁶ You exact pledges from your fellows without reason, And leave them naked, stripped of their clothes;

ו כִּי־תַחְבֹּל אַחֶיךָ חִנָּם וּבִגְדֵי עֲרוּמִּים תַּפְשִׁיט:

⁷ You do not give the thirsty water to drink; You deny bread to the hungry.

ז לֹא־מַיִם עָיֵף תַּשְׁקֶה וּמֵרָעֵב תִּמְנַע־לָחֶם:

⁸ The land belongs to the strong; The privileged occupy it.

ח וְאִישׁ זְרוֹעַ לוֹ הָאָרֶץ וּנְשׂוּא פָנִים יֵשֶׁב בָּהּ:

⁹ You have sent away widows empty-handed; The strength of the fatherless is broken.

ט אַלְמָנוֹת שִׁלַּחְתָּ רֵיקָם וּזְרֹעוֹת יְתֹמִים יְדֻכָּא:

¹⁰ Therefore snares are all around you, And sudden terrors frighten you,

י עַל־כֵּן סְבִיבוֹתֶיךָ פַחִים וִיבַהֶלְךָ פַּחַד פִּתְאֹם:

¹¹ Or darkness, so you cannot see; A flood of waters covers you.

יא אוֹ־חֹשֶׁךְ לֹא־תִרְאֶה וְשִׁפְעַת־מַיִם תְּכַסֶּךָּ:

¹² *Hashem* is in the heavenly heights; See the highest stars, how lofty!

יב הֲלֹא־אֱלוֹהַּ גֹּבַהּ שָׁמָיִם וּרְאֵה רֹאשׁ כּוֹכָבִים כִּי־רָמּוּ:

¹³ You say, "What can *Hashem* know? Can He govern through the dense cloud?

יג וְאָמַרְתָּ מַה־יָּדַע אֵל הַבְעַד עֲרָפֶל יִשְׁפּוֹט:

¹⁴ The clouds screen Him so He cannot see As He moves about the circuit of heaven."

יד עָבִים סֵתֶר־לוֹ וְלֹא יִרְאֶה וְחוּג שָׁמַיִם יִתְהַלָּךְ:

¹⁵ Have you observed the immemorial path That evil men have trodden;

טו הַאֹרַח עוֹלָם תִּשְׁמֹר אֲשֶׁר דָּרְכוּ מְתֵי־אָוֶן:

¹⁶ How they were shriveled up before their time And their foundation poured out like a river?

טז אֲשֶׁר־קֻמְּטוּ וְלֹא־עֵת נָהָר יוּצַק יְסוֹדָם:

¹⁷ They said to *Hashem*, "Leave us alone; What can *Shaddai* do about it?"

יז הָאֹמְרִים לָאֵל סוּר מִמֶּנּוּ וּמַה־יִּפְעַל שַׁדַּי לָמוֹ:

¹⁸ But it was He who filled their houses with good things. (The thoughts of the wicked are beyond me!)

יח וְהוּא מִלֵּא בָתֵּיהֶם טוֹב וַעֲצַת רְשָׁעִים רָחֲקָה מֶנִּי:

---

righteousness dwelt. But now [it is filled with] murderers" (1:21). While a righteous person might believe that his observance of the formal commandments is what brings *Hashem* close to him, what *Hashem* desires most is kindness to other human beings. The chapter in *Yeshayahu* continues: "I will restore your magistrates as of old, and your counselors as of yore… *Tzion* shall be saved in the judgment; Her repentant ones, in the retribution." (1:26–27). It is through kindness, righteousness and justice towards others that the redemption of *Tzion* will come.

Job

¹⁹ The righteous, seeing it, rejoiced; The innocent laughed with scorn.

יט יִרְא֤וּ צַדִּיקִ֣ים וְיִשְׂמָ֑חוּ וְ֝נָקִ֗י יִלְעַג־לָֽמוֹ׃

²⁰ Surely their substance was destroyed, And their remnant consumed by fire.

כ אִם־לֹ֣א נִכְחַ֣ד קִימָ֑נוּ וְ֝יִתְרָ֗ם אָ֣כְלָה אֵֽשׁ׃

²¹ Be close to Him and wholehearted; Good things will come to you thereby.

כא הַסְכֶּן־נָ֣א עִמּ֣וֹ וּשְׁלָ֑ם בָּ֝הֶ֗ם תְּֽבוֹאַתְךָ֥ טוֹבָֽה׃

²² Accept instruction from His mouth; Lay up His words in your heart.

כב קַח־נָ֣א מִפִּ֣יו תּוֹרָ֑ה וְשִׂ֥ים אֲ֝מָרָ֗יו בִּלְבָבֶֽךָ׃

²³ If you return to *Shaddai* you will be restored, If you banish iniquity from your tent;

כג אִם־תָּשׁ֣וּב עַד־שַׁ֭דַּי תִּבָּנֶ֑ה תַּרְחִ֥יק עַ֝וְלָ֗ה מֵאׇהֳלֶֽךָ׃

²⁴ If you regard treasure as dirt, Ophir-gold as stones of the wadi,

כד וְשִׁית־עַל־עָפָ֥ר בָּ֑צֶר וּבְצ֖וּר נְחָלִ֣ים אוֹפִֽיר׃

²⁵ And *Shaddai* be your treasure And precious silver for you,

כה וְהָיָ֣ה שַׁדַּ֣י בְּצָרֶ֑יךָ וְכֶ֖סֶף תּוֹעָפ֣וֹת לָֽךְ׃

²⁶ When you seek the favor of *Shaddai*, And lift up your face to *Hashem*,

כו כִּי־אָ֗ז עַל־שַׁדַּ֥י תִּתְעַנָּ֑ג וְתִשָּׂ֖א אֶל־אֱל֣וֹהַּ פָּנֶֽיךָ׃

²⁷ You will pray to Him, and He will listen to you, And you will pay your vows.

כז תַּעְתִּ֣יר אֵ֭לָיו וְיִשְׁמָעֶ֑ךָּ וּנְדָרֶ֥יךָ תְשַׁלֵּֽם׃

²⁸ You will decree and it will be fulfilled, And light will shine upon your affairs.

כח וְֽתִגְזַר־א֭וֹמֶר וְיָ֣קׇם לָ֑ךְ וְעַל־דְּ֝רָכֶ֗יךָ נָ֣גַֽהּ אֽוֹר׃

²⁹ When others sink low, you will say it is pride; For He saves the humble.

כט כִּֽי־הִ֭שְׁפִּילוּ וַתֹּ֣אמֶר גֵּוָ֑ה וְשַׁ֖ח עֵינַ֣יִם יוֹשִֽׁעַ׃

³⁰ He will deliver the guilty; He will be delivered through the cleanness of your hands.

ל יְֽמַלֵּ֥ט אִֽי־נָקִ֑י וְ֝נִמְלַ֗ט בְּבֹ֣ר כַּפֶּֽיךָ׃

23 ¹ *Iyov* said in reply:

כג א וַיַּ֥עַן אִיּ֗וֹב וַיֹּאמַֽר׃

² Today again my complaint is bitter; My strength is spent on account of my groaning.

ב גַּם־הַ֭יּוֹם מְרִ֣י שִׂחִ֑י יָ֝דִ֗י כָּבְדָ֥ה עַל־אַנְחָתִֽי׃

³ Would that I knew how to reach Him, How to get to His dwelling-place.

ג מִֽי־יִתֵּ֣ן יָ֭דַעְתִּי וְאֶמְצָאֵ֑הוּ אָ֝ב֗וֹא עַד־תְּכוּנָתֽוֹ׃

⁴ I would set out my case before Him And fill my mouth with arguments.

ד אֶעֶרְכָ֣ה לְפָנָ֣יו מִשְׁפָּ֑ט וּ֝פִ֗י אֲמַלֵּ֥א תוֹכָחֽוֹת׃

⁵ I would learn what answers He had for me And know how He would reply to me.

ה אֵ֭דְעָה מִלִּ֣ים יַעֲנֵ֑נִי וְ֝אָבִ֗ינָה מַה־יֹּ֥אמַר לִֽי׃

⁶ Would He contend with me overbearingly? Surely He would not accuse me!

ו הַבְּרׇב־כֹּ֭חַ יָרִ֣יב עִמָּדִ֑י לֹ֥א אַךְ־ה֝֗וּא יָשִׂ֥ם בִּֽי׃

⁷ There the upright would be cleared by Him, And I would escape forever from my judge.

ז שָׁ֗ם יָשָׁ֥ר נוֹכָ֣ח עִמּ֑וֹ וַאֲפַלְּטָ֥ה לָ֝נֶ֗צַח מִשֹּׁפְטִֽי׃

8 But if I go East – He is not there; West – I still do not perceive Him;

הֵן קֶדֶם אֶהֱלֹךְ וְאֵינֶנּוּ וְאָחוֹר וְלֹא־אָבִין לוֹ:

HAYN KE-dem e-he-LOKH v'-ay-NE-nu v'-a-KHOR v'-LO a-VEEN LO

9 North – since He is concealed, I do not behold Him; South – He is hidden, and I cannot see Him.

שְׂמֹאול בַּעֲשֹׂתוֹ וְלֹא־אָחַז יַעְטֹף יָמִין וְלֹא אֶרְאֶה:

10 But He knows the way I take; Would He assay me, I should emerge pure as gold.

כִּי־יָדַע דֶּרֶךְ עִמָּדִי בְּחָנַנִי כַּזָּהָב אֵצֵא:

11 I have followed in His tracks, Kept His way without swerving,

בַּאֲשֻׁרוֹ אָחֲזָה רַגְלִי דַּרְכּוֹ שָׁמַרְתִּי וְלֹא־אָט:

12 I have not deviated from what His lips commanded; I have treasured His words more than my daily bread.

מִצְוַת שְׂפָתָיו וְלֹא אָמִישׁ מֵחֻקִּי צָפַנְתִּי אִמְרֵי־פִיו:

13 He is one; who can dissuade Him? Whatever He desires, He does.

וְהוּא בְאֶחָד וּמִי יְשִׁיבֶנּוּ וְנַפְשׁוֹ אִוְּתָה וַיָּעַשׂ:

14 For He will bring my term to an end, But He has many more such at His disposal.

כִּי יַשְׁלִים חֻקִּי וְכָהֵנָּה רַבּוֹת עִמּוֹ:

15 Therefore I am terrified at His presence; When I consider, I dread Him.

עַל־כֵּן מִפָּנָיו אֶבָּהֵל אֶתְבּוֹנֵן וְאֶפְחַד מִמֶּנּוּ:

16 *Hashem* has made me fainthearted; *Shaddai* has terrified me.

וְאֵל הֵרַךְ לִבִּי וְשַׁדַּי הִבְהִילָנִי:

17 Yet I am not cut off by the darkness; He has concealed the thick gloom from me.

כִּי־לֹא נִצְמַתִּי מִפְּנֵי־חֹשֶׁךְ וּמִפָּנַי כִּסָּה־אֹפֶל:

24 1 Why are times for judgment not reserved by *Shaddai*? Even those close to Him cannot foresee His actions.

מַדּוּעַ מִשַּׁדַּי לֹא־נִצְפְּנוּ עִתִּים וִידְעוֹ [וְיֹדְעָיו] לֹא־חָזוּ יָמָיו:

ma-DU-a mi-sha-DAI lo nitz-p'-NU i-TEEM v'-yo-d'-AV lo KHA-zu ya-MAV

2 People remove boundary-stones; They carry off flocks and pasture them;

גְּבֻלוֹת יַשִּׂיגוּ עֵדֶר גָּזְלוּ וַיִּרְעוּ:

IDF soldier praying at the Western Wall

23:8 But if I go East – He is not there Throughout the book, *Iyov*'s bitterness at God's apparent abandonment of him has been very noticeable. Until now it seemed that *Iyov* was upset because he knew that he did not deserve the punishment he received. Now, however, he expresses concern over his distance from *Hashem*. For a God-fearing person, distance from *Hashem* is unbearable. Similarly, when *Yeshayahu* proclaims to the inhabitants of *Yerushalayim*: "Though you pray at length, I will not listen." (1:15), this was meant to motivate them towards repentance. As a truly righteous man, *Iyov* could bear a test from the Almighty, but he cannot bear the lack of response to his prayers.

24:1 Even those close to Him cannot foresee His actions A careful reading shows that *Iyov* is not complaining about his punishment, but about the fact that he cannot see the end of his suffering. Similarly, in *Sefer Tehillim* (44:24), the People of Israel complain to God about their long exile from the Land of Israel: "Rouse Yourself; why do You sleep, O *Hashem*? Awaken, do not reject us forever." They cannot bear the seemingly endless exile from their homeland. It is always much easier to suffer if the end is in sight.

³ They lead away the donkeys of the fatherless, And seize the widow's bull as a pledge;

ג חֲמוֹר יְתוֹמִים יִנְהָגוּ יַחְבְּלוּ שׁוֹר אַלְמָנָה:

⁴ They chase the needy off the roads; All the poor of the land are forced into hiding.

ד יַטּוּ אֶבְיוֹנִים מִדָּרֶךְ יַחַד חֻבְּאוּ עֲנִיֵּי־אָרֶץ:

⁵ Like the wild asses of the wilderness, They go about their tasks, seeking food; The wilderness provides each with food for his lads;

ה הֵן פְּרָאִים בַּמִּדְבָּר יָצְאוּ בְּפָעֳלָם מְשַׁחֲרֵי לַטָּרֶף עֲרָבָה לוֹ לֶחֶם לַנְּעָרִים:

⁶ They harvest fodder in the field, And glean the late grapes in the vineyards of the wicked.

ו בַּשָּׂדֶה בְּלִילוֹ יקצירו [יִקְצוֹרוּ] וְכֶרֶם רָשָׁע יְלַקֵּשׁוּ:

⁷ They pass the night naked for lack of clothing, They have no covering against the cold;

ז עָרוֹם יָלִינוּ מִבְּלִי לְבוּשׁ וְאֵין כְּסוּת בַּקָּרָה:

⁸ They are drenched by the mountain rains, And huddle against the rock for lack of shelter.

ח מִזֶּרֶם הָרִים יִרְטָבוּ וּמִבְּלִי מַחְסֶה חִבְּקוּ־צוּר:

⁹ They snatch the fatherless infant from the breast, And seize the child of the poor as a pledge.

ט יִגְזְלוּ מִשֹּׁד יָתוֹם וְעַל־עָנִי יַחְבֹּלוּ:

¹⁰ They go about naked for lack of clothing, And, hungry, carry sheaves;

י עָרוֹם הִלְּכוּ בְּלִי לְבוּשׁ וּרְעֵבִים נָשְׂאוּ עֹמֶר:

¹¹ Between rows [of olive trees] they make oil, And, thirsty, they tread the winepresses.

יא בֵּין־שׁוּרֹתָם יַצְהִירוּ יְקָבִים דָּרְכוּ וַיִּצְמָאוּ:

¹² Men groan in the city; The souls of the dying cry out; Yet *Hashem* does not regard it as a reproach.

יב מֵעִיר מְתִים יִנְאָקוּ וְנֶפֶשׁ־חֲלָלִים תְּשַׁוֵּעַ וֶאֱלוֹהַּ לֹא־יָשִׂים תִּפְלָה:

¹³ They are rebels against the light; They are strangers to its ways, And do not stay in its path.

יג הֵמָּה הָיוּ בְּמֹרְדֵי־אוֹר לֹא־הִכִּירוּ דְרָכָיו וְלֹא יָשְׁבוּ בִּנְתִיבֹתָיו:

¹⁴ The murderer arises in the evening To kill the poor and needy, And at night he acts the thief.

יד לָאוֹר יָקוּם רוֹצֵחַ יִקְטָל־עָנִי וְאֶבְיוֹן וּבַלַּיְלָה יְהִי כַגַּנָּב:

¹⁵ The eyes of the adulterer watch for twilight, Thinking, "No one will glimpse me then." He masks his face.

טו וְעֵין נֹאֵף שָׁמְרָה נֶשֶׁף לֵאמֹר לֹא־תְשׁוּרֵנִי עָיִן וְסֵתֶר פָּנִים יָשִׂים:

¹⁶ In the dark they break into houses; By day they shut themselves in; They do not know the light.

טז חָתַר בַּחֹשֶׁךְ בָּתִּים יוֹמָם חִתְּמוּ־לָמוֹ לֹא־יָדְעוּ אוֹר:

¹⁷ For all of them morning is darkness; It is then that they discern the terror of darkness.

יז כִּי יַחְדָּו בֹּקֶר לָמוֹ צַלְמָוֶת כִּי־יַכִּיר בַּלְהוֹת צַלְמָוֶת:

¹⁸ May they be flotsam on the face of the water; May their portion in the land be cursed; May none turn aside by way of their vineyards.

יח קַל־הוּא עַל־פְּנֵי־מַיִם תְּקֻלַּל חֶלְקָתָם בָּאָרֶץ לֹא־יִפְנֶה דֶּרֶךְ כְּרָמִים:

¹⁹ May drought and heat snatch away their snow waters, And Sheol, those who have sinned.

יט צִיָּה גַם־חֹם יִגְזְלוּ מֵימֵי־שֶׁלֶג שְׁאוֹל חָטָאוּ:

²⁰ May the womb forget him; May he be sweet to the worms; May he be no longer remembered; May wrongdoers be broken like a tree.

כ יִשְׁכָּחֵהוּ רֶחֶם מְתָקוֹ רִמָּה עוֹד לֹא־יִזָּכֵר וַתִּשָּׁבֵר כָּעֵץ עַוְלָה:

²¹ May he consort with a barren woman who bears no child, Leave his widow deprived of good.

כא רֹעֶה עֲקָרָה לֹא תֵלֵד וְאַלְמָנָה לֹא יְיֵטִיב:

²² Though he has the strength to seize bulls, May he live with no assurance of survival.

כב וּמָשַׁךְ אַבִּירִים בְּכֹחוֹ יָקוּם וְלֹא־יַאֲמִין בַּחַיִּין:

²³ Yet [*Hashem*] gives him the security on which he relies, And keeps watch over his affairs.

כג יִתֶּן־לוֹ לָבֶטַח וְיִשָּׁעֵן וְעֵינֵיהוּ עַל־דַּרְכֵיהֶם:

²⁴ Exalted for a while, let them be gone; Be brought low, and shrivel like mallows, And wither like the heads of grain.

כד רוֹמּוּ מְּעַט וְאֵינֶנּוּ וְהֻמְּכוּ כַּכֹּל יִקָּפְצוּן וּכְרֹאשׁ שִׁבֹּלֶת יִמָּלוּ:

²⁵ Surely no one can confute me, Or prove that I am wrong.

כה וְאִם־לֹא אֵפוֹ מִי יַכְזִיבֵנִי וְיָשֵׂם לְאַל מִלָּתִי:

25 ¹ Bildad the Shuhite said in reply:

כה א וַיַּעַן בִּלְדַּד הַשֻּׁחִי וַיֹּאמַר:

² Dominion and dread are His; He imposes peace in His heights.

ב הַמְשֵׁל וָפַחַד עִמּוֹ עֹשֶׂה שָׁלוֹם בִּמְרוֹמָיו:

ham-SHAYL va-FA-khad i-MO o-SEH sha-LOM bim-ro-MAV

³ Can His troops be numbered? On whom does His light not shine?

ג הֲיֵשׁ מִסְפָּר לִגְדוּדָיו וְעַל־מִי לֹא־יָקוּם אוֹרֵהוּ:

⁴ How can man be in the right before *Hashem*? How can one born of woman be cleared of guilt?

ד וּמַה־יִּצְדַּק אֱנוֹשׁ עִם־אֵל וּמַה־יִּזְכֶּה יְלוּד אִשָּׁה:

⁵ Even the moon is not bright, And the stars are not pure in His sight.

ה הֵן עַד־יָרֵחַ וְלֹא יַאֲהִיל וְכוֹכָבִים לֹא־זַכּוּ בְעֵינָיו:

⁶ How much less man, a worm, The son-of-man, a maggot.

ו אַף כִּי־אֱנוֹשׁ רִמָּה וּבֶן־אָדָם תּוֹלֵעָה:

26 ¹ Then *Iyov* said in reply:

כו א וַיַּעַן אִיּוֹב וַיֹּאמַר:

² You would help without having the strength; You would deliver with arms that have no power.

ב מֶה־עָזַרְתָּ לְלֹא־כֹחַ הוֹשַׁעְתָּ זְרוֹעַ לֹא־עֹז:

meh a-ZAR-ta l'-lo KHO-akh ho-SHA-ta z'-RO-a lo OZ

שמים **25:2 He imposes peace in His heights** The words *oseh shalom bimromav* (עשה שלום במרומיו), 'He imposes peace in His heights,' form the first part of a well-known Jewish prayer: "He who imposes peace in His heights, may He make peace upon us and upon all Israel. Now respond: *Amen.*" The medieval commentator *Rashi* explains that the word for 'heaven,' *shamayim* (שמים), is derived from the words *aish* (אש), 'fire,' and *mayim* (מים), 'water,' as the two came together in harmony to make up the heavens

A fiery sky over the Mediterranean Sea

(Genesis 1:8). This prayer representing hope for peace in this world is recited at the end of the *Amidah*, the central prayer of the Jewish liturgy. At times it seems that just as fire and water cannot coexist, mankind will never be able to live together harmoniously. Nevertheless, we beseech *Hashem* to make peace on earth just He has made peace between fire and water in the heavens.

26:2 You would deliver with arms that have no power *Iyov* acknowledges that while *Bildad*'s intentions are good, in reality his words are of no assistance since they do not provide any comfort. Though *Bildad* and *Iyov*'s other friends are trying to help, *Iyov* finds their statements very hurtful. It is often difficult to find the right words to comfort a grieving friend. In Jewish practice, a traditional formula is said when trying

³ Without having the wisdom, you offer advice And freely give your counsel.

ג מַה־יָּעַצְתָּ לְּלֹא חָכְמָה וְתוּשִׁיָּה לָרֹב הוֹדָעְתָּ:

⁴ To whom have you addressed words? Whose breath issued from you?

ד אֶת־מִי הִגַּדְתָּ מִלִּין וְנִשְׁמַת־מִי יָצְאָה מִמֶּךָּ:

⁵ The shades tremble Beneath the waters and their denizens.

ה הָרְפָאִים יְחוֹלָלוּ מִתַּחַת מַיִם וְשֹׁכְנֵיהֶם:

⁶ Sheol is naked before Him; Abaddon has no cover.

ו עָרוֹם שְׁאוֹל נֶגְדּוֹ וְאֵין כְּסוּת לָאֲבַדּוֹן:

⁷ He it is who stretched out Zaphon over chaos, Who suspended earth over emptiness.

ז נֹטֶה צָפוֹן עַל־תֹּהוּ תֹּלֶה אֶרֶץ עַל־בְּלִי־מָה:

⁸ He wrapped up the waters in His clouds; Yet no cloud burst under their weight.

ח צֹרֵר־מַיִם בְּעָבָיו וְלֹא־נִבְקַע עָנָן תַּחְתָּם:

⁹ He shuts off the view of His throne, Spreading His cloud over it.

ט מְאַחֵז פְּנֵי־כִסֵּה פַּרְשֵׁז עָלָיו עֲנָנוֹ:

¹⁰ He drew a boundary on the surface of the waters, At the extreme where light and darkness meet.

י חֹק־חָג עַל־פְּנֵי־מָיִם עַד־תַּכְלִית אוֹר עִם־חֹשֶׁךְ:

¹¹ The pillars of heaven tremble, Astounded at His blast.

יא עַמּוּדֵי שָׁמַיִם יְרוֹפָפוּ וְיִתְמְהוּ מִגַּעֲרָתוֹ:

¹² By His power He stilled the sea; By His skill He struck down Rahab.

יב בְּכֹחוֹ רָגַע הַיָּם ובתובנתו [וּבִתְבוּנָתוֹ] מָחַץ רָהַב:

¹³ By His wind the heavens were calmed; His hand pierced the Elusive Serpent.

יג בְּרוּחוֹ שָׁמַיִם שִׁפְרָה חֹלֲלָה יָדוֹ נָחָשׁ בָּרִיחַ:

¹⁴ These are but glimpses of His rule, The mere whisper that we perceive of Him; Who can absorb the thunder of His mighty deeds?

יד הֶן־אֵלֶּה קְצוֹת דרכו [דְּרָכָיו] וּמַה־שֵּׁמֶץ דָּבָר נִשְׁמַע־בּוֹ וְרַעַם גבורתו [גְּבוּרוֹתָיו] מִי יִתְבּוֹנָן:

27 ¹ *Iyov* again took up his theme and said:

כז א וַיֹּסֶף אִיּוֹב שְׂאֵת מְשָׁלוֹ וַיֹּאמַר:

² By *Hashem* who has deprived me of justice! By *Shaddai* who has embittered my life!

ב חַי־אֵל הֵסִיר מִשְׁפָּטִי וְשַׁדַּי הֵמַר נַפְשִׁי:

³ As long as there is life in me, And *Hashem*'s breath is in my nostrils,

ג כִּי־כָל־עוֹד נִשְׁמָתִי בִי וְרוּחַ אֱלוֹהַּ בְּאַפִּי:

⁴ My lips will speak no wrong, Nor my tongue utter deceit.

ד אִם־תְּדַבֵּרְנָה שְׂפָתַי עַוְלָה וּלְשׁוֹנִי אִם־יֶהְגֶּה רְמִיָּה:

to comfort a mourner: "May the Omnipresent comfort you among the mourners of *Tzion* and *Yerushalayim*." Since *Hashem* is the only One who can truly understand the suffering of the individual, and the only One who can really bring comfort, we call upon Him to comfort the mourner. The

An Israeli soldier mourns over fallen comrades

Hebrew word for 'Omnipresent' is *hamakom* (המקום), which literally means 'the place.' We pray that *Hashem* comforts the mourner, and that the mourner recognize God's presence even in the difficult place in which he currently finds himself.

המקום

5 Far be it from me to say you are right; Until I die I will maintain my integrity.

ה חָלִילָה לִּי אִם־אַצְדִּיק אֶתְכֶם עַד־אֶגְוָע לֹא־אָסִיר תֻּמָּתִי מִמֶּנִּי:

6 I persist in my righteousness and will not yield; I shall be free of reproach as long as I live.

ו בְּצִדְקָתִי הֶחֱזַקְתִּי וְלֹא אַרְפֶּהָ לֹא־יֶחֱרַף לְבָבִי מִיָּמָי:

7 May my enemy be as the wicked; My assailant, as the wrongdoer.

ז יְהִי כְרָשָׁע אֹיְבִי וּמִתְקוֹמְמִי כְעַוָּל:

8 For what hope has the impious man when he is cut down, When *Hashem* takes away his life?

ח כִּי מַה־תִּקְוַת חָנֵף כִּי יִבְצָע כִּי יֵשֶׁל אֱלוֹהַּ נַפְשׁוֹ:

9 Will *Hashem* hear his cry When trouble comes upon him,

ט הַצַעֲקָתוֹ יִשְׁמַע אֵל כִּי־תָבוֹא עָלָיו צָרָה:

ha-tza-a-ka-TO yish-MA AYL kee ta-VO a-LAV tza-RAH

10 When he seeks the favor of *Shaddai*, Calls upon *Hashem* at all times?

י אִם־עַל־שַׁדַּי יִתְעַנָּג יִקְרָא אֱלוֹהַּ בְּכָל־עֵת:

11 I will teach you what is in *Hashem*'s power, And what is with *Shaddai* I will not conceal.

יא אוֹרֶה אֶתְכֶם בְּיַד־אֵל אֲשֶׁר עִם־שַׁדַּי לֹא אֲכַחֵד:

12 All of you have seen it, So why talk nonsense?

יב הֵן־אַתֶּם כֻּלְּכֶם חֲזִיתֶם וְלָמָּה־זֶּה הֶבֶל תֶּהְבָּלוּ:

13 This is the evil man's portion from *Hashem*, The lot that the ruthless receive from *Shaddai*:

יג זֶה חֵלֶק־אָדָם רָשָׁע עִם־אֵל וְנַחֲלַת עָרִיצִים מִשַּׁדַּי יִקָּחוּ:

14 Should he have many sons – they are marked for the sword; His descendants will never have their fill of bread;

יד אִם־יִרְבּוּ בָנָיו לְמוֹ־חָרֶב וְצֶאֱצָאָיו לֹא יִשְׂבְּעוּ־לָחֶם:

15 Those who survive him will be buried in a plague, And their widows will not weep;

טו שְׂרִידוֹ [שְׂרִידָיו] בַּמָּוֶת יִקָּבֵרוּ וְאַלְמְנֹתָיו לֹא תִבְכֶּינָה:

16 Should he pile up silver like dust, Lay up clothing like dirt –

טז אִם־יִצְבֹּר כֶּעָפָר כָּסֶף וְכַחֹמֶר יָכִין מַלְבּוּשׁ:

17 He may lay it up, but the righteous will wear it, And the innocent will share the silver.

יז יָכִין וְצַדִּיק יִלְבָּשׁ וְכֶסֶף נָקִי יַחֲלֹק:

18 The house he built is like a bird's nest, Like the booth a watchman makes.

יח בָּנָה כָעָשׁ בֵּיתוֹ וּכְסֻכָּה עָשָׂה נֹצֵר:

19 He lies down, a rich man, with [his wealth] intact; When he opens his eyes it is gone.

יט עָשִׁיר יִשְׁכַּב וְלֹא יֵאָסֵף עֵינָיו פָּקַח וְאֵינֶנּוּ:

27:9 Will *Hashem* hear his cry In this chapter, *Iyov* indicates that his colleagues who came to comfort him have instead brought about the opposite effect. Contemporary Bible scholar Amos Hakham explains that *Iyov* is so hurt by his friends that he calls them his enemies. He declares that even *Hashem* will ignore their cries when they call out for help, since in trying to defend God, they have misrepresented Him and also offended their fellow. One must be careful with the words he chooses to comfort those who are grieving, for it is easy to cause pain and distress while intending to console. Sometimes remaining silent, as the friends did for the first seven days they sat with *Iyov*, is really the best response.

Blowing the shofar, a form of calling out to God on *Rosh Hashana*

20 Terror overtakes him like a flood; A storm wind makes off with him by night.

כ תְּשִׂיגֵהוּ כַמַּיִם בַּלָּהֹות לַיְלָה גְּנָבַתּוּ סוּפָֽה׃

21 The east wind carries him far away, and he is gone; It sweeps him from his place.

כא יִשָּׂאֵהוּ קָדִים וְיֵלַךְ וִישָׂעֲרֵהוּ מִמְּקֹמֽו׃

22 Then it hurls itself at him without mercy; He tries to escape from its force.

כב וְיַשְׁלֵךְ עָלָיו וְלֹא יַחְמֹל מִיָּדֹו בָּרֹוחַ יִבְרָֽח׃

23 It claps its hands at him, And whistles at him from its place.

כג יִשְׂפֹּק עָלֵימֹו כַפֵּימֹו וְיִשְׁרֹק עָלָיו מִמְּקֹמֽו׃

28 1 There is a mine for silver, And a place where gold is refined.

כח א כִּי יֵשׁ לַכֶּסֶף מֹוצָא וּמָקֹום לַזָּהָב יָזֹֽקּוּ׃

2 Iron is taken out of the earth, And copper smelted from rock.

ב בַּרְזֶל מֵעָפָר יֻקָּח וְאֶבֶן יָצוּק נְחוּשָֽׁה׃

3 He sets bounds for darkness; To every limit man probes, To rocks in deepest darkness.

ג קֵץ שָׂם לַחֹשֶׁךְ וּלְכָל־תַּכְלִית הוּא חֹוקֵר אֶבֶן אֹפֶל וְצַלְמָֽוֶת׃

4 They open up a shaft far from where men live, [In places] forgotten by wayfarers, Destitute of men, far removed.

ד פָּרַץ נַחַל מֵעִם־גָּר הַנִּשְׁכָּחִים מִנִּי־רָגֶל דַּלּוּ מֵאֱנֹושׁ נָֽעוּ׃

5 Earth, out of which food grows, Is changed below as if into fire.

ה אֶרֶץ מִמֶּנָּה יֵצֵא־לָחֶם וְתַחְתֶּיהָ נֶהְפַּךְ כְּמֹו־אֵֽשׁ׃

6 Its rocks are a source of sapphires; It contains gold dust too.

ו מְקֹום־סַפִּיר אֲבָנֶיהָ וְעַפְרֹת זָהָב לֹֽו׃

7 No bird of prey knows the path to it; The falcon's eye has not gazed upon it.

ז נָתִיב לֹא־יְדָעֹו עָיִט וְלֹא שְׁזָפַתּוּ עֵין אַיָּֽה׃

8 The proud beasts have not reached it; The lion has not crossed it.

ח לֹא־הִדְרִיכֻהוּ בְנֵי־שָׁחַץ לֹא־עָדָה עָלָיו שָֽׁחַל׃

9 Man sets his hand against the flinty rock And overturns mountains by the roots.

ט בַּחַלָּמִישׁ שָׁלַח יָדֹו הָפַךְ מִשֹּׁרֶשׁ הָרִֽים׃

10 He carves out channels through rock; His eyes behold every precious thing.

י בַּצּוּרֹות יְאֹרִים בִּקֵּעַ וְכָל־יְקָר רָאֲתָה עֵינֹֽו׃

11 He dams up the sources of the streams So that hidden things may be brought to light.

יא מִבְּכִי נְהָרֹות חִבֵּשׁ וְתַעֲלֻמָהּ יֹצִא אֹֽור׃

12 But where can wisdom be found; Where is the source of understanding?

יב וְהַחָכְמָה מֵאַיִן תִּמָּצֵא וְאֵי זֶה מְקֹום בִּינָֽה׃

13 No man can set a value on it; It cannot be found in the land of the living.

יג לֹא־יָדַע אֱנֹושׁ עֶרְכָּהּ וְלֹא תִמָּצֵא בְּאֶרֶץ הַֽחַיִּֽים׃

14 The deep says, "It is not in me"; The sea says, "I do not have it."

יד תְּהֹום אָמַר לֹא בִי־הִיא וְיָם אָמַר אֵין עִמָּדִֽי׃

15 It cannot be bartered for gold; Silver cannot be paid out as its price.

טו לֹא־יֻתַּן סְגֹור תַּחְתֶּיהָ וְלֹא יִשָּׁקֵל כֶּסֶף מְחִירָֽהּ׃

16 The finest gold of Ophir cannot be weighed against it, Nor precious onyx, nor sapphire.

טז לֹא־תְסֻלֶּה בְּכֶתֶם אוֹפִיר בְּשֹׁהַם יָקָר וְסַפִּיר:

17 Gold or glass cannot match its value, Nor vessels of fine gold be exchanged for it.

יז לֹא־יַעַרְכֶנָּה זָהָב וּזְכוֹכִית וּתְמוּרָתָהּ כְּלִי־פָז:

18 Coral and crystal cannot be mentioned with it; A pouch of wisdom is better than rubies.

יח רָאמוֹת וְגָבִישׁ לֹא יִזָּכֵר וּמֶשֶׁךְ חָכְמָה מִפְּנִינִים:

*ra-MOT v'-ga-VEESH LO yi-za-KHAYR u-ME-shekh
khokh-MAH mi-p'-nee-NEEM*

19 Topaz from Nubia cannot match its value; Pure gold cannot be weighed against it.

יט לֹא־יַעַרְכֶנָּה פִּטְדַת־כּוּשׁ בְּכֶתֶם טָהוֹר לֹא תְסֻלֶּה:

20 But whence does wisdom come? Where is the source of understanding?

כ וְהַחָכְמָה מֵאַיִן תָּבוֹא וְאֵי זֶה מְקוֹם בִּינָה:

21 It is hidden from the eyes of all living Concealed from the fowl of heaven.

כא וְנֶעֶלְמָה מֵעֵינֵי כָל־חָי וּמֵעוֹף הַשָּׁמַיִם נִסְתָּרָה:

22 Abaddon and Death say, "We have only a report of it."

כב אֲבַדּוֹן וָמָוֶת אָמְרוּ בְּאָזְנֵינוּ שָׁמַעְנוּ שִׁמְעָהּ:

23 *Hashem* understands the way to it; He knows its source;

כג אֱלֹהִים הֵבִין דַּרְכָּהּ וְהוּא יָדַע אֶת־מְקוֹמָהּ:

24 For He sees to the ends of the earth, Observes all that is beneath the heavens.

כד כִּי־הוּא לִקְצוֹת־הָאָרֶץ יַבִּיט תַּחַת כָּל־הַשָּׁמַיִם יִרְאֶה:

25 When He fixed the weight of the winds, Set the measure of the waters;

כה לַעֲשׂוֹת לָרוּחַ מִשְׁקָל וּמַיִם תִּכֵּן בְּמִדָּה:

26 When He made a rule for the rain And a course for the thunderstorms,

כו בַּעֲשֹׂתוֹ לַמָּטָר חֹק וְדֶרֶךְ לַחֲזִיז קֹלוֹת:

27 Then He saw it and gauged it; He measured it and probed it.

כז אָז רָאָהּ וַיְסַפְּרָהּ הֱכִינָהּ וְגַם־חֲקָרָהּ:

28 He said to man, "See! Fear of *Hashem* is wisdom; To shun evil is understanding."

כח וַיֹּאמֶר לָאָדָם הֵן יִרְאַת אֲדֹנָי הִיא חָכְמָה וְסוּר מֵרָע בִּינָה:

Rubies

28:18 A pouch of wisdom is better than rubies In several places, the Bible uses the ruby as an example of something precious. *Sefer Mishlei* (31:10) describes the worth of the "woman of valor" as "far beyond that of rubies," and in this verse the value of wisdom is described as "better than rubies." Rabbi Menachem Mendel Schneerson, the twentieth century leader of the Chabad-Lubavitch Hasidic movement, once told former Haifa mayor Arie Gurel: "In Haifa, there is a sea. One shouldn't become intimidated by something that is deep. This is the uniqueness of Haifa: It has a sea and there is a valley and in the valley are precious stones and gems. The Holy One, Blessed Be He, did a wondrous thing; He concealed them in the depths of the earth, and in any case, in the depth of the river." Based on that conversation, a company called Shefa Yamim was started for the purpose of searching for precious stones near Haifa. Over the years, Shefa Yamim has discovered diamonds and other precious stones hidden in the Land of Israel, among them rubies.

29 ¹ *Iyov* again took up his theme and said:

ויֹּסֶף אִיּוֹב שְׂאֵת מְשָׁלוֹ וַיֹּאמַר: א **כט**

² O that I were as in months gone by, In the days when *Hashem* watched over me,

מִי־יִתְּנֵנִי כְיַרְחֵי־קֶדֶם כִּימֵי אֱלוֹהַּ יִשְׁמְרֵנִי: ב

³ When His lamp shone over my head, When I walked in the dark by its light,

בְּהִלּוֹ נֵרוֹ עֲלֵי רֹאשִׁי לְאוֹרוֹ אֵלֶךְ חֹשֶׁךְ: ג

⁴ When I was in my prime, When *Hashem*'s company graced my tent,

כַּאֲשֶׁר הָיִיתִי בִּימֵי חָרְפִּי בְּסוֹד אֱלוֹהַּ עֲלֵי אָהֳלִי: ד

⁵ When *Shaddai* was still with me, When my lads surrounded me,

בְּעוֹד שַׁדַּי עִמָּדִי סְבִיבוֹתַי נְעָרָי: ה

⁶ When my feet were bathed in cream, And rocks poured out streams of oil for me.

בִּרְחֹץ הֲלִיכַי בְּחֵמָה וְצוּר יָצוּק עִמָּדִי פַּלְגֵי־שָׁמֶן: ו

⁷ When I passed through the city gates To take my seat in the square,

בְּצֵאתִי שַׁעַר עֲלֵי־קָרֶת בָּרְחוֹב אָכִין מוֹשָׁבִי: ז

⁸ Young men saw me and hid, Elders rose and stood;

רָאוּנִי נְעָרִים וְנֶחְבָּאוּ וִישִׁישִׁים קָמוּ עָמָדוּ: ח

⁹ Nobles held back their words; They clapped their hands to their mouths.

שָׂרִים עָצְרוּ בְמִלִּים וְכַף יָשִׂימוּ לְפִיהֶם: ט

¹⁰ The voices of princes were hushed; Their tongues stuck to their palates.

קוֹל־נְגִידִים נֶחְבָּאוּ וּלְשׁוֹנָם לְחִכָּם דָּבֵקָה: י

¹¹ The ear that heard me acclaimed me; The eye that saw, commended me.

כִּי אֹזֶן שָׁמְעָה וַתְּאַשְּׁרֵנִי וְעַיִן רָאֲתָה וַתְּעִידֵנִי: יא

¹² For I saved the poor man who cried out, The orphan who had none to help him.

כִּי־אֲמַלֵּט עָנִי מְשַׁוֵּעַ וְיָתוֹם וְלֹא־עֹזֵר לוֹ: יב

¹³ I received the blessing of the lost; I gladdened the heart of the widow.

בִּרְכַּת אֹבֵד עָלַי תָּבֹא וְלֵב אַלְמָנָה אַרְנִן: יג

¹⁴ I clothed myself in righteousness and it robed me; Justice was my cloak and turban.

צֶדֶק לָבַשְׁתִּי וַיִּלְבָּשֵׁנִי כִּמְעִיל וְצָנִיף מִשְׁפָּטִי: יד

¹⁵ I was eyes to the blind And feet to the lame.

עֵינַיִם הָיִיתִי לַעִוֵּר וְרַגְלַיִם לַפִּסֵּחַ אָנִי: טו

¹⁶ I was a father to the needy, And I looked into the case of the stranger.

אָב אָנֹכִי לָאֶבְיוֹנִים וְרִב לֹא־יָדַעְתִּי אֶחְקְרֵהוּ: טז

¹⁷ I broke the jaws of the wrongdoer, And I wrested prey from his teeth.

וָאֲשַׁבְּרָה מְתַלְּעוֹת עַוָּל וּמִשִּׁנָּיו אַשְׁלִיךְ טָרֶף: יז

¹⁸ I thought I would end my days with my family, And be as long-lived as the phoenix,

וָאֹמַר עִם־קִנִּי אֶגְוָע וְכַחוֹל אַרְבֶּה יָמִים: יח

¹⁹ My roots reaching water, And dew lying on my branches;

שָׁרְשִׁי פָתוּחַ אֱלֵי־מָיִם וְטַל יָלִין בִּקְצִירִי: יט

²⁰ My vigor refreshed, My bow ever new in my hand.

כְּבוֹדִי חָדָשׁ עִמָּדִי וְקַשְׁתִּי בְּיָדִי תַחֲלִיף: כ

²¹ Men would listen to me expectantly, And wait for my counsel.

לִי־שָׁמְעוּ וְיִחֵלּוּ וְיִדְּמוּ לְמוֹ עֲצָתִי: כא

²² After I spoke they had nothing to say; My words were as drops [of dew] upon them.

כב אַחֲרֵי דְבָרִי לֹא יִשְׁנוּ וְעָלֵימוֹ תִּטֹּף מִלָּתִי:

²³ They waited for me as for rain, For the late rain, their mouths open wide.

כג וְיִחֲלוּ כַמָּטָר לִי וּפִיהֶם פָּעֲרוּ לְמַלְקוֹשׁ:

²⁴ When I smiled at them, they would not believe it; They never expected a sign of my favor.

כד אֶשְׂחַק אֲלֵהֶם לֹא יַאֲמִינוּ וְאוֹר פָּנַי לֹא יַפִּילוּן:

²⁵ I decided their course and presided over them; I lived like a king among his troops, Like one who consoles mourners.

כה אֶבְחַר דַּרְכָּם וְאֵשֵׁב רֹאשׁ וְאֶשְׁכּוֹן כְּמֶלֶךְ בַּגְּדוּד כַּאֲשֶׁר אֲבֵלִים יְנַחֵם:

ev-KHAR dar-KAM v'-ay-SHAYV ROSH v'-esh-KON k'-ME-lekh ba-g'-DUD ka-a-SHER a-vay-LEEM y'-na-KHAYM

30 ¹ But now those younger than I deride me, [Men] whose fathers I would have disdained to put among my sheep dogs.

ל א וְעַתָּה שָׂחֲקוּ עָלַי צְעִירִים מִמֶּנִּי לְיָמִים אֲשֶׁר־מָאַסְתִּי אֲבוֹתָם לָשִׁית עִם־כַּלְבֵי צֹאנִי:

² Of what use to me is the strength of their hands? All their vigor is gone.

ב גַּם־כֹּחַ יְדֵיהֶם לָמָּה לִּי עָלֵימוֹ אָבַד כָּלַח:

³ Wasted from want and starvation, They flee to a parched land, To the gloom of desolate wasteland.

ג בְּחֶסֶר וּבְכָפָן גַּלְמוּד הַעֹרְקִים צִיָּה אֶמֶשׁ שׁוֹאָה וּמְשֹׁאָה:

⁴ They pluck saltwort and wormwood; The roots of broom are their food.

ד הַקֹּטְפִים מַלּוּחַ עֲלֵי־שִׂיחַ וְשֹׁרֶשׁ רְתָמִים לַחְמָם:

⁵ Driven out from society, They are cried at like a thief.

ה מִן־גֵּו יְגֹרָשׁוּ יָרִיעוּ עָלֵימוֹ כַּגַּנָּב:

⁶ They live in the gullies of wadis, In holes in the ground, and in rocks,

ו בַּעֲרוּץ נְחָלִים לִשְׁכֹּן חֹרֵי עָפָר וְכֵפִים:

⁷ Braying among the bushes, Huddling among the nettles,

ז בֵּין־שִׂיחִים יִנְהָקוּ תַּחַת חָרוּל יְסֻפָּחוּ:

⁸ Scoundrels, nobodies, Stricken from the earth.

ח בְּנֵי־נָבָל גַּם־בְּנֵי בְלִי־שֵׁם נִכְּאוּ מִן־הָאָרֶץ:

⁹ Now I am the butt of their gibes; I have become a byword to them.

ט וְעַתָּה נְגִינָתָם הָיִיתִי וָאֱהִי לָהֶם לְמִלָּה:

¹⁰ They abhor me; they keep their distance from me; They do not withhold spittle from my face.

י תִּעֲבוּנִי רָחֲקוּ מֶנִּי וּמִפָּנַי לֹא־חָשְׂכוּ רֹק:

29:25 I lived like a king among his troops *Iyov* notes that he was able to comfort the mourners and to deal fairly with the poor and widows because he was respected among them. It is relatively easy to be merciful and kind from a high position. Perhaps part of *Iyov's* test is to learn that his kindness should not be contingent on his feelings of superiority. Compassion and sensitivity to others is built into the nature of the Land of Israel, where the Sabbatical year (*Sh'mitta*) is observed every seven years, to remember and provide for the needy and less fortunate (see Leviticus 25, 6–7).

An Israeli farmer looks out on his field during the Sabbatical year

Job

11 Because *Hashem* has disarmed and humbled me,
They have thrown off restraint in my presence.

יא כִּי־יתרו [יִתְרִי] פִּתַּח וַיְעַנֵּנִי וְרֶסֶן מִפָּנַי
שִׁלֵּחוּ:

12 Mere striplings assail me at my right hand: They
put me to flight; They build their roads for my ruin.

יב עַל־יָמִין פִּרְחַח יָקוּמוּ רַגְלַי שִׁלֵּחוּ
וַיָּסֹלּוּ עָלַי אָרְחוֹת אֵידָם:

13 They tear up my path; They promote my fall,
Although it does them no good.

יג נָתְסוּ נְתִיבָתִי לְהַוָּתִי יֹעִילוּ לֹא עֹזֵר
לָמוֹ:

14 They come as through a wide breach; They roll in
like raging billows.

יד כְּפֶרֶץ רָחָב יֶאֱתָיוּ תַּחַת שֹׁאָה
הִתְגַּלְגָּלוּ:

15 Terror tumbles upon me; It sweeps away my honor
like the wind; My dignity vanishes like a cloud.

טו הָהְפַּךְ עָלַי בַּלָּהוֹת תִּרְדֹּף כָּרוּחַ נְדִבָתִי
וּכְעָב עָבְרָה יְשֻׁעָתִי:

16 So now my life runs out; Days of misery have taken
hold of me.

טז וְעַתָּה עָלַי תִּשְׁתַּפֵּךְ נַפְשִׁי יֹאחֲזוּנִי
יְמֵי־עֹנִי:

17 By night my bones feel gnawed; My sinews never
rest.

יז לַיְלָה עֲצָמַי נִקַּר מֵעָלָי וְעֹרְקַי לֹא
יִשְׁכָּבוּן:

18 With great effort I change clothing; The neck of my
tunic fits my waist.

יח בְּרָב־כֹּחַ יִתְחַפֵּשׂ לְבוּשִׁי כְּפִי כֻתָּנְתִּי
יַאַזְרֵנִי:

19 He regarded me as clay, I have become like dust
and ashes.

יט הֹרָנִי לַחֹמֶר וָאֶתְמַשֵּׁל כֶּעָפָר וָאֵפֶר:

ho-RA-nee la-KHO-mer va-et-ma-SHAYL ke-a-FAR va-AY-fer

20 I cry out to You, but You do not answer me; I wait,
but You do [not] consider me.

כ אֲשַׁוַּע אֵלֶיךָ וְלֹא תַעֲנֵנִי עָמַדְתִּי
וַתִּתְבֹּנֶן בִּי:

21 You have become cruel to me; With Your powerful
hand You harass me.

כא תֵּהָפֵךְ לְאַכְזָר לִי בְּעֹצֶם יָדְךָ תִשְׂטְמֵנִי:

22 You lift me up and mount me on the wind; You
make my courage melt.

כב תִּשָּׂאֵנִי אֶל־רוּחַ תַּרְכִּיבֵנִי וּתְמֹגְגֵנִי
תשוה [תֻּשִׁיָּה:]

23 I know You will bring me to death, The house
assigned for all the living.

כג כִּי־יָדַעְתִּי מָוֶת תְּשִׁיבֵנִי וּבֵית מוֹעֵד
לְכָל־חָי:

24 Surely He would not strike at a ruin If, in calamity,
one cried out to Him.

כד אַךְ לֹא־בְעִי יִשְׁלַח־יָד אִם־בְּפִידוֹ לָהֶן
שׁוּעַ:

30:19 I have become like dust and ashes *Iyov* expresses his modesty with the same words used by *Avraham* when he beseeched *Hashem* to save the cities of Sodom and Gomorrah: "I am but dust and ashes" (Genesis 18:27). Because of *Avraham's* genuine sense of modesty, he is granted the Land of Israel as an eternal inheritance for his descendants. When they follow in the path of their father *Avraham* and carry themselves with humility, the Children of Israel in turn merit living peacefully in the land. However, when they are filled with pride, they stray from *Hashem*, follow other gods and are then punished with exile from the land. *Yeshayahu* declares that during the time of the ultimate redemption, arrogance and pride will be eradicated from among the Children of Israel: "Man's haughty look shall be brought low, And the pride of mortals shall be humbled. None but *Hashem* shall be exalted in that day" (Isaiah 2:11).

A dust storm at the Large Crater in the Negev desert

Job

²⁵ Did I not weep for the unfortunate? Did I not grieve for the needy?

כה אִם־לֹא בָכִיתִי לִקְשֵׁה־יֹום עָגְמָה נַפְשִׁי לָאֶבְיֹון:

²⁶ I looked forward to good fortune, but evil came; I hoped for light, but darkness came.

כו כִּי טֹוב קִוִּיתִי וַיָּבֹא רָע וַאֲיַחֲלָה לְאֹור וַיָּבֹא אֹפֶל:

²⁷ My bowels are in turmoil without respite; Days of misery confront me.

כז מֵעַי רֻתְּחוּ וְלֹא־דָמּוּ קִדְּמֻנִי יְמֵי־עֹנִי:

²⁸ I walk about in sunless gloom; I rise in the assembly and cry out.

כח קֹדֵר הִלַּכְתִּי בְּלֹא חַמָּה קַמְתִּי בַקָּהָל אֲשַׁוֵּעַ:

²⁹ I have become a brother to jackals, A companion to ostriches.

כט אָח הָיִיתִי לְתַנִּים וְרֵעַ לִבְנֹות יַעֲנָה:

³⁰ My skin, blackened, is peeling off me; My bones are charred by the heat.

ל עֹורִי שָׁחַר מֵעָלָי וְעַצְמִי־חָרָה מִנִּי־חֹרֶב:

³¹ So my lyre is given over to mourning, My pipe, to accompany weepers.

לא וַיְהִי לְאֵבֶל כִּנֹּרִי וְעֻגָבִי לְקֹול בֹּכִים:

31 ¹ I have covenanted with my eyes Not to gaze on a maiden.

לא א בְּרִית כָּרַתִּי לְעֵינָי וּמָה אֶתְבֹּונֵן עַל־בְּתוּלָה:

² What fate is decreed by *Hashem* above? What lot, by *Shaddai* in the heights?

ב וּמֶה חֵלֶק אֱלֹוהַּ מִמָּעַל וְנַחֲלַת שַׁדַּי מִמְּרֹמִים:

³ Calamity is surely for the iniquitous; Misfortune, for the worker of mischief.

ג הֲלֹא־אֵיד לְעַוָּל וְנֵכֶר לְפֹעֲלֵי אָוֶן:

⁴ Surely He observes my ways, Takes account of my every step.

ד הֲלֹא־הוּא יִרְאֶה דְרָכָי וְכָל־צְעָדַי יִסְפֹּור:

⁵ Have I walked with worthless men, Or my feet hurried to deceit?

ה אִם־הָלַכְתִּי עִם־שָׁוְא וַתַּחַשׁ עַל־מִרְמָה רַגְלִי:

⁶ Let Him weigh me on the scale of righteousness; Let *Hashem* ascertain my integrity.

ו יִשְׁקְלֵנִי בְמֹאזְנֵי־צֶדֶק וְיֵדַע אֱלֹוהַּ תֻּמָּתִי:

⁷ If my feet have strayed from their course, My heart followed after my eyes, And a stain sullied my hands,

ז אִם תִּטֶּה אַשֻּׁרִי מִנִּי הַדֶּרֶךְ וְאַחַר עֵינַי הָלַךְ לִבִּי וּבְכַפַּי דָּבַק מְאוּם:

⁸ May I sow, but another reap, May the growth of my field be uprooted!

ח אֶזְרְעָה וְאַחֵר יֹאכֵל וְצֶאֱצָאַי יְשֹׁרָשׁוּ:

⁹ If my heart was ravished by the wife of my neighbor, And I lay in wait at his door,

ט אִם־נִפְתָּה לִבִּי עַל־אִשָּׁה וְעַל־פֶּתַח רֵעִי אָרָבְתִּי:

¹⁰ May my wife grind for another, May others kneel over her!

י תִּטְחַן לְאַחֵר אִשְׁתִּי וְעָלֶיהָ יִכְרְעוּן אֲחֵרִין:

¹¹ For that would have been debauchery, A criminal offense,

יא כִּי־הוּא [הִיא] זִמָּה והיא [וְהוּא] עָוֹן פְּלִילִים:

¹² A fire burning down to Abaddon, Consuming the roots of all my increase.

יב כִּי אֵשׁ הִיא עַד־אֲבַדֹּון תֹּאכֵל וּבְכָל־תְּבוּאָתִי תְשָׁרֵשׁ:

Job

¹³ Did I ever brush aside the case of my servants, man or maid, When they made a complaint against me?

יג אִם־אֶמְאַס מִשְׁפַּט עַבְדִּי וַאֲמָתִי בְּרִבָם עִמָּדִי:

¹⁴ What then should I do when *Hashem* arises; When He calls me to account, what should I answer Him?

יד וּמָה אֶעֱשֶׂה כִּי־יָקוּם אֵל וְכִי־יִפְקֹד מָה אֲשִׁיבֶנּוּ:

¹⁵ Did not He who made me in my mother's belly make him? Did not One form us both in the womb?

טו הֲלֹא־בַבֶּטֶן עֹשֵׂנִי עָשָׂהוּ וַיְכֻנֶנּוּ בָּרֶחֶם אֶחָד:

¹⁶ Did I deny the poor their needs, Or let a widow pine away,

טז אִם־אֶמְנַע מֵחֵפֶץ דַּלִּים וְעֵינֵי אַלְמָנָה אֲכַלֶּה:

¹⁷ By eating my food alone, The fatherless not eating of it also?

יז וְאֹכַל פִּתִּי לְבַדִּי וְלֹא־אָכַל יָתוֹם מִמֶּנָּה:

¹⁸ Why, from my youth he grew up with me as though I were his father; Since I left my mother's womb I was her guide.

יח כִּי מִנְּעוּרַי גְּדֵלַנִי כְאָב וּמִבֶּטֶן אִמִּי אַנְחֶנָּה:

¹⁹ I never saw an unclad wretch, A needy man without clothing,

יט אִם־אֶרְאֶה אוֹבֵד מִבְּלִי לְבוּשׁ וְאֵין כְּסוּת לָאֶבְיוֹן:

²⁰ Whose loins did not bless me As he warmed himself with the shearings of my sheep.

כ אִם־לֹא בֵרְכוּנִי חֲלָצוֹ [חֲלָצָיו] וּמִגֵּז כְּבָשַׂי יִתְחַמָּם:

²¹ If I raised my hand against the fatherless, Looking to my supporters in the gate,

כא אִם־הֲנִיפוֹתִי עַל־יָתוֹם יָדִי כִּי־אֶרְאֶה בַשַּׁעַר עֶזְרָתִי:

²² May my arm drop off my shoulder; My forearm break off at the elbow.

כב כְּתֵפִי מִשִּׁכְמָה תִפּוֹל וְאֶזְרֹעִי מִקָּנָה תִשָּׁבֵר:

²³ For I am in dread of *Hashem*-sent calamity; I cannot bear His threat.

כג כִּי פַחַד אֵלַי אֵיד אֵל וּמִשְּׂאֵתוֹ לֹא אוּכָל:

²⁴ Did I put my reliance on gold, Or regard fine gold as my bulwark?

כד אִם־שַׂמְתִּי זָהָב כִּסְלִי וְלַכֶּתֶם אָמַרְתִּי מִבְטַחִי:

²⁵ Did I rejoice in my great wealth, In having attained plenty?

כה אִם־אֶשְׂמַח כִּי־רַב חֵילִי וְכִי־כַבִּיר מָצְאָה יָדִי:

²⁶ If ever I saw the light shining, The moon on its course in full glory,

כו אִם־אֶרְאֶה אוֹר כִּי יָהֵל וְיָרֵחַ יָקָר הֹלֵךְ:

²⁷ And I secretly succumbed, And my hand touched my mouth in a kiss,

כז וַיִּפְתְּ בַּסֵּתֶר לִבִּי וַתִּשַּׁק יָדִי לְפִי:

²⁸ That, too, would have been a criminal offense, For I would have denied *Hashem* above.

כח גַּם־הוּא עָוֹן פְּלִילִי כִּי־כִחַשְׁתִּי לָאֵל מִמָּעַל:

²⁹ Did I rejoice over my enemy's misfortune? Did I thrill because evil befell him?

כט אִם־אֶשְׂמַח בְּפִיד מְשַׂנְאִי וְהִתְעֹרַרְתִּי כִּי־מְצָאוֹ רָע:

³⁰ I never let my mouth sin By wishing his death in a curse.

ל וְלֹא־נָתַתִּי לַחֲטֹא חִכִּי לִשְׁאֹל בְּאָלָה נַפְשׁוֹ:

³¹ (Indeed, the men of my clan said, "We would consume his flesh insatiably!")

לא אִם־לֹא אָמְרוּ מְתֵי אָהֳלִי מִי־יִתֵּן מִבְּשָׂרוֹ לֹא נִשְׂבָּע:

³² No sojourner spent the night in the open; I opened my doors to the road.

לב בַּחוּץ לֹא־יָלִין גֵּר דְּלָתַי לָאֹרַח אֶפְתָּח:

³³ Did I hide my transgressions like *Adam*, Bury my wrongdoing in my bosom,

לג אִם־כִּסִּיתִי כְאָדָם פְּשָׁעָי לִטְמוֹן בְּחֻבִּי עֲוֹנִי:

³⁴ That I should [now] fear the great multitude, And am shattered by the contempt of families, So that I keep silent and do not step outdoors?

לד כִּי אֶעֱרוֹץ הָמוֹן רַבָּה וּבוּז־מִשְׁפָּחוֹת יְחִתֵּנִי וָאֶדֹּם לֹא־אֵצֵא פָתַח:

³⁵ O that I had someone to give me a hearing; O that *Shaddai* would reply to my writ, Or my accuser draw up a true bill!

לה מִי יִתֶּן־לִי שֹׁמֵעַ לִי הֶן־תָּוִי שַׁדַּי יַעֲנֵנִי וְסֵפֶר כָּתַב אִישׁ רִיבִי:

³⁶ I would carry it on my shoulder; Tie it around me for a wreath.

לו אִם־לֹא עַל־שִׁכְמִי אֶשָּׂאֶנּוּ אֶעֶנְדֶנּוּ עֲטָרוֹת לִי:

³⁷ I would give him an account of my steps, Offer it as to a commander.

לז מִסְפַּר צְעָדַי אַגִּידֶנּוּ כְּמוֹ־נָגִיד אֲקָרֲבֶנּוּ:

³⁸ If my land cries out against me, Its furrows weep together;

לח אִם־עָלַי אַדְמָתִי תִזְעָק וְיַחַד תְּלָמֶיהָ יִבְכָּיוּן:

³⁹ If I have eaten its produce without payment, And made its [rightful] owners despair,

לט אִם־כֹּחָהּ אָכַלְתִּי בְלִי־כָסֶף וְנֶפֶשׁ בְּעָלֶיהָ הִפָּחְתִּי:

⁴⁰ May nettles grow there instead of wheat; Instead of barley, stinkweed! The words of *Iyov* are at an end.

מ תַּחַת חִטָּה יֵצֵא חוֹחַ וְתַחַת־שְׂעֹרָה בָאְשָׁה תַּמּוּ דִּבְרֵי אִיּוֹב:

*TA-khat khi-TAH yay-TZAY KHO-akh v'-TA-khat
s'-o-RAH vo-SHAH TA-mu div-RAY i-YOV*

32 ¹ These three men ceased replying to *Iyov*, for he considered himself right.

לב א וַיִּשְׁבְּתוּ שְׁלֹשֶׁת הָאֲנָשִׁים הָאֵלֶּה מֵעֲנוֹת אֶת־אִיּוֹב כִּי הוּא צַדִּיק בְּעֵינָיו:

² Then Elihu son of Barachel the Buzite, of the family of *Ram*, was angry – angry at *Iyov* because he thought himself right against *Hashem*.

ב וַיִּחַר אַף אֱלִיהוּא בֶן־בַּרַכְאֵל הַבּוּזִי מִמִּשְׁפַּחַת רָם בְּאִיּוֹב חָרָה אַפּוֹ עַל־צַדְּקוֹ נַפְשׁוֹ מֵאֱלֹהִים:

³ He was angry as well at his three friends, because they found no reply, but merely condemned *Iyov*.

ג וּבִשְׁלֹשֶׁת רֵעָיו חָרָה אַפּוֹ עַל אֲשֶׁר לֹא־מָצְאוּ מַעֲנֶה וַיַּרְשִׁיעוּ אֶת־אִיּוֹב:

31:40 The words of *Iyov* are at an end These words depict *Iyov's* exhaustion. After his long peroration lamenting his many misfortunes and speculating as to their possible causes, *Iyov* suddenly gives up. He no longer has the strength to fight or the energy to protest. *Iyov* spends a lot of time and emotional energy trying to make sense of his suffering. Due to his intense suffering, it was difficult for *Iyov* to recognize, as King *Shlomo* did, the truth that "For whom *Hashem* loves, He rebukes" (Proverbs 3:12). Often, suffering is brought upon a person as a mark of God's love, while He abandons those for whom He has no regard to the whims of chance. King *David* also realizes that sometimes suffering is really a gift, when he says "Happy is the man whom You discipline, *Hashem*," (Psalms 94:12). This idea is reflected in a well-known statement by Rabbi Simeon Bar Yochai (*Berachot* 5a): "Three gifts were given by God through suffering; *Torah*, the Land of Israel, and the world to come." The righteous are able to perceive that suffering paves the way to bearing the greatest gifts of God to His people.

An Israeli flag flies beside a decommissioned Israeli tank in the Golan Heights

4 Elihu waited out *Iyov*'s speech, for they were all older than he.

ד וֶאֱלִיהוּ חִכָּה אֶת־אִיּוֹב בִּדְבָרִים כִּי זְקֵנִים־הֵמָּה מִמֶּנּוּ לְיָמִים:

5 But when Elihu saw that the three men had nothing to reply, he was angry.

ה וַיַּרְא אֱלִיהוּ כִּי אֵין מַעֲנֶה בְּפִי שְׁלֹשֶׁת הָאֲנָשִׁים וַיִּחַר אַפּוֹ:

6 Then Elihu son of Barachel the Buzite said in reply: I have but few years, while you are old; Therefore I was too awestruck and fearful To hold forth among you.

ו וַיַּעַן אֱלִיהוּ בֶן־בַּרַכְאֵל הַבּוּזִי וַיֹּאמַר צָעִיר אֲנִי לְיָמִים וְאַתֶּם יְשִׁישִׁים עַל־כֵּן זָחַלְתִּי וָאִירָא מֵחַוֺּת דֵּעִי אֶתְכֶם:

va-YA-an e-lee-HU ven ba-rakh-AYL ha-bu-ZEE va-yo-MAR
tza-EER a-NEE l'-ya-MEEM v'-a-TEM y'-shee-SHEEM al KAYN
za-KHAL-tee va-ee-RA may-kha-VOT day-EE et-KHEM

7 I thought, "Let age speak; Let advanced years declare wise things."

ז אָמַרְתִּי יָמִים יְדַבֵּרוּ וְרֹב שָׁנִים יֹדִיעוּ חָכְמָה:

8 But truly it is the spirit in men, The breath of *Shaddai*, that gives them understanding.

ח אָכֵן רוּחַ־הִיא בֶאֱנוֹשׁ וְנִשְׁמַת שַׁדַּי תְּבִינֵם:

9 It is not the aged who are wise, The elders, who understand how to judge.

ט לֹא־רַבִּים יֶחְכָּמוּ וּזְקֵנִים יָבִינוּ מִשְׁפָּט:

10 Therefore I say, "Listen to me; I too would hold forth."

י לָכֵן אָמַרְתִּי שִׁמְעָה־לִּי אֲחַוֶּה דֵּעִי אַף־אָנִי:

11 Here I have waited out your speeches, I have given ear to your insights, While you probed the issues;

יא הֵן הוֹחַלְתִּי לְדִבְרֵיכֶם אָזִין עַד־תְּבוּנֹתֵיכֶם עַד־תַּחְקְרוּן מִלִּין:

12 But as I attended to you, I saw that none of you could argue with *Iyov*, Or offer replies to his statements.

יב וְעָדֵיכֶם אֶתְבּוֹנָן וְהִנֵּה אֵין לְאִיּוֹב מוֹכִיחַ עוֹנֶה אֲמָרָיו מִכֶּם:

13 I fear you will say, "We have found the wise course; *Hashem* will defeat him, not man."

יג פֶּן־תֹּאמְרוּ מָצָאנוּ חָכְמָה אֵל יִדְּפֶנּוּ לֹא־אִישׁ:

14 He did not set out his case against me, Nor shall I use your reasons to reply to him.

יד וְלֹא־עָרַךְ אֵלַי מִלִּין וּבְאִמְרֵיכֶם לֹא אֲשִׁיבֶנּוּ:

15 They have been broken and can no longer reply; Words fail them.

טו חַתּוּ לֹא־עָנוּ עוֹד הֶעְתִּיקוּ מֵהֶם מִלִּים:

16 I have waited till they stopped speaking, Till they ended and no longer replied.

טז וְהוֹחַלְתִּי כִּי־לֹא יְדַבֵּרוּ כִּי עָמְדוּ לֹא־עָנוּ עוֹד:

32:6 I have but few years, while you are old By allowing *Iyov*'s other friends to speak first and expressing his own opinion only afterwards, Elihu seems to be giving great respect to his elders. However, we quickly learn that his deference is just a show. Not only does he disagree with the others, but he even scolds them. This lack of concern for appropriate behavior is also clear in his condemnatory and unsympathetic stance towards *Iyov*. However, *Malachi* states that before the ultimate redemption occurs: "He shall reconcile parents with children and children with their parents, so that, when I come, I do not strike the whole land with utter destruction." (3:24). According to the Bible, the way to bring hope and happiness to the world, and to build up the Land of Israel, is by the young honoring their elders, in accordance with the fifth commandment.

A father and son walk hand in hand in a city park in Israel

17 Now I also would have my say; I too would like to hold forth,

יז אַעֲנֶה אַף־אֲנִי חֶלְקִי אֲחַוֶּה דֵעִי אַף־אָנִי:

18 For I am full of words; The wind in my belly presses me.

יח כִּי מָלֵתִי מִלִּים הֱצִיקַתְנִי רוּחַ בִּטְנִי:

19 My belly is like wine not yet opened, Like jugs of new wine ready to burst.

יט הִנֵּה־בִטְנִי כְּיַיִן לֹא־יִפָּתֵחַ כְּאֹבוֹת חֲדָשִׁים יִבָּקֵעַ:

20 Let me speak, then, and get relief; Let me open my lips and reply.

כ אֲדַבְּרָה וְיִרְוַח־לִי אֶפְתַּח שְׂפָתַי וְאֶעֱנֶה:

21 I would not show regard for any man, Or temper my speech for anyone's sake;

כא אַל־נָא אֶשָּׂא פְנֵי־אִישׁ וְאֶל־אָדָם לֹא אֲכַנֶּה:

22 For I do not know how to temper my speech – My Maker would soon carry me oV!

כב כִּי לֹא יָדַעְתִּי אֲכַנֶּה כִּמְעַט יִשָּׂאֵנִי עֹשֵׂנִי:

33 1 But now, *Iyov*, listen to my words, Give give ear to all that I say.

לג א וְאוּלָם שְׁמַע־נָא אִיּוֹב מִלָּי וְכָל־דְּבָרַי הַאֲזִינָה:

2 Now I open my lips; My tongue forms words in my mouth.

ב הִנֵּה־נָא פָּתַחְתִּי פִי דִּבְּרָה לְשׁוֹנִי בְחִכִּי:

3 My words bespeak the uprightness of my heart; My lips utter insight honestly.

ג יֹשֶׁר־לִבִּי אֲמָרָי וְדַעַת שְׂפָתַי בָּרוּר מִלֵּלוּ:

4 The spirit of *Hashem* formed me; The breath of *Shaddai* sustains me.

ד רוּחַ־אֵל עָשָׂתְנִי וְנִשְׁמַת שַׁדַּי תְּחַיֵּנִי:

5 If you can, answer me; Argue against me, take your stand.

ה אִם־תּוּכַל הֲשִׁיבֵנִי עֶרְכָה לְפָנַי הִתְיַצָּבָה:

6 You and I are the same before *Hashem*; I too was nipped from clay.

ו הֵן־אֲנִי כְפִיךָ לָאֵל מֵחֹמֶר קֹרַצְתִּי גַם־אָנִי:

7 ou are not overwhelmed by fear of me; My pressure does not weigh heavily on you.

ז הִנֵּה אֵמָתִי לֹא תְבַעֲתֶךָּ וְאַכְפִּי עָלֶיךָ לֹא־יִכְבָּד:

8 Indeed, you have stated in my hearing, I heard the words spoken,

ח אַךְ אָמַרְתָּ בְאָזְנָי וְקוֹל מִלִּין אֶשְׁמָע:

9 "I am guiltless, free from transgression; I am innocent, without iniquity.

ט זַךְ אֲנִי בְּלִי פָשַׁע חַף אָנֹכִי וְלֹא עָוֹן לִי:

10 But He finds reasons to oppose me, Considers me His enemy.

י הֵן תְּנוּאוֹת עָלַי יִמְצָא יַחְשְׁבֵנִי לְאוֹיֵב לוֹ:

11 He puts my feet in stocks, Watches all my ways."

יא יָשֵׂם בַּסַּד רַגְלָי יִשְׁמֹר כָּל־אָרְחֹתָי:

12 In this you are not right; I will answer you: *Hashem* is greater than any man.

יב הֶן־זֹאת לֹא־צָדַקְתָּ אֶעֱנֶךָּ כִּי־יִרְבֶּה אֱלוֹהַּ מֵאֱנוֹשׁ:

13 Why do you complain against Him That He does not reply to any of man's charges?

יג מַדּוּעַ אֵלָיו רִיבוֹתָ כִּי כָל־דְּבָרָיו לֹא־יַעֲנֶה:

14 For *Hashem* speaks time and again – Though man does not perceive it –

יד כִּי־בְאַחַת יְדַבֶּר־אֵל וּבִשְׁתַּיִם לֹא יְשׁוּרֶנָּה:

¹⁵ In a dream, a night vision, When deep sleep falls on men, While they slumber on their beds.

טו בַּחֲלוֹם חֶזְיוֹן לַיְלָה בִּנְפֹל תַּרְדֵּמָה עַל־אֲנָשִׁים בִּתְנוּמוֹת עֲלֵי מִשְׁכָּב:

¹⁶ Then He opens men's understanding, And by disciplining them leaves His signature

טז אָז יִגְלֶה אֹזֶן אֲנָשִׁים וּבְמֹסָרָם יַחְתֹּם:

¹⁷ To turn man away from an action, To suppress pride in man.

יז לְהָסִיר אָדָם מַעֲשֶׂה וְגֵוָה מִגֶּבֶר יְכַסֶּה:

¹⁸ He spares him from the Pit, His person, from perishing by the sword.

יח יַחְשֹׂךְ נַפְשׁוֹ מִנִּי־שָׁחַת וְחַיָּתוֹ מֵעֲבֹר בַּשָּׁלַח:

¹⁹ He is reproved by pains on his bed, And the trembling in his bones is constant.

יט וְהוּכַח בְּמַכְאוֹב עַל־מִשְׁכָּבוֹ וְרִיב [וְרוֹב] עֲצָמָיו אֵתָן:

²⁰ He detests food; Fine food [is repulsive] to him.

כ וְזִהֲמַתּוּ חַיָּתוֹ לָחֶם וְנַפְשׁוֹ מַאֲכַל תַּאֲוָה:

²¹ His flesh wastes away till it cannot be seen, And his bones are rubbed away till they are invisible.

כא יִכֶל בְּשָׂרוֹ מֵרֹאִי ושפי [וְשֻׁפּוּ] עַצְמוֹתָיו לֹא רֻאּוּ:

²² He comes close to the Pit, His life [verges] on death.

כב וַתִּקְרַב לַשַּׁחַת נַפְשׁוֹ וְחַיָּתוֹ לַמְמִתִים:

²³ If he has a representative, One advocate against a thousand To declare the man's uprightness,

כג אִם־יֵשׁ עָלָיו מַלְאָךְ מֵלִיץ אֶחָד מִנִּי־אָלֶף לְהַגִּיד לְאָדָם יָשְׁרוֹ:

²⁴ Then He has mercy on him and decrees, "Redeem him from descending to the Pit, For I have obtained his ransom;

כד וַיְחֻנֶּנּוּ וַיֹּאמֶר פְּדָעֵהוּ מֵרֶדֶת שָׁחַת מָצָאתִי כֹפֶר:

²⁵ Let his flesh be healthier than in his youth; Let him return to his younger days."

כה רֻטֲפַשׁ בְּשָׂרוֹ מִנֹּעַר יָשׁוּב לִימֵי עֲלוּמָיו:

²⁶ He prays to *Hashem* and is accepted by Him; He enters His presence with shouts of joy, For He requites a man for his righteousness.

כו יֶעְתַּר אֶל־אֱלוֹהַּ וַיִּרְצֵהוּ וַיַּרְא פָּנָיו בִּתְרוּעָה וַיָּשֶׁב לֶאֱנוֹשׁ צִדְקָתוֹ:

²⁷ He declares to men, "I have sinned; I have perverted what was right; But I was not paid back for it."

כז יָשֹׁר עַל־אֲנָשִׁים וַיֹּאמֶר חָטָאתִי וְיָשָׁר הֶעֱוֵיתִי וְלֹא־שָׁוָה לִי:

ya-SHOR al a-na-SHEEM va-YO-mer kha-TA-tee
v'-ya-SHAR he-e-VAY-tee v'lo SHA-vah LEE

33:27 I have sinned In order for a person to be forgiven and his soul to be redeemed (verse 28), he must repent his sins and return from his evil ways. This is true for individuals, and applies equally on a national level. The Bible tells us that after the Children of Israel have sinned and are scattered among the nations of the world, it is through repentance that they will merit redemption and return to their land: "You will return to *Hashem* your God, and you and your children will heed His command… then *Hashem* your God will restore your fortunes and take you back in love… And *Hashem* your God will bring you to the land that your fathers possessed, and you shall possess it" (Deuteronomy 30:2–5). It is through repentance that they will return to the Land of Israel and rebuild the *Beit Hamikdash* in *Yerushalayim*, the spiritual center of the world. Only then will we be able to truly bask in God's glory.

Thousands gather at the Western Wall to recite the penitential prayers recited before and during the Ten Days of Repentance

28 He redeemed him from passing into the Pit; He will enjoy the light.

כח פָּדָה נַפְשִׁי [נַפְשׁוֹ] מֵעֲבֹר בַּשָּׁחַת וְחַיָּתִי [וְחַיָּתוֹ] בָּאוֹר תִּרְאֶה:

29 Truly, *Hashem* does all these things Two or three times to a man,

כט הֶן־כָּל־אֵלֶּה יִפְעַל־אֵל פַּעֲמַיִם שָׁלוֹשׁ עִם־גָּבֶר:

30 To bring him back from the Pit, That he may bask in the light of life.

ל לְהָשִׁיב נַפְשׁוֹ מִנִּי־שָׁחַת לֵאוֹר בְּאוֹר הַחַיִּים:

31 Pay heed, *Iyov*, and hear me; Be still, and I will speak;

לא הַקְשֵׁב אִיּוֹב שְׁמַע־לִי הַחֲרֵשׁ וְאָנֹכִי אֲדַבֵּר:

32 If you have what to say, answer me; Speak, for I am eager to vindicate you.

לב אִם־יֵשׁ־מִלִּין הֲשִׁיבֵנִי דַּבֵּר כִּי־חָפַצְתִּי צַדְּקֶךָּ:

33 But if not, you listen to me; Be still, and I will teach you wisdom.

לג אִם־אַיִן אַתָּה שְׁמַע־לִי הַחֲרֵשׁ וַאֲאַלֶּפְךָ חָכְמָה:

34 ¹ Elihu said in reply:

א וַיַּעַן אֱלִיהוּא וַיֹּאמַר: לד

2 Listen, O wise men, to my words; You who have knowledge, give ear to me.

ב שִׁמְעוּ חֲכָמִים מִלָּי וְיֹדְעִים הַאֲזִינוּ לִי:

shim-U kha-kha-MEEM mi-LAI v'-yo-d'-EEM ha-a-ZEE-nu LEE

3 For the ear tests arguments As the palate tastes food.

ג כִּי־אֹזֶן מִלִּין תִּבְחָן וְחֵךְ יִטְעַם לֶאֱכֹל:

4 Let us decide for ourselves what is just; Let us know among ourselves what is good.

ד מִשְׁפָּט נִבְחֲרָה־לָּנוּ נֵדְעָה בֵינֵינוּ מַה־טּוֹב:

5 For *Iyov* has said, "I am right; *Hashem* has deprived me of justice.

ה כִּי־אָמַר אִיּוֹב צָדַקְתִּי וְאֵל הֵסִיר מִשְׁפָּטִי:

6 I declare the judgment against me false; My arrow-wound is deadly, though I am free from transgression."

ו עַל־מִשְׁפָּטִי אֲכַזֵּב אָנוּשׁ חִצִּי בְלִי־פָשַׁע:

7 What man is like *Iyov*, Who drinks mockery like water;

ז מִי־גֶבֶר כְּאִיּוֹב יִשְׁתֶּה־לַּעַג כַּמָּיִם:

8 Who makes common cause with evildoers, And goes with wicked men?

ח וְאָרַח לְחֶבְרָה עִם־פֹּעֲלֵי אָוֶן וְלָלֶכֶת עִם־אַנְשֵׁי־רֶשַׁע:

9 For he says, "Man gains nothing When he is in *Hashem*'s favor."

ט כִּי־אָמַר לֹא יִסְכָּן־גָּבֶר בִּרְצֹתוֹ עִם־אֱלֹהִים:

Heaven and earth at Timna Park in the Negev desert

34:2 Listen, O wise men, to my words Elihu calls on the wise men and those who have knowledge to 'listen' or 'hear', and also to 'give ear'. This pair of synonyms appear together in a number of places in the Bible, most prominently in *Sefer Devarim* 32:1. That verse introduces a song in which *Hashem* calls on heaven and earth to be the eternal witnesses to the covenant He has made with the Jewish people. If Israel follows His commandments, they will live peacefully in the land. If, however, they over-indulge, become morally corrupt and abandon the Lord, they will be sent into exile. The prophet *Yeshayahu* also calls on heaven and earth with these same words (Isaiah 1:2).

¹⁰ Therefore, men of understanding, listen to me; Wickedness be far from *Hashem*, Wrongdoing, from *Shaddai*!

¹¹ For He pays a man according to his actions, And provides for him according to his conduct;

¹² For *Hashem* surely does not act wickedly; *Shaddai* does not pervert justice.

¹³ Who placed the earth in His charge? Who ordered the entire world?

¹⁴ If He but intends it, He can call back His spirit and breath;

¹⁵ All flesh would at once expire, And mankind return to dust.

¹⁶ If you would understand, listen to this; Give ear to what I say.

¹⁷ Would one who hates justice govern? Would you condemn the Just Mighty One?

¹⁸ Would you call a king a scoundrel, Great men, wicked?

¹⁹ He is not partial to princes; The noble are not preferred to the wretched; For all of them are the work of His hands.

²⁰ Some die suddenly in the middle of the night; People are in turmoil and pass on; Even great men are removed – not by human hands.

²¹ For His eyes are upon a man's ways; He observes his every step.

²² Neither darkness nor gloom offers A hiding-place for evildoers.

²³ He has no set time for man To appear before *Hashem* in judgment.

²⁴ He shatters mighty men without number And sets others in their place.

²⁵ Truly, He knows their deeds; Night is over, and they are crushed.

²⁶ He strikes them down with the wicked Where people can see,

²⁷ Because they have been disloyal to Him And have not understood any of His ways;

י לָכֵן אַנְשֵׁי לֵבָב שִׁמְעוּ לִי חָלִלָה לָאֵל מֵרֶשַׁע וְשַׁדַּי מֵעָוֶל:

יא כִּי פֹעַל אָדָם יְשַׁלֶּם־לוֹ וּכְאֹרַח אִישׁ יַמְצִאֶנּוּ:

יב אַף־אָמְנָם אֵל לֹא־יַרְשִׁיעַ וְשַׁדַּי לֹא־יְעַוֵּת מִשְׁפָּט:

יג מִי־פָקַד עָלָיו אָרְצָה וּמִי שָׂם תֵּבֵל כֻּלָּהּ:

יד אִם־יָשִׂים אֵלָיו לִבּוֹ רוּחוֹ וְנִשְׁמָתוֹ אֵלָיו יֶאֱסֹף:

טו יִגְוַע כָּל־בָּשָׂר יָחַד וְאָדָם עַל־עָפָר יָשׁוּב:

טז וְאִם־בִּינָה שִׁמְעָה־זֹּאת הַאֲזִינָה לְקוֹל מִלָּי:

יז הַאַף שׂוֹנֵא מִשְׁפָּט יַחֲבוֹשׁ וְאִם־צַדִּיק כַּבִּיר תַּרְשִׁיעַ:

יח הַאֲמֹר לְמֶלֶךְ בְּלִיָּעַל רָשָׁע אֶל־נְדִיבִים:

יט אֲשֶׁר לֹא־נָשָׂא פְּנֵי שָׂרִים וְלֹא נִכַּר־שׁוֹעַ לִפְנֵי־דָל כִּי־מַעֲשֵׂה יָדָיו כֻּלָּם:

כ רֶגַע יָמֻתוּ וַחֲצוֹת לָיְלָה יְגֹעֲשׁוּ עָם וְיַעֲבֹרוּ וְיָסִירוּ אַבִּיר לֹא בְיָד:

כא כִּי־עֵינָיו עַל־דַּרְכֵי־אִישׁ וְכָל־צְעָדָיו יִרְאֶה:

כב אֵין־חֹשֶׁךְ וְאֵין צַלְמָוֶת לְהִסָּתֶר שָׁם פֹּעֲלֵי אָוֶן:

כג כִּי לֹא עַל־אִישׁ יָשִׂים עוֹד לַהֲלֹךְ אֶל־אֵל בַּמִּשְׁפָּט:

כד יָרֹעַ כַּבִּירִים לֹא־חֵקֶר וַיַּעֲמֵד אֲחֵרִים תַּחְתָּם:

כה לָכֵן יַכִּיר מַעְבָּדֵיהֶם וְהָפַךְ לַיְלָה וְיִדַּכָּאוּ:

כו תַּחַת־רְשָׁעִים סְפָקָם בִּמְקוֹם רֹאִים:

כז אֲשֶׁר עַל־כֵּן סָרוּ מֵאַחֲרָיו וְכָל־דְּרָכָיו לֹא הִשְׂכִּילוּ:

איוב
פרק לה

28 Thus He lets the cry of the poor come before Him; He listens to the cry of the needy.

כח לְהָבִיא עָלָיו צַעֲקַת־דָּל וְצַעֲקַת עֲנִיִּים יִשְׁמָע:

29 When He is silent, who will condemn? If He hides His face, who will see Him, Be it nation or man?

כט וְהוּא יַשְׁקִט וּמִי יַרְשִׁעַ וְיַסְתֵּר פָּנִים וּמִי יְשׁוּרֶנּוּ וְעַל־גּוֹי וְעַל־אָדָם יָחַד:

30 The impious man rule no more, Nor do those who ensnare the people.

ל מִמְּלֹךְ אָדָם חָנֵף מִמֹּקְשֵׁי עָם:

31 Has he said to *Hashem*, "I will bear [my punishment] and offend no more.

לא כִּי־אֶל־אֵל הֶאָמַר נָשָׂאתִי לֹא אֶחְבֹּל:

32 What I cannot see You teach me. If I have done iniquity, I shall not do so again"?

לב בִּלְעֲדֵי אֶחֱזֶה אַתָּה הֹרֵנִי אִם־עָוֶל פָּעַלְתִּי לֹא אֹסִיף:

33 Should He requite as you see fit? But you have despised [Him]! You must decide, not I; Speak what you know.

לג הֲמֵעִמְּךָ יְשַׁלְמֶנָּה כִּי־מָאַסְתָּ כִּי־אַתָּה תִבְחַר וְלֹא־אָנִי וּמַה־יָדַעְתָּ דַבֵּר:

34 Men of understanding say to me, Wise men who hear me,

לד אַנְשֵׁי לֵבָב יֹאמְרוּ לִי וְגֶבֶר חָכָם שֹׁמֵעַ לִי:

35 "*Iyov* does not speak with knowledge; His words lack understanding."

לה אִיּוֹב לֹא־בְדַעַת יְדַבֵּר וּדְבָרָיו לֹא בְהַשְׂכֵּיל:

36 Would that *Iyov* were tried to the limit For answers which befit sinful men.

לו אָבִי יִבָּחֵן אִיּוֹב עַד־נֶצַח עַל־תְּשֻׁבֹת בְּאַנְשֵׁי־אָוֶן:

37 He adds to his sin; He increases his transgression among us; He multiplies his statements against *Hashem*.

לז כִּי יֹסִיף עַל־חַטָּאתוֹ פֶּשַׁע בֵּינֵינוּ יִסְפּוֹק וְיֶרֶב אֲמָרָיו לָאֵל:

35 1 Elihu said in reply:

לה א וַיַּעַן אֱלִיהוּ וַיֹּאמַר:

2 Do you think it just To say, "I am right against *Hashem*"?

ב הֲזֹאת חָשַׁבְתָּ לְמִשְׁפָּט אָמַרְתָּ צִדְקִי מֵאֵל:

3 If you ask how it benefits you, "What have I gained from not sinning?"

ג כִּי־תֹאמַר מַה־יִּסְכָּן־לָךְ מָה־אֹעִיל מֵחַטָּאתִי:

4 I shall give you a reply, You, along with your friends.

ד אֲנִי אֲשִׁיבְךָ מִלִּין וְאֶת־רֵעֶיךָ עִמָּךְ:

5 Behold the heavens and see; Look at the skies high above you.

ה הַבֵּט שָׁמַיִם וּרְאֵה וְשׁוּר שְׁחָקִים גָּבְהוּ מִמֶּךָּ:

6 If you sin, what do you do to Him? If your transgressions are many, How do you affect Him?

ו אִם־חָטָאתָ מַה־תִּפְעָל־בּוֹ וְרַבּוּ פְשָׁעֶיךָ מַה־תַּעֲשֶׂה־לּוֹ:

7 If you are righteous, What do you give Him; What does He receive from your hand?

ז אִם־צָדַקְתָּ מַה־תִּתֶּן־לוֹ אוֹ מַה־מִיָּדְךָ יִקָּח:

8 Your wickedness affects men like yourself; Your righteousness, mortals.

ח לְאִישׁ־כָּמוֹךָ רִשְׁעֶךָ וּלְבֶן־אָדָם צִדְקָתֶךָ:

9 Because of contention the oppressed cry out; They shout because of the power of the great.

ט מֵרֹב עֲשׁוּקִים יַזְעִיקוּ יְשַׁוְּעוּ מִזְּרוֹעַ רַבִּים:

Job

10 But none says, "Where is my God, my Maker, Who gives strength in the night;

י וְלֹא־אָמַר אַיֵּה אֱלוֹהַּ עֹשָׂי נֹתֵן זְמִרוֹת בַּלָּיְלָה:

v'-LO a-MAR a-YAY e-LO-ah o-SAI no-TAYN z'-mee-ROT ba-LAI-lah

11 Who gives us more knowledge than the beasts of the earth, Makes us wiser than the birds of the sky?"

יא מַלְּפֵנוּ מִבַּהֲמוֹת אָרֶץ וּמֵעוֹף הַשָּׁמַיִם יְחַכְּמֵנוּ:

12 Then they cry out, but He does not respond Because of the arrogance of evil men.

יב שָׁם יִצְעֲקוּ וְלֹא יַעֲנֶה מִפְּנֵי גְּאוֹן רָעִים:

13 Surely it is false that *Hashem* does not listen, That *Shaddai* does not take note of it.

יג אַךְ־שָׁוְא לֹא־יִשְׁמַע אֵל וְשַׁדַּי לֹא יְשׁוּרֶנָּה:

14 Though you say, "You do not take note of it," The case is before Him; So wait for Him.

יד אַף כִּי־תֹאמַר לֹא תְשׁוּרֶנּוּ דִּין לְפָנָיו וּתְחוֹלֵל לוֹ:

15 But since now it does not seem so, He vents his anger; He does not realize that it may be long drawn out.

טו וְעַתָּה כִּי־אַיִן פָּקַד אַפּוֹ וְלֹא־יָדַע בַּפַּשׁ מְאֹד:

16 Hence *Iyov* mouths empty words, And piles up words without knowledge.

טז וְאִיּוֹב הֶבֶל יִפְצֶה־פִּיהוּ בִּבְלִי־דַעַת מִלִּין יַכְבִּר:

36 1 Then Elihu spoke once more.

לו א וַיֹּסֶף אֱלִיהוּא וַיֹּאמַר:

2 Wait a little and let me hold forth; There is still more to say for *Hashem*.

ב כַּתַּר־לִי זְעֵיר וַאֲחַוֶּךָּ כִּי עוֹד לֶאֱלוֹהַּ מִלִּים:

3 I will make my opinions widely known; I will justify my Maker.

ג אֶשָּׂא דֵעִי לְמֵרָחוֹק וּלְפֹעֲלִי אֶתֵּן־צֶדֶק:

4 In truth, my words are not false; A man of sound opinions is before you.

ד כִּי־אָמְנָם לֹא־שֶׁקֶר מִלָּי תְּמִים דֵּעוֹת עִמָּךְ:

5 See, *Hashem* is mighty; He is not contemptuous; He is mighty in strength and mind.

ה הֶן־אֵל כַּבִּיר וְלֹא יִמְאָס כַּבִּיר כֹּחַ לֵב:

6 He does not let the wicked live; He grants justice to the lowly.

ו לֹא־יְחַיֶּה רָשָׁע וּמִשְׁפַּט עֲנִיִּים יִתֵּן:

7 He does not withdraw His eyes from the righteous; With kings on thrones He seats them forever, and they are exalted.

ז לֹא־יִגְרַע מִצַּדִּיק עֵינָיו וְאֶת־מְלָכִים לַכִּסֵּא וַיֹּשִׁיבֵם לָנֶצַח וַיִּגְבָּהוּ:

A ripe pomegranate tree: autumn in Israel

Job

35:10 Who gives strength in the night The Hebrew word for 'strength' in this verse is *zemirot* (זמירות). This word generally means 'songs', but its root (ז-מ-ר) also has another meaning: To prune a tree and remove its extraneous branches. The connection between these words is not initially obvious, but as the "mother of all languages," Hebrew words often get to the very essence of the object they are describing. A tree thrives when its heavy branches and extraneous foliage are clipped, so that it can most effectively apply its nutritional resources. Though it may seem that cutting a tree weakens it, this process actually strengthens it. Similarly, music is not merely a collection of randomly collected notes. To be left with a beautiful song, one must "prune" extraneous sounds. This same principle can be applied to our lives; in order to properly strengthen ourselves and transform our entire existence into holy song, we must remove the burdensome elements of our character.

זמר

8 If they are bound in shackles And caught in trammels of affliction,

ח וְאִם־אֲסוּרִים בַּזִּקִּים יִלָּכְדוּן בְּחַבְלֵי־עֹנִי:

9 He declares to them what they have done, And that their transgressions are excessive;

ט וַיַּגֵּד לָהֶם פָּעֳלָם וּפִשְׁעֵיהֶם כִּי יִתְגַּבָּרוּ:

10 He opens their understanding by discipline, And orders them back from mischief.

י וַיִּגֶל אָזְנָם לַמּוּסָר וַיֹּאמֶר כִּי־יְשֻׁבוּן מֵאָוֶן:

11 If they will serve obediently, They shall spend their days in happiness, Their years in delight.

יא אִם־יִשְׁמְעוּ וְיַעֲבֹדוּ יְכַלּוּ יְמֵיהֶם בַּטּוֹב וּשְׁנֵיהֶם בַּנְּעִימִים:

12 But if they are not obedient, They shall perish by the sword, Die for lack of understanding.

יב וְאִם־לֹא יִשְׁמְעוּ בְּשֶׁלַח יַעֲבֹרוּ וְיִגְוְעוּ כִּבְלִי־דָעַת:

13 But the impious in heart become enraged; They do not cry for help when He afflicts them.

יג וְחַנְפֵי־לֵב יָשִׂימוּ אָף לֹא יְשַׁוְּעוּ כִּי אֲסָרָם:

14 They die in their youth; [Expire] among the depraved.

יד תָּמֹת בַּנֹּעַר נַפְשָׁם וְחַיָּתָם בַּקְּדֵשִׁים:

15 He rescues the lowly from their affliction, And opens their understanding through distress.

טו יְחַלֵּץ עָנִי בְעָנְיוֹ וְיִגֶל בַּלַּחַץ אָזְנָם:

16 Indeed, He draws you away from the brink of distress To a broad place where there is no constraint; Your table is laid out with rich food.

טז וְאַף הֲסִיתְךָ מִפִּי־צָר רַחַב לֹא־מוּצָק תַּחְתֶּיהָ וְנַחַת שֻׁלְחָנְךָ מָלֵא דָשֶׁן:

17 You are obsessed with the case of the wicked man, But the justice of the case will be upheld.

יז וְדִין־רָשָׁע מָלֵאתָ דִּין וּמִשְׁפָּט יִתְמֹכוּ:

18 Let anger at his affluence not mislead you; Let much bribery not turn you aside.

יח כִּי־חֵמָה פֶּן־יְסִיתְךָ בְסָפֶק וְרָב־כֹּפֶר אַל־יַטֶּךָּ:

19 Will your limitless wealth avail you, All your powerful efforts?

יט הֲיַעֲרֹךְ שׁוּעֲךָ לֹא בְצָר וְכֹל מַאֲמַצֵּי־כֹחַ:

20 Do not long for the night When peoples vanish where they are.

כ אַל־תִּשְׁאַף הַלָּיְלָה לַעֲלוֹת עַמִּים תַּחְתָּם:

21 Beware! Do not turn to mischief; Because of that you have been tried by affliction.

כא הִשָּׁמֶר אַל־תֵּפֶן אֶל־אָוֶן כִּי־עַל־זֶה בָּחַרְתָּ מֵעֹנִי:

22 See, *Hashem* is beyond reach in His power; Who governs like Him?

כב הֶן־אֵל יַשְׂגִּיב בְּכֹחוֹ מִי כָמֹהוּ מוֹרֶה:

23 Who ever reproached Him for His conduct? Who ever said, "You have done wrong"?

כג מִי־פָקַד עָלָיו דַּרְכּוֹ וּמִי־אָמַר פָּעַלְתָּ עַוְלָה:

24 Remember, then, to magnify His work, Of which men have sung,

כד זְכֹר כִּי־תַשְׂגִּיא פָעֳלוֹ אֲשֶׁר שֹׁרְרוּ אֲנָשִׁים:

25 Which all men have beheld, Men have seen, from a distance.

כה כָּל־אָדָם חָזוּ־בוֹ אֱנוֹשׁ יַבִּיט מֵרָחוֹק:

26 See, *Hashem* is greater than we can know; The number of His years cannot be counted.

כו הֶן־אֵל שַׂגִּיא וְלֹא נֵדָע מִסְפַּר שָׁנָיו וְלֹא־חֵקֶר:

Job

27 He forms the droplets of water, Which cluster into rain, from His mist.

כז כִּי יְגָרַע נִטְפֵי־מָיִם יָזֹקּוּ מָטָר לְאֵדֽוֹ׃

28 The skies rain; They pour down on all mankind.

כח אֲשֶׁר־יִזְּלוּ שְׁחָקִים יִרְעֲפוּ עֲלֵי אָדָם רָֽב׃

29 Can one, indeed, contemplate the expanse of clouds, The thunderings from His pavilion?

כט אַף אִם־יָבִין מִפְרְשֵׂי־עָב תְּשֻׁאוֹת סֻכָּתֽוֹ׃

30 See, He spreads His lightning over it; It fills the bed of the sea.

ל הֵן־פָּרַשׂ עָלָיו אוֹרוֹ וְשָׁרְשֵׁי הַיָּם כִּסָּֽה׃

31 By these things He controls peoples; He gives food in abundance.

לא כִּי־בָם יָדִין עַמִּים יִתֶּן־אֹכֶל לְמַכְבִּֽיר׃

kee VAM ya-DEEN a-MEEM yi-TEN O-khel l'-makh-BEER

32 Lightning fills His hands; He orders it to hit the mark.

לב עַל־כַּפַּיִם כִּסָּה־אוֹר וַיְצַו עָלֶיהָ בְמַפְגִּֽיעַ׃

33 Its noise tells of Him. The kindling of anger against iniquity.

לג יַגִּיד עָלָיו רֵעוֹ מִקְנֶה אַף עַל־עוֹלֶֽה׃

37 ¹ Because of this, too, my heart quakes, And leaps from its place.

לז א אַף־לְזֹאת יֶחֱרַד לִבִּי וְיִתַּר מִמְּקוֹמֽוֹ׃

² Just listen to the noise of His rumbling, To the sound that comes out of His mouth.

ב שִׁמְעוּ שָׁמוֹעַ בְּרֹגֶז קֹלוֹ וְהֶגֶה מִפִּיו יֵצֵֽא׃

³ He lets it loose beneath the entire heavens – His lightning, to the ends of the earth.

ג תַּחַת־כָּל־הַשָּׁמַיִם יִשְׁרֵהוּ וְאוֹרוֹ עַל־כַּנְפוֹת הָאָֽרֶץ׃

⁴ After it, He lets out a roar; He thunders in His majestic voice. No one can find a trace of it by the time His voice is heard.

ד אַחֲרָיו יִשְׁאַג־קוֹל יַרְעֵם בְּקוֹל גְּאוֹנוֹ וְלֹא יְעַקְּבֵם כִּי־יִשָּׁמַע קוֹלֽוֹ׃

a-kha-RAV yish-AG KOL yar-AYM b'-KOL g'-o-NO
v'-LO y'-ak-VAYM kee yi-sha-MA ko-LO

⁵ *Hashem* thunders marvelously with His voice; He works wonders that we cannot understand.

ה יַרְעֵם אֵל בְּקוֹלוֹ נִפְלָאוֹת עֹשֶׂה גְדֹלוֹת וְלֹא נֵדָֽע׃

Rain falls on a vineyard in the Golan Heights

36:31 He gives food in abundance *Hashem* uses His control over nature to punish people and to reward them. If He judges mankind favorably, then He will provide "food in abundance." This is especially true in the Land of Israel, as expressed in *Sefer Devarim* (11:13–17). God says that if the Children of Israel perform good deeds and follow His commands, He will reward them with rain at the proper times, which will produce bountiful crops. Conversely, drought and famine are the punishments for national sin. It is important to recognize that while rain and drought are seemingly natural phenomena, they are actually *Hashem's* vehicle for reward and punishment, and for communicating with His children.

37:4 After it, He lets out a roar In this verse, the majestic voice of God roars, proclaiming His justice and goodness to all creatures. The Divine voice is often described in the Bible as a roar, frequently as an expression of His anger. In ancient Israel, lions were commonly found in the forested areas of the country. The lion is therefore often used as a metaphor in the Bible. Though the lion's roar is frightening, it serves as a warning to its prey that the lion is present, and clever prey can escape. So too, God communicates with His children to warn them to correct their ways before it is too late.

⁶ He commands the snow, "Fall to the ground!" And the downpour of rain, His mighty downpour of rain,

ו כִּי לַשֶּׁלֶג יֹאמַר הֱוֵא אָרֶץ וְגֶשֶׁם מָטָר וְגֶשֶׁם מִטְרוֹת עֻזּוֹ:

⁷ Is as a sign on every man's hand, That all men may know His doings.

ז בְּיַד־כָּל־אָדָם יַחְתּוֹם לָדַעַת כָּל־אַנְשֵׁי מַעֲשֵׂהוּ:

⁸ Then the beast enters its lair, And remains in its den.

ח וַתָּבֹא חַיָּה בְמוֹ־אָרֶב וּבִמְעוֹנֹתֶיהָ תִשְׁכֹּן:

⁹ The storm wind comes from its chamber, And the cold from the constellations.

ט מִן־הַחֶדֶר תָּבוֹא סוּפָה וּמִמְּזָרִים קָרָה:

¹⁰ By the breath of *Hashem* ice is formed, And the expanse of water becomes solid.

י מִנִּשְׁמַת־אֵל יִתֶּן־קָרַח וְרֹחַב מַיִם בְּמוּצָק:

¹¹ He also loads the clouds with moisture And scatters His lightning-clouds.

יא אַף־בְּרִי יַטְרִיחַ עָב יָפִיץ עֲנַן אוֹרוֹ:

¹² He keeps turning events by His stratagems, That they might accomplish all that He commands them Throughout the inhabited earth,

יב וְהוּא מְסִבּוֹת מִתְהַפֵּךְ בְּתַחְבּוּלֹתָו [בְּתַחְבּוּלֹתָיו] לְפָעֳלָם כֹּל אֲשֶׁר יְצַוֵּם עַל־פְּנֵי תֵבֵל אָרְצָה:

¹³ Causing each of them to happen to His land, Whether as a scourge or as a blessing.

יג אִם־לְשֵׁבֶט אִם־לְאַרְצוֹ אִם־לְחֶסֶד יַמְצִאֵהוּ:

¹⁴ Give ear to this, *Iyov*; Stop to consider the marvels of *Hashem*.

יד הַאֲזִינָה זֹּאת אִיּוֹב עֲמֹד וְהִתְבּוֹנֵן נִפְלְאוֹת אֵל:

¹⁵ Do you know what charge *Hashem* lays upon them When His lightning-clouds shine?

טו הֲתֵדַע בְּשׂוּם־אֱלוֹהַּ עֲלֵיהֶם וְהוֹפִיעַ אוֹר עֲנָנוֹ:

¹⁶ Do you know the marvels worked upon the expanse of clouds By Him whose understanding is perfect,

טז הֲתֵדַע עַל־מִפְלְשֵׂי־עָב מִפְלְאוֹת תְּמִים דֵּעִים:

¹⁷ Why your clothes become hot When the land is becalmed by the south wind?

יז אֲשֶׁר־בְּגָדֶיךָ חַמִּים בְּהַשְׁקִט אֶרֶץ מִדָּרוֹם:

¹⁸ Can you help him stretch out the heavens, Firm as a mirror of cast metal?

יח תַּרְקִיעַ עִמּוֹ לִשְׁחָקִים חֲזָקִים כִּרְאִי מוּצָק:

¹⁹ Inform us, then, what we may say to Him; We cannot argue because [we are in] darkness.

יט הוֹדִיעֵנוּ מַה־נֹּאמַר לוֹ לֹא־נַעֲרֹךְ מִפְּנֵי־חֹשֶׁךְ:

²⁰ Is anything conveyed to Him when I speak? Can a man say anything when he is confused?

כ הַיְסֻפַּר־לוֹ כִּי אֲדַבֵּר אִם־אָמַר אִישׁ כִּי יְבֻלָּע:

²¹ Now, then, one cannot see the sun, Though it be bright in the heavens, Until the wind comes and clears them [of clouds].

כא וְעַתָּה לֹא רָאוּ אוֹר בָּהִיר הוּא בַּשְּׁחָקִים וְרוּחַ עָבְרָה וַתְּטַהֲרֵם:

²² By the north wind the golden rays emerge; The splendor about *Hashem* is awesome.

כב מִצָּפוֹן זָהָב יֶאֱתֶה עַל־אֱלוֹהַּ נוֹרָא הוֹד:

²³ Shaddai – we cannot attain to Him; He is great in power and justice And abundant in righteousness; He does not torment.

כג שַׁדַּי לֹא־מְצָאנֻהוּ שַׂגִּיא־כֹחַ וּמִשְׁפָּט וְרֹב־צְדָקָה לֹא יְעַנֶּה:

²⁴ Therefore, men are in awe of Him Whom none of the wise can perceive.

כד לָכֵן יְרֵאוּהוּ אֲנָשִׁים לֹא־יִרְאֶה כָּל־חַכְמֵי־לֵב:

38 ¹ Then *Hashem* replied to *Iyov* out of the tempest and said:

לח א וַיַּעַן־יְהֹוָה אֶת־אִיּוֹב מִן הסערה [מִן־הַסְּעָרָה] וַיֹּאמַר:

² Who is this who darkens counsel, Speaking without knowledge?

ב מִי זֶה מַחְשִׁיךְ עֵצָה בְמִלִּין בְּלִי־דָעַת:

³ Gird your loins like a man; I will ask and you will inform Me.

ג אֱזָר־נָא כְגֶבֶר חֲלָצֶיךָ וְאֶשְׁאָלְךָ וְהוֹדִיעֵנִי:

⁴ Where were you when I laid the earth's foundations? Speak if you have understanding.

ד אֵיפֹה הָיִיתָ בְּיָסְדִי־אָרֶץ הַגֵּד אִם־יָדַעְתָּ בִינָה:

ay-FOH ha-YEE-ta b'-yos-DEE A-retz ha-GAYD im ya-DA-ta vee-NAH

⁵ Do you know who fixed its dimensions Or who measured it with a line?

ה מִי־שָׂם מְמַדֶּיהָ כִּי תֵדָע אוֹ מִי־נָטָה עָלֶיהָ קָּו:

⁶ Onto what were its bases sunk? Who set its cornerstone

ו עַל־מָה אֲדָנֶיהָ הָטְבָּעוּ אוֹ מִי־יָרָה אֶבֶן פִּנָּתָהּ:

⁷ When the morning stars sang together And all the divine beings shouted for joy?

ז בְּרָן־יַחַד כּוֹכְבֵי בֹקֶר וַיָּרִיעוּ כָּל־בְּנֵי אֱלֹהִים:

⁸ Who closed the sea behind doors When it gushed forth out of the womb,

ח וַיָּסֶךְ בִּדְלָתַיִם יָם בְּגִיחוֹ מֵרֶחֶם יֵצֵא:

⁹ When I clothed it in clouds, Swaddled it in dense clouds,

ט בְּשׂוּמִי עָנָן לְבֻשׁוֹ וַעֲרָפֶל חֲתֻלָּתוֹ:

¹⁰ When I made breakers My limit for it, And set up its bar and doors,

י וָאֶשְׁבֹּר עָלָיו חֻקִּי וָאָשִׂים בְּרִיחַ וּדְלָתָיִם:

¹¹ And said, "You may come so far and no farther; Here your surging waves will stop"?

יא וָאֹמַר עַד־פֹּה תָבוֹא וְלֹא תֹסִיף וּפֹא־יָשִׁית בִּגְאוֹן גַּלֶּיךָ:

¹² Have you ever commanded the day to break, Assigned the dawn its place,

יב הֲמִיָּמֶיךָ צִוִּיתָ בֹּקֶר ידעתה [יִדַּעְתָּ] השחר [הַשַּׁחַר] מְקֹמוֹ:

¹³ So that it seizes the corners of the earth And shakes the wicked out of it?

יג לֶאֱחֹז בְּכַנְפוֹת הָאָרֶץ וְיִנָּעֲרוּ רְשָׁעִים מִמֶּנָּה:

Appreciating nature in Eilat

38:4 Where were you when I laid the earth's foundations? In this chapter, *Hashem* finally responds to *Iyov's* questioning of His justice. He says that since *Iyov* was not around when God created the world, he cannot possibly understand the way in which He runs the world. Rabbi Judah Halevi, in his book *The Kuzari*, suggests that precisely because man was not around to witness the creation of the world, *Hashem* introduces Himself in the first of the ten commandments as the God who took the Children of Israel out of Egypt, rather than the God who created the world (Exodus 20:2). The people could not relate to God as creator, since they did not explicitly know him as such. However, the Exodus, which was experienced by the entire Nation of Israel, proved God's existence to them beyond a shadow of a doubt. Furthermore, *Ramban* explains that *Hashem's* manipulation of nature during the Exodus proves that He is indeed the Creator of the natural order of the world, and that He continues to be involved in the running of the world and the lives of His people.

¹⁴ It changes like clay under the seal Till [its hues] are fixed like those of a garment.

יד תִּתְהַפֵּךְ כְּחֹמֶר חוֹתָם וְיִתְיַצְּבוּ כְּמוֹ לְבוּשׁ:

¹⁵ Their light is withheld from the wicked, And the upraised arm is broken.

טו וְיִמָּנַע מֵרְשָׁעִים אוֹרָם וּזְרוֹעַ רָמָה תִּשָּׁבֵר:

¹⁶ Have you penetrated to the sources of the sea, Or walked in the recesses of the deep?

טז הֲבָאתָ עַד־נִבְכֵי־יָם וּבְחֵקֶר תְּהוֹם הִתְהַלָּכְתָּ:

¹⁷ Have the gates of death been disclosed to you? Have you seen the gates of deep darkness?

יז הֲנִגְלוּ לְךָ שַׁעֲרֵי־מָוֶת וְשַׁעֲרֵי צַלְמָוֶת תִּרְאֶה:

¹⁸ Have you surveyed the expanses of the earth? If you know of these – tell Me.

יח הִתְבֹּנַנְתָּ עַד־רַחֲבֵי־אָרֶץ הַגֵּד אִם־יָדַעְתָּ כֻלָּהּ:

¹⁹ Which path leads to where light dwells, And where is the place of darkness,

יט אֵי־זֶה הַדֶּרֶךְ יִשְׁכָּן־אוֹר וְחֹשֶׁךְ אֵי־זֶה מְקֹמוֹ:

²⁰ That you may take it to its domain And know the way to its home?

כ כִּי תִקָּחֶנּוּ אֶל־גְּבוּלוֹ וְכִי־תָבִין נְתִיבוֹת בֵּיתוֹ:

²¹ Surely you know, for you were born then, And the number of your years is many!

כא יָדַעְתָּ כִּי־אָז תִּוָּלֵד וּמִסְפַּר יָמֶיךָ רַבִּים:

²² Have you penetrated the vaults of snow, Seen the vaults of hail,

כב הֲבָאתָ אֶל־אֹצְרוֹת שָׁלֶג וְאֹצְרוֹת בָּרָד תִּרְאֶה:

²³ Which I have put aside for a time of adversity, For a day of war and battle?

כג אֲשֶׁר־חָשַׂכְתִּי לְעֶת־צָר לְיוֹם קְרָב וּמִלְחָמָה:

²⁴ By what path is the west wind dispersed, The east wind scattered over the earth?

כד אֵי־זֶה הַדֶּרֶךְ יֵחָלֶק אוֹר יָפֵץ קָדִים עֲלֵי־אָרֶץ:

²⁵ Who cut a channel for the torrents And a path for the thunderstorms,

כה מִי־פִלַּג לַשֶּׁטֶף תְּעָלָה וְדֶרֶךְ לַחֲזִיז קֹלוֹת:

²⁶ To rain down on uninhabited land, On the wilderness where no man is,

כו לְהַמְטִיר עַל־אֶרֶץ לֹא־אִישׁ מִדְבָּר לֹא־אָדָם בּוֹ:

²⁷ To saturate the desolate wasteland, And make the crop of grass sprout forth?

כז לְהַשְׂבִּיעַ שֹׁאָה וּמְשֹׁאָה וּלְהַצְמִיחַ מֹצָא דֶשֶׁא:

²⁸ Does the rain have a father? Who begot the dewdrops?

כח הֲיֵשׁ־לַמָּטָר אָב אוֹ מִי־הוֹלִיד אֶגְלֵי־טָל:

²⁹ From whose belly came forth the ice? Who gave birth to the frost of heaven?

כט מִבֶּטֶן מִי יָצָא הַקָּרַח וּכְפֹר שָׁמַיִם מִי יְלָדוֹ:

³⁰ Water congeals like stone, And the surface of the deep compacts.

ל כָּאֶבֶן מַיִם יִתְחַבָּאוּ וּפְנֵי תְהוֹם יִתְלַכָּדוּ:

³¹ Can you tie cords to Pleiades Or undo the reins of Orion?

לא הַתְקַשֵּׁר מַעֲדַנּוֹת כִּימָה אוֹ־מֹשְׁכוֹת כְּסִיל תְּפַתֵּחַ:

³² Can you lead out Mazzaroth in its season, Conduct the Bear with her sons?

לב הֲתֹצִיא מַזָּרוֹת בְּעִתּוֹ וְעַיִשׁ עַל־בָּנֶיהָ תַנְחֵם:

33 Do you know the laws of heaven Or impose its authority on earth?

לג הֲיָדַעְתָּ חֻקּוֹת שָׁמָיִם אִם־תָּשִׂים מִשְׁטָרוֹ בָאָרֶץ׃

34 Can you send up an order to the clouds For an abundance of water to cover you?

לד הֲתָרִים לָעָב קוֹלֶךָ וְשִׁפְעַת־מַיִם תְּכַסֶּךָּ׃

35 Can you dispatch the lightning on a mission And have it answer you, "I am ready"?

לה הַתְשַׁלַּח בְּרָקִים וְיֵלֵכוּ וְיֹאמְרוּ לְךָ הִנֵּנוּ׃

36 Who put wisdom in the hidden parts? Who gave understanding to the mind?

לו מִי־שָׁת בַּטֻּחוֹת חָכְמָה אוֹ מִי־נָתַן לַשֶּׂכְוִי בִינָה׃

37 Who is wise enough to give an account of the heavens? Who can tilt the bottles of the sky,

לז מִי־יְסַפֵּר שְׁחָקִים בְּחָכְמָה וְנִבְלֵי שָׁמַיִם מִי יַשְׁכִּיב׃

38 Whereupon the earth melts into a mass, And its clods stick together.

לח בְּצֶקֶת עָפָר לַמּוּצָק וּרְגָבִים יְדֻבָּקוּ׃

39 Can you hunt prey for the lion, And satisfy the appetite of the king of beasts?

לט הֲתָצוּד לְלָבִיא טָרֶף וְחַיַּת כְּפִירִים תְּמַלֵּא׃

40 They crouch in their dens, Lie in ambush in their lairs.

מ כִּי־יָשֹׁחוּ בַמְּעוֹנוֹת יֵשְׁבוּ בַסֻּכָּה לְמוֹ־אָרֶב׃

41 Who provides food for the raven When his young cry out to *Hashem* And wander about without food?

מא מִי יָכִין לָעֹרֵב צֵידוֹ כִּי־יְלָדָו [יְלָדָיו] אֶל־אֵל יְשַׁוֵּעוּ יִתְעוּ לִבְלִי־אֹכֶל׃

39 1 Do you know the season when the mountain goats give birth? Can you mark the time when the hinds calve?

לט א הֲיָדַעְתָּ עֵת לֶדֶת יַעֲלֵי־סָלַע חֹלֵל אַיָּלוֹת תִּשְׁמֹר׃

2 Can you count the months they must complete? Do you know the season they give birth,

ב תִּסְפֹּר יְרָחִים תְּמַלֶּאנָה וְיָדַעְתָּ עֵת לִדְתָּנָה׃

3 When they couch to bring forth their offspring, To deliver their young?

ג תִּכְרַעְנָה יַלְדֵיהֶן תְּפַלַּחְנָה חֶבְלֵיהֶם תְּשַׁלַּחְנָה׃

4 Their young are healthy; they grow up in the open; They leave and return no more.

ד יַחְלְמוּ בְנֵיהֶם יִרְבּוּ בַבָּר יָצְאוּ וְלֹא־שָׁבוּ לָמוֹ׃

5 Who sets the wild ass free? Who loosens the bonds of the onager,

ה מִי־שִׁלַּח פֶּרֶא חָפְשִׁי וּמֹסְרוֹת עָרוֹד מִי פִתֵּחַ׃

6 Whose home I have made the wilderness, The salt land his dwelling-place?

ו אֲשֶׁר־שַׂמְתִּי עֲרָבָה בֵיתוֹ וּמִשְׁכְּנוֹתָיו מְלֵחָה׃

7 He scoffs at the tumult of the city, Does not hear the shouts of the driver.

ז יִשְׂחַק לַהֲמוֹן קִרְיָה תְּשֻׁאוֹת נוֹגֵשׂ לֹא יִשְׁמָע׃

8 He roams the hills for his pasture; He searches for any green thing.

ח יְתוּר הָרִים מִרְעֵהוּ וְאַחַר כָּל־יָרוֹק יִדְרוֹשׁ׃

9 Would the wild ox agree to serve you? Would he spend the night at your crib?

ט הֲיֹאבֶה רֵּים עָבְדֶךָ אִם־יָלִין עַל־אֲבוּסֶךָ׃

10 Can you hold the wild ox by ropes to the furrow? Would he plow up the valleys behind you?

י הֲתִקְשָׁר־רֵים בְּתֶלֶם עֲבֹתוֹ אִם־יְשַׂדֵּד עֲמָקִים אַחֲרֶיךָ׃

11 Would you rely on his great strength And leave your toil to him?

יא הֲתִבְטַח־בּוֹ כִּי־רַב כֹּחוֹ וְתַעֲזֹב אֵלָיו יְגִיעֶךָ׃

¹² Would you trust him to bring in the seed And gather it in from your threshing floor?

הֲתַאֲמִין בּוֹ כִּי־יָשׁוב [יָשִׁיב] זַרְעֶךָ וְגָרְנְךָ יֶאֱסֹף:

¹³ The wing of the ostrich beats joyously; Are her pinions and plumage like the stork's?

כְּנַף־רְנָנִים נֶעֱלָסָה אִם־אֶבְרָה חֲסִידָה וְנֹצָה:

k'-naf r'-na-NEEM ne-e-LA-sah im ev-RAH kha-see-DAH v'-no-TZAH

¹⁴ She leaves her eggs on the ground, Letting them warm in the dirt,

כִּי־תַעֲזֹב לָאָרֶץ בֵּצֶיהָ וְעַל־עָפָר תְּחַמֵּם:

¹⁵ Forgetting they may be crushed underfoot, Or trampled by a wild beast.

וַתִּשְׁכַּח כִּי־רֶגֶל תְּזוּרֶהָ וְחַיַּת הַשָּׂדֶה תְּדוּשֶׁהָ:

¹⁶ Her young are cruelly abandoned as if they were not hers; Her labor is in vain for lack of concern.

הִקְשִׁיחַ בָּנֶיהָ לְּלֹא־לָהּ לְרִיק יְגִיעָהּ בְּלִי־פָחַד:

¹⁷ For *Hashem* deprived her of wisdom, Gave her no share of understanding,

כִּי־הִשָּׁהּ אֱלוֹהַּ חָכְמָה וְלֹא־חָלַק לָהּ בַּבִּינָה:

¹⁸ Else she would soar on high, Scoffing at the horse and its rider.

כָּעֵת בַּמָּרוֹם תַּמְרִיא תִּשְׂחַק לַסּוּס וּלְרֹכְבוֹ:

¹⁹ Do you give the horse his strength? Do you clothe his neck with a mane?

הֲתִתֵּן לַסּוּס גְּבוּרָה הֲתַלְבִּישׁ צַוָּארוֹ רַעְמָה:

²⁰ Do you make him quiver like locusts, His majestic snorting [spreading] terror?

הֲתַרְעִישֶׁנּוּ כָּאַרְבֶּה הוֹד נַחְרוֹ אֵימָה:

²¹ He paws with force, he runs with vigor, Charging into battle.

יַחְפְּרוּ בָעֵמֶק וְיָשִׂישׂ בְּכֹחַ יֵצֵא לִקְרַאת־נָשֶׁק:

²² He scoffs at fear; he cannot be frightened; He does not recoil from the sword.

יִשְׂחַק לְפַחַד וְלֹא יֵחָת וְלֹא־יָשׁוּב מִפְּנֵי־חָרֶב:

²³ A quiverful of arrows whizzes by him, And the flashing spear and the javelin.

עָלָיו תִּרְנֶה אַשְׁפָּה לַהַב חֲנִית וְכִידוֹן:

²⁴ Trembling with excitement, he swallows the land; He does not turn aside at the blast of the trumpet.

בְּרַעַשׁ וְרֹגֶז יְגַמֶּא־אָרֶץ וְלֹא־יַאֲמִין כִּי־קוֹל שׁוֹפָר:

²⁵ As the trumpet sounds, he says, "Aha!" From afar he smells the battle, The roaring and shouting of the officers.

בְּדֵי שֹׁפָר יֹאמַר הֶאָח וּמֵרָחוֹק יָרִיחַ מִלְחָמָה רַעַם שָׂרִים וּתְרוּעָה:

39:13 The wing of the ostrich beats joyously The Land of Israel used to be home to wild ostriches, until they became extinct in the region as a result of hunting. In fact, in 2006, four ancient ostrich eggs, thought to be at least 5,000 years old, were found in the Sharon region, just north of *Tel Aviv*. Because they were common in ancient Israel, ostriches are mentioned in a number of places in the Bible. Verses 13–18 make mention of the cruelty of the ostrich, which leaves its eggs to be trampled and is callous to its young (see also Lamentations 4:3). The ostrich is also listed among the non-kosher birds that are forbidden to be eaten (Leviticus 11:16 and Deuteronomy 14:15).

An ostrich in Southern Israel

Job

26 Is it by your wisdom that the hawk grows pinions, Spreads his wings to the south?

כו הֲמִבִּינָתְךָ יַאֲבֶר־נֵץ יִפְרֹשׂ כנפו [כְּנָפָיו] לְתֵימָן:

27 Does the eagle soar at your command, Building his nest high,

כז אִם־עַל־פִּיךָ יַגְבִּיהַּ נָשֶׁר וְכִי יָרִים קִנּוֹ:

28 Dwelling in the rock, Lodging upon the fastness of a jutting rock?

כח סֶלַע יִשְׁכֹּן וְיִתְלֹנָן עַל־שֶׁן־סֶלַע וּמְצוּדָה:

29 From there he spies out his food; From afar his eyes see it.

כט מִשָּׁם חָפַר־אֹכֶל לְמֵרָחוֹק עֵינָיו יַבִּיטוּ:

30 His young gulp blood; Where the slain are, there is he.

ל ואפרחו [וְאֶפְרֹחָיו] יְעַלְעוּ־דָם וּבַאֲשֶׁר חֲלָלִים שָׁם הוּא:

40 1 *Hashem* said in reply to *Iyov*.

מ א וַיַּעַן יְהוָה אֶת־אִיּוֹב וַיֹּאמַר:

2 Shall one who should be disciplined complain against *Shaddai*? He who arraigns *Hashem* must respond.

ב הֲרֹב עִם־שַׁדַּי יִסּוֹר מוֹכִיחַ אֱלוֹהַּ יַעֲנֶנָּה:

3 *Iyov* said in reply to *Hashem*:

ג וַיַּעַן אִיּוֹב אֶת־יְהוָה וַיֹּאמַר:

4 See, I am of small worth; what can I answer You? I clap my hand to my mouth.

ד הֵן קַלֹּתִי מָה אֲשִׁיבֶךָּ יָדִי שַׂמְתִּי לְמוֹ־פִי:

5 I have spoken once, and will not reply; Twice, and will do so no more.

ה אַחַת דִּבַּרְתִּי וְלֹא אֶעֱנֶה וּשְׁתַּיִם וְלֹא אוֹסִיף:

6 Then *Hashem* replied to *Iyov* out of the tempest and said:

ו וַיַּעַן־יְהוָה אֶת־אִיּוֹב מנ סערה [מִן] [סְעָרָה] וַיֹּאמַר:

7 Gird your loins like a man; I will ask, and you will inform Me.

ז אֱזָר־נָא כְגֶבֶר חֲלָצֶיךָ אֶשְׁאָלְךָ וְהוֹדִיעֵנִי:

8 Would you impugn My justice? Would you condemn Me that you may be right?

ח הַאַף תָּפֵר מִשְׁפָּטִי תַּרְשִׁיעֵנִי לְמַעַן תִּצְדָּק:

ha-AF ta-FAYR mish-pa-TEE tar-shee-AY-nee l'-MA-an titz-DAK

9 Have you an arm like *Hashem*'s? Can you thunder with a voice like His?

ט וְאִם־זְרוֹעַ כָּאֵל לָךְ וּבְקוֹל כָּמֹהוּ תַרְעֵם:

40:8 Would you condemn Me that you may be right? The Sages of the Talmud (*Bava Batra* 15a) try to determine the time period in which *Iyov* lived. Although some opinions have him living during the period of the Exodus from Egypt (see commentary to 2:7), another suggests that he was among the Babylonian exiles who returned to the Land of Israel after the destruction of the first *Beit Hamikdash*. The identification of *Iyov* with the generation that experienced the destruction of the Temple and exile from *Eretz Yisrael* is fitting. Throughout the book, *Iyov* struggles with the reality that he is suffering, though seemingly righteous. He challenges God's justice, trying to make sense of the age-old question about why bad things happen to good people. Likewise, the Jews at the time of the exile also struggled to understand why they deserved to suffer as they did (see Ezekiel 18). Though the Jews sinned and *Iyov* did not, his personal suffering is seen as emblematic of the suffering of the Nation of Israel.

Memorial to the Deportees at Yad Vashem, Israel's Holocaust Remembrance Center

¹⁰ Deck yourself now with grandeur and eminence; Clothe yourself in glory and majesty.

י עֲדֵה נָא גָאוֹן וָגֹבַהּ וְהוֹד וְהָדָר תִּלְבָּשׁ:

¹¹ Scatter wide your raging anger; See every proud man and bring him low.

יא הָפֵץ עֶבְרוֹת אַפֶּךָ וּרְאֵה כָל־גֵּאֶה וְהַשְׁפִּילֵהוּ:

¹² See every proud man and humble him, And bring them down where they stand.

יב רְאֵה כָל־גֵּאֶה הַכְנִיעֵהוּ וַהֲדֹךְ רְשָׁעִים תַּחְתָּם:

¹³ Bury them all in the earth; Hide their faces in obscurity.

יג טָמְנֵם בֶּעָפָר יָחַד פְּנֵיהֶם חֲבֹשׁ בַּטָּמוּן:

¹⁴ Then even I would praise you For the triumph your right hand won you.

יד וְגַם־אֲנִי אוֹדֶךָּ כִּי־תוֹשִׁעַ לְךָ יְמִינֶךָ:

¹⁵ Take now behemoth, whom I made as I did you; He eats grass, like the cattle.

טו הִנֵּה־נָא בְהֵמוֹת אֲשֶׁר־עָשִׂיתִי עִמָּךְ חָצִיר כַּבָּקָר יֹאכֵל:

¹⁶ His strength is in his loins, His might in the muscles of his belly.

טז הִנֵּה־נָא כֹחוֹ בְמָתְנָיו וְאֹנוֹ בִּשְׁרִירֵי בִטְנוֹ:

¹⁷ He makes his tail stand up like a cedar; The sinews of his thighs are knit together.

יז יַחְפֹּץ זְנָבוֹ כְמוֹ־אָרֶז גִּידֵי פַחֲדָו [פַחֲדָיו] יְשֹׂרָגוּ:

¹⁸ His bones are like tubes of bronze, His limbs like iron rods.

יח עֲצָמָיו אֲפִיקֵי נְחוּשָׁה גְּרָמָיו כִּמְטִיל בַּרְזֶל:

¹⁹ He is the first of *Hashem*'s works; Only his Maker can draw the sword against him.

יט הוּא רֵאשִׁית דַּרְכֵי־אֵל הָעֹשׂוֹ יַגֵּשׁ חַרְבּוֹ:

²⁰ The mountains yield him produce, Where all the beasts of the field play.

כ כִּי־בוּל הָרִים יִשְׂאוּ־לוֹ וְכָל־חַיַּת הַשָּׂדֶה יְשַׂחֲקוּ־שָׁם:

²¹ He lies down beneath the lotuses, In the cover of the swamp reeds.

כא תַּחַת־צֶאֱלִים יִשְׁכָּב בְּסֵתֶר קָנֶה וּבִצָּה:

²² The lotuses embower him with shade; The willows of the brook surround him.

כב יְסֻכֻּהוּ צֶאֱלִים צִלֲלוֹ יְסֻבּוּהוּ עַרְבֵי־נָחַל:

²³ He can restrain the river from its rushing; He is confident the stream will gush at his command.

כג הֵן יַעֲשֹׁק נָהָר לֹא יַחְפּוֹז יִבְטַח כִּי־יָגִיחַ יַרְדֵּן אֶל־פִּיהוּ:

²⁴ Can he be taken by his eyes? Can his nose be pierced by hooks?

כד בְּעֵינָיו יִקָּחֶנּוּ בְּמוֹקְשִׁים יִנְקָב־אָף:

²⁵ Can you draw out Leviathan by a fishhook? Can you press down his tongue by a rope?

כה תִּמְשֹׁךְ לִוְיָתָן בְּחַכָּה וּבְחֶבֶל תַּשְׁקִיעַ לְשֹׁנוֹ:

²⁶ Can you put a ring through his nose, Or pierce his jaw with a barb?

כו הֲתָשִׂים אַגְמוֹן בְּאַפּוֹ וּבְחוֹחַ תִּקּוֹב לֶחֱיוֹ:

²⁷ Will he plead with you at length? Will he speak soft words to you?

כז הֲיַרְבֶּה אֵלֶיךָ תַּחֲנוּנִים אִם־יְדַבֵּר אֵלֶיךָ רַכּוֹת:

²⁸ Will he make an agreement with you To be taken as your lifelong slave?

כח הֲיִכְרֹת בְּרִית עִמָּךְ תִּקָּחֶנּוּ לְעֶבֶד עוֹלָם:

²⁹ Will you play with him like a bird, And tie him down for your girls?

כט הַתְשַׂחֶק־בּוֹ כַּצִּפּוֹר וְתִקְשְׁרֶנּוּ לְנַעֲרוֹתֶיךָ:

³⁰ Shall traders traffic in him? Will he be divided up among merchants?

ל יִכְרוּ עָלָיו חַבָּרִים יֶחֱצוּהוּ בֵּין כְּנַעֲנִים:

³¹ Can you fill his skin with darts Or his head with fish-spears?

לא הַתְמַלֵּא בְשֻׂכּוֹת עוֹרוֹ וּבְצִלְצַל דָּגִים רֹאשׁוֹ:

³² Lay a hand on him, And you will never think of battle again.

לב שִׂים־עָלָיו כַּפֶּךָ זְכֹר מִלְחָמָה אַל־תּוֹסַף:

41 ¹ See, any hope [of capturing] him must be disappointed; One is prostrated by the very sight of him.

מא א הֵן־תֹּחַלְתּוֹ נִכְזָבָה הֲגַם אֶל־מַרְאָיו יֻטָל:

² There is no one so fierce as to rouse him; Who then can stand up to Me?

ב לֹא־אַכְזָר כִּי יְעוּרֶנּוּ וּמִי הוּא לְפָנַי יִתְיַצָּב:

³ Whoever confronts Me I will requite, For everything under the heavens is Mine.

ג מִי הִקְדִּימַנִי וַאֲשַׁלֵּם תַּחַת כָּל־הַשָּׁמַיִם לִי־הוּא:

⁴ I will not be silent concerning him Or the praise of his martial exploits.

ד לֹא־[לוֹ] אַחֲרִישׁ בַּדָּיו וּדְבַר־גְּבוּרוֹת וְחִין עֶרְכּוֹ:

⁵ Who can uncover his outer garment? Who can penetrate the folds of his jowls?

ה מִי־גִלָּה פְּנֵי לְבוּשׁוֹ בְּכֶפֶל רִסְנוֹ מִי יָבוֹא:

⁶ Who can pry open the doors of his face? His bared teeth strike terror.

ו דַּלְתֵי פָנָיו מִי פִתֵּחַ סְבִיבוֹת שִׁנָּיו אֵימָה:

⁷ His protective scales are his pride, Locked with a binding seal.

ז גַּאֲוָה אֲפִיקֵי מָגִנִּים סָגוּר חוֹתָם צָר:

⁸ One scale touches the other; Not even a breath can enter between them.

ח אֶחָד בְּאֶחָד יִגַּשׁוּ וְרוּחַ לֹא־יָבוֹא בֵינֵיהֶם:

⁹ Each clings to each; They are interlocked so they cannot be parted.

ט אִישׁ־בְּאָחִיהוּ יְדֻבָּקוּ יִתְלַכְּדוּ וְלֹא יִתְפָּרָדוּ:

¹⁰ His sneezings flash lightning, And his eyes are like the glimmerings of dawn.

י עֲטִישֹׁתָיו תָּהֶל אוֹר וְעֵינָיו כְּעַפְעַפֵּי־שָׁחַר:

¹¹ Firebrands stream from his mouth; Fiery sparks escape.

יא מִפִּיו לַפִּידִים יַהֲלֹכוּ כִּידוֹדֵי אֵשׁ יִתְמַלָּטוּ:

mi-PEEV la-pee-DEEM ya-ha-LO-khu kee-DO-day AYSH yit-ma-LA-tu

¹² Out of his nostrils comes smoke As from a steaming, boiling cauldron.

יב מִנְּחִירָיו יֵצֵא עָשָׁן כְּדוּד נָפוּחַ וְאַגְמֹן:

Reading from the *Torah* at the Western Wall

41:11 Firebrands stream from his mouth This verse recalls the description of the revelation at Mount Sinai, in which *Hashem* revealed Himself with fire: "All the people witnessed the thunder and lightning" (Exodus 20:15). *Iyov* is echoing a theme repeated in this book, by indicating that God's glory is defined not just by the fact that He created the world and continues to rule it absolutely, but also on account of the giving of the *Torah*. The Jewish people worship God not just because He created the world, but because He intervened directly on their behalf by giving them the Law and because He is constantly involved in the day-to-day wellbeing of His people.

¹³ His breath ignites coals; Flames blaze from his mouth.

¹⁴ Strength resides in his neck; Power leaps before him.

¹⁵ The layers of his flesh stick together; He is as though cast hard; he does not totter.

¹⁶ His heart is cast hard as a stone, Hard as the nether millstone.

¹⁷ Divine beings are in dread as he rears up; As he crashes down, they cringe.

¹⁸ No sword that overtakes him can prevail, Nor spear, nor missile, nor lance.

¹⁹ He regards iron as straw, Bronze, as rotted wood.

²⁰ No arrow can put him to flight; Slingstones turn into stubble for him.

²¹ Clubs are regarded as stubble; He scoffs at the quivering javelin.

²² His underpart is jagged shards; It spreads a threshing-sledge on the mud.

²³ He makes the depths seethe like a cauldron; He makes the sea [boil] like an ointment-pot.

²⁴ His wake is a luminous path; He makes the deep seem white-haired.

²⁵ There is no one on land who can dominate him, Made as he is without fear.

²⁶ He sees all that is haughty; He is king over all proud beasts.

42 ¹ *Iyov* said in reply to *Hashem*:

² I know that You can do everything, That nothing you propose is impossible for You.

³ Who is this who obscures counsel without knowledge? Indeed, I spoke without understanding Of things beyond me, which I did not know.

⁴ Hear now, and I will speak; I will ask, and You will inform me.

⁵ I had heard You with my ears, But now I see You with my eyes;

⁶ Therefore, I recant and relent, Being but dust and ashes.

יג נַפְשׁוֹ גֶּחָלִים תְּלַהֵט וְלַהַב מִפִּיו יֵצֵא:

יד בְּצַוָּארוֹ יָלִין עֹז וּלְפָנָיו תָּדוּץ דְּאָבָה:

טו מַפְּלֵי בְשָׂרוֹ דָבֵקוּ יָצוּק עָלָיו בַּל־יִמּוֹט:

טז לִבּוֹ יָצוּק כְּמוֹ־אָבֶן וְיָצוּק כְּפֶלַח תַּחְתִּית:

יז מִשֵּׂתוֹ יָגוּרוּ אֵלִים מִשְּׁבָרִים יִתְחַטָּאוּ:

יח מַשִּׂיגֵהוּ חֶרֶב בְּלִי תָקוּם חֲנִית מַסָּע וְשִׁרְיָה:

יט יַחְשֹׁב לְתֶבֶן בַּרְזֶל לְעֵץ רִקָּבוֹן נְחוּשָׁה:

כ לֹא־יַבְרִיחֶנּוּ בֶן־קָשֶׁת לְקַשׁ נֶהְפְּכוּ־לוֹ אַבְנֵי־קָלַע:

כא כְּקַשׁ נֶחְשְׁבוּ תוֹתָח וְיִשְׂחַק לְרַעַשׁ כִּידוֹן:

כב תַּחְתָּיו חַדּוּדֵי חָרֶשׂ יִרְפַּד חָרוּץ עֲלֵי־טִיט:

כג יַרְתִּיחַ כַּסִּיר מְצוּלָה יָם יָשִׂים כַּמֶּרְקָחָה:

כד אַחֲרָיו יָאִיר נָתִיב יַחְשֹׁב תְּהוֹם לְשֵׂיבָה:

כה אֵין־עַל־עָפָר מָשְׁלוֹ הֶעָשׂוּ לִבְלִי־חָת:

כו אֶת־כָּל־גָּבֹהַּ יִרְאֶה הוּא מֶלֶךְ עַל־כָּל־בְּנֵי־שָׁחַץ:

מב א וַיַּעַן אִיּוֹב אֶת־יְהוָה וַיֹּאמַר:

ב ידעת [יָדַעְתִּי] כִּי־כֹל תּוּכָל וְלֹא־יִבָּצֵר מִמְּךָ מְזִמָּה:

ג מִי זֶה מַעְלִים עֵצָה בְּלִי דָעַת לָכֵן הִגַּדְתִּי וְלֹא אָבִין נִפְלָאוֹת מִמֶּנִּי וְלֹא אֵדָע:

ד שְׁמַע־נָא וְאָנֹכִי אֲדַבֵּר אֶשְׁאָלְךָ וְהוֹדִיעֵנִי:

ה לְשֵׁמַע־אֹזֶן שְׁמַעְתִּיךָ וְעַתָּה עֵינִי רָאָתְךָ:

ו עַל־כֵּן אֶמְאַס וְנִחַמְתִּי עַל־עָפָר וָאֵפֶר:

⁷ After *Hashem* had spoken these words to *Iyov*, *Hashem* said to Eliphaz the Temanite, "I am incensed at you and your two friends, for you have not spoken the truth about Me as did My servant *Iyov*.

ז וַיְהִ֗י אַחַ֨ר דִּבֶּ֧ר יְהֹוָ֛ה אֶת־הַדְּבָרִ֥ים הָאֵ֖לֶּה אֶל־אִיּ֑וֹב וַיֹּ֣אמֶר יְהֹוָה֮ אֶל־אֱלִיפַ֣ז הַתֵּימָנִי֒ חָרָ֤ה אַפִּי֙ בְךָ֔ וּבִשְׁנֵ֣י רֵעֶ֔יךָ כִּ֠י לֹ֣א דִבַּרְתֶּ֥ם אֵלַ֛י נְכוֹנָ֖ה כְּעַבְדִּ֥י אִיּֽוֹב:

⁸ Now take seven bulls and seven rams and go to My servant *Iyov* and sacrifice a burnt offering for yourselves. And let *Iyov*, My servant, pray for you; for to him I will show favor and not treat you vilely, since you have not spoken the truth about Me as did My servant *Iyov*."

ח וְעַתָּ֡ה קְחֽוּ־לָכֶ֣ם שִׁבְעָֽה־פָרִים֩ וְשִׁבְעָ֨ה אֵילִ֜ים וּלְכ֣וּ ׀ אֶל־עַבְדִּ֣י אִיּ֗וֹב וְהַֽעֲלִיתֶ֣ם עוֹלָה֮ בַּֽעַדְכֶם֒ וְאִיּ֣וֹב עַבְדִּ֗י יִתְפַּלֵּ֣ל עֲלֵיכֶ֔ם כִּ֚י אִם־פָּנָ֣יו אֶשָּׂ֔א לְבִלְתִּ֛י עֲשׂ֥וֹת עִמָּכֶ֖ם נְבָלָ֑ה כִּ֠י לֹ֣א דִבַּרְתֶּ֥ם אֵלַ֛י נְכוֹנָ֖ה כְּעַבְדִּ֥י אִיּֽוֹב:

v'-a-TAH k'-KHU la-KHEM shiv-AH fa-REEM v'-shiv-AH ay-LEEM ul-KHU el av-DEE i-YOV v'-ha-a-lee-TEM o-LAH ba-ad-KHEM v'-i-YOV av-DEE yit-pa-LAYL a-lay-KHEM KEE im pa-NAV e-SA l'-vil-TEE a-SOT i-ma-KHEM n'-va-LAH KEE LO di-bar-TEM ay-LAI n'-kho-NAH k'-av-DEE i-YOV

⁹ Eliphaz the Temanite and Bildad the Shuhite and Zophar the Naamathite went and did as *Hashem* had told them, and *Hashem* showed favor to *Iyov*.

ט וַיֵּֽלְכ֞וּ אֱלִיפַ֣ז הַתֵּֽימָנִ֗י וּבִלְדַּד֙ הַשּׁ֣וּחִ֔י צֹפַ֖ר הַנַּֽעֲמָתִ֑י וַיַּֽעֲשׂ֔וּ כַּֽאֲשֶׁ֛ר דִּבֶּ֥ר אֲלֵיהֶ֖ם יְהֹוָ֑ה וַיִּשָּׂ֥א יְהֹוָ֖ה אֶת־פְּנֵ֥י אִיּֽוֹב:

¹⁰ *Hashem* restored *Iyov*'s fortunes when he prayed on behalf of his friends, and *Hashem* gave *Iyov* twice what he had before.

י וַֽיהֹוָ֗ה שָׁ֚ב אֶת־שְׁבִ֣ית [שְׁב֣וּת] אִיּ֔וֹב בְּהִֽתְפַּֽלְל֖וֹ בְּעַ֣ד רֵעֵ֑הוּ וַיֹּ֧סֶף יְהֹוָ֛ה אֶת־כָּל־אֲשֶׁ֥ר לְאִיּ֖וֹב לְמִשְׁנֶֽה:

¹¹ All his brothers and sisters and all his former friends came to him and had a meal with him in his house. They consoled and comforted him for all the misfortune that *Hashem* had brought upon him. Each gave him one *kesita* and each one gold ring.

יא וַיָּבֹ֣אוּ אֵ֠לָיו כָּל־אֶחָ֨יו וְכָל־אַחְיֹתָ֜יו [אַחְיוֹתָ֗יו] וְכָל־יֹֽדְעָיו֮ לְפָנִים֒ וַיֹּֽאכְל֨וּ עִמּ֣וֹ לֶחֶם֮ בְּבֵיתוֹ֒ וַיָּנֻ֣דוּ ל֗וֹ וַיְנַֽחֲמ֣וּ אֹת֔וֹ עַ֚ל כָּל־הָ֣רָעָ֔ה אֲשֶׁר־הֵבִ֥יא יְהֹוָ֖ה עָלָ֑יו וַיִּתְּנוּ־ל֗וֹ אִ֚ישׁ קְשִׂיטָ֣ה אֶחָ֔ת וְאִ֕ישׁ נֶ֖זֶם זָהָ֥ב אֶחָֽד:

¹² Thus *Hashem* blessed the latter years of *Iyov*'s life more than the former. He had fourteen thousand sheep, six thousand camels, one thousand yoke of oxen, and one thousand she-asses.

יב וַֽיהֹוָ֗ה בֵּרַ֛ךְ אֶת־אַֽחֲרִ֥ית אִיּ֖וֹב מֵרֵֽאשִׁת֑וֹ וַֽיְהִי־ל֡וֹ אַרְבָּעָה֩ עָשָׂ֨ר אֶ֜לֶף צֹ֗אן וְשֵׁ֤שֶׁת אֲלָפִים֙ גְּמַלִּ֔ים וְאֶֽלֶף־צֶ֥מֶד בָּקָ֖ר וְאֶ֥לֶף אֲתוֹנֽוֹת:

¹³ He also had seven sons and three daughters.

יג וַֽיְהִי־ל֛וֹ שִׁבְעָ֥נָ֥ה בָנִ֖ים וְשָׁל֥וֹשׁ בָּנֽוֹת:

Job

42:8 And let *Iyov*, My servant, pray for you By praying for his friends who have sinned *Iyov* ultimately demonstrates compassion, thereby walking in the footsteps of *Avraham*. In *Sefer Bereishit* (chapter 20), *Avraham*'s wife *Sara* is taken by Abimelech, king of the Philistines, who thought she was *Avraham*'s sister. After Abimelech is punished and *Sara* is returned, *Avraham* prays for the Philistine king's return to good health and the amelioration of the punishment *Hashem* had inflicted upon him. The inclination to be kind and forgiving is one of the reasons *Avraham* merited the Land of Israel as a permanent inheritance for himself and his descendants. By emulating these traits of kindness and compassion *Iyov* proves his righteousness, even in the face of his pain and suffering.

Rabbi Tuly Weisz celebrating Hanukkah with Holocaust survivors

¹⁴ The first he named Jemimah, the second Keziah, and the third Keren-happuch.

¹⁵ Nowhere in the land were women as beautiful as *Iyov*'s daughters to be found. Their father gave them estates together with their brothers.

¹⁶ Afterward, *Iyov* lived one hundred and forty years to see four generations of sons and grandsons.

¹⁷ So *Iyov* died old and contented.

יד וַיִּקְרָ֞א שֵׁם־הָֽאַחַת֙ יְמִימָ֔ה וְשֵׁ֥ם הַשֵּׁנִ֖ית קְצִיעָ֑ה וְשֵׁ֥ם הַשְּׁלִישִׁ֖ית קֶ֥רֶן הַפּֽוּךְ:

טו וְלֹ֨א נִמְצָ֜א נָשִׁ֥ים יָפ֛וֹת כִּבְנ֥וֹת אִיּ֖וֹב בְּכָל־הָאָ֑רֶץ וַיִּתֵּ֨ן לָהֶ֧ם אֲבִיהֶ֛ם נַחֲלָ֖ה בְּת֥וֹךְ אֲחֵיהֶֽם:

טז וַיְחִ֤י אִיּוֹב֙ אַֽחֲרֵי־זֹ֔את מֵאָ֥ה וְאַרְבָּעִ֖ים שָׁנָ֑ה ויִרא [וַיִּרְאֶ֗ה] אֶת־בָּנָיו֙ וְאֶת־בְּנֵ֣י בָנָ֔יו אַרְבָּעָ֖ה דֹּרֽוֹת:

יז וַיָּ֣מָת אִיּ֔וֹב זָקֵ֖ן וּשְׂבַ֥ע יָמִֽים:

List of Transliterated Words in *The Israel Bible*

The following is a list of nouns which have been transliterated into Hebrew in the English translation and commentary of *The Israel Bible*:

Hebrew Name	English Name	Pronunciation	Hebrew
Achan	Achan	a-KHAN	עָכָן
Achav	Ahab	akh-AV	אַחְאָב
Achaz	Ahaz	a-KHAZ	אָחָז
Achazyahu	Ahaziah	a-khaz-YA-hu	אֲחַזְיָהוּ
Achiezer	Ahiezer	a-khee-E-zer	אֲחִיעֶזֶר
Achihud	Ahihud	a-khee-HUD	אֲחִיהוּד
Achikam	Ahikam	a-khee-KAM	אֲחִיקָם
Achilud	Ahilud	a-khee-LUD	אֲחִילוּד
Achimelech	Ahimelech	a-khee-ME-lekh	אֲחִימֶלֶךְ
Achira	Ahira	a-khee-RA	אֲחִירַע
Achisamach	Ahisamach	a-khee-sa-MAKH	אֲחִיסָמָךְ
Achitofel	Ahithophel	a-khee-TO-fel	אֲחִיתֹפֶל
Achituv	Ahitub	a-khee-TUV	אֲחִיטוּב
Achiya	Ahijah	a-khi-YAH	אֲחִיָּה
Adam	Adam	a-DAM	אָדָם
Adar	Adar	a-DAR	אֲדָר
Adoniyahu	Adonijah	a-do-ni-YA-hu	אֲדֹנִיָּהוּ
Adulam	Adullam	a-du-LAM	עֲדֻלָּם
Agur	Agur	a-GUR	אָגוּר
Aharon	Aaron	a-ha-RON	אַהֲרֹן
Amasa	Amasa	a-ma-SA	עֲמָשָׂא
Amatzya	Amaziah	a-matz-YAH	אֲמַצְיָה
Amen	Amen	a-MAYN	אָמֵן
Amiel	Ammiel	a-mee-AYL	עַמִּיאֵל
Aminadav	Amminadab	a-mee-na-DAV	עַמִּינָדָב
Amitai	Amittai	a-mi-TAI	אֲמִתַּי
Amnon	Amnon	am-NON	אַמְנֹן

Hebrew Name	English Name	Pronunciation	Hebrew
Amon	Amon	a-MON	אָמוֹן
Amos	Amos	a-MOS	עָמוֹס
Amotz	Amoz	a-MOTZ	אָמוֹץ
Amram	Amram	am-RAM	עַמְרָם
Anatot	Anathoth	a-na-TOT	עֲנָתוֹת
Aron	Ark	a-RON	אָרוֹן
Aron HaBrit	Ark of the Covenant	a-RON ha-b'-REET	אֲרוֹן הַבְּרִית
Arpachshad	Arpachshad	ar-pakh-SHAD	אַרְפַּכְשַׁד
Asa	Asa	a-SA	אָסָא
Asael	Asahel	a-sah-AYL	עֲשָׂהאֵל
Asaf	Asaph	a-SAF	אָסָף
Ashdod	Ashdod	ash-DOD	אַשְׁדּוֹד
Asher	Asher	a-SHAYR	אָשֵׁר
Ashkelon	Ashkelon	ash-k'-LON	אַשְׁקְלוֹן
Atalya	Athaliah	a-tal-YAH	עֲתַלְיָה
Avdon	Abdon	av-DON	עַבְדּוֹן
Avichayil	Abihail	a-vee-KHA-yil	אֲבִיחַיִל
Avidan	Abidan	a-vee-DAN	אֲבִידָן
Avigail	Abigail	a-vee-GA-yil	אֲבִיגַיִל
Avihu	Abihu	a-vee-HU	אֲבִיהוּא
Avimelech	Abimelech	a-vee-ME-lekh	אֲבִימֶלֶךְ
Avinadav	Abinadab	a-vee-na-DAV	אֲבִינָדָב
Aviram	Abiram	a-vee-RAM	אֲבִירָם
Avishai	Abishai	a-vee-SHAI	אֲבִישַׁי
Aviya	Abijah	a-vi-YAH	אֲבִיָּה
Aviyam	Abijam	a-vi-YAM	אֲבִיָּם
Avner	Abner	av-NAYR	אַבְנֵר
Avraham	Abraham	av-ra-HAM	אַבְרָהָם
Avram	Abram	av-RAM	אַבְרָם
Avshalom	Absalom	av-sha-LOM	אַבְשָׁלוֹם
Azarya	Azariah	a-zar-YAH	עֲזַרְיָה
Azeika	Azekah	a-zay-KAH	עֲזֵקָה
Azza	Gaza	a-ZAH	עַזָּה

Hebrew Name	English Name	Pronunciation	Hebrew
B'nei Yisrael	The Children of Israel	b'-NAY yis-ra-AYL	בְּנֵי יִשְׂרָאֵל
Barak	Barak	ba-rakh-AYL	בָּרָק
Baruch	Baruch	ba-RUKH	בָּרוּךְ
Barzilai	Barzillai	bar-zi-LAI	בַּרְזִלַּי
Basha	Baasa	ba-SHA	בַּעְשָׁא
Batsheva	Bath-sheba	bat-SHE-va	בַּת־שֶׁבַע
Be'er Sheva	Beer-sheba	b'-AYR SHE-va	בְּאֵר שֶׁבַע
Be'eri	Beeri	b'-ay-REE	בְּאֵרִי
Beit Aven	Beth-aven	bayt A-ven	בֵּית אָוֶן
Beit El	Beth-el	bayt el	בֵּית אֵל
Beit Hamikdash	Temple	bayt ha-mik-DASH	בֵּית הַמִּקְדָּשׁ
Beit Lechem	Beth-lehem	bayt LE-khem	בֵּית לָחֶם
Beit Shean	Beth-shean	bayt sh'-AN	בֵּית שְׁאָן
Beit Shemesh	Beth-shemesh	bayt SHE-mesh	בֵּית שָׁמֶשׁ
Berechya	Berechiah	be-rekh-YAH	בֶּרֶכְיָה
Betzalel	Bezalel	b'-tzal-AYL	בְּצַלְאֵל
Bilha	Bilhah	bil-HAH	בִּלְהָה
Binyamin	Benjamin	bin-ya-MIN	בִּנְיָמִין
Boaz	Boaz	BO-az	בֹּעַז
Buki	Bukki	bu-KEE	בֻּקִּי
Buzi	Buzi	bu-ZEE	בּוּזִי
Carmel	Carmel	kar-MEL	כַּרְמֶל
Chachalya	Hacaliah	kha-khal-YAH	חֲכַלְיָה
Chagai	Haggai	kha-GAI	חַגַּי
Chana	Hannah	kha-NAH	חַנָּה
Chanamel	Hanamel	kha-nam-AYL	חֲנַמְאֵל
Chanani	Hanani	kha-NA-nee	חֲנָנִי
Chananya	Hananiah	kha-nan-YAH	חֲנַנְיָה
Chaniel	Hanniel	kha-nee-AYL	חַנִּיאֵל
Chanoch	Enoch	kha-NOKH	חֲנוֹךְ
Chava	Eve	kha-VAH	חַוָּה
Chavakuk	Habakkuk	kha-va-KUK	חֲבַקּוּק
Chermon	Hermon	kher-MON	חֶרְמוֹן

Hebrew Name	English Name	Pronunciation	Hebrew
Chetzron	Hezron	khetz-RON	חֶצְרוֹן
Chever	Heber	KHE-ver	חֶבֶר
Chevron	Hebron	khev-RON	חֶבְרוֹן
Chilkiyahu	Hilkiah	khil-ki-YA-hu	חִלְקִיָּהוּ
Chizkiyahu	Hezekiah	khiz-ki-YA-hu	חִזְקִיָּהוּ
Chofni	Hophni	khof-NEE	חָפְנִי
Chogla	Hoglah	khog-LAH	חָגְלָה
Chulda	Hulda	khul-DAH	חֻלְדָּה
Chur	Hur	Khur	חוּר
Dan	Dan	Dan	דָּן
Daniel	Daniel	da-ni-YAYL	דָּנִיֵּאל
Datan	Dathan	da-TAN	דָּתָן
David	David	da-VID	דָּוִד
Devora	Deborah	d'-vo-RAH	דְּבוֹרָה
Dina	Dinah	DEE-nah	דִּינָה
Doeg Ha'adomi	Doeg the Edomite	do-AYG ha-a-do-MEE	דּוֹאֵג הָאֲדֹמִי
Efraim	Ephraim	ef-RA-yim	אֶפְרַיִם
Efrat	Ephrat	ef-RAT	אֶפְרָתָה
Efrat	Ephrathah	ef-RA-tah	אֶפְרָתָה
Ehud	Ehud	ay-HUD	אֵהוּד
Eila	Elah	AY-lah	אֵלָה
Eilon	Elon	ay-LON	אֵילוֹן
Ein Gedi	En-gedi	ayn GE-dee	עֵין גֶּדִי
Elazar	Eleazar	el-a-ZAR	אֶלְעָזָר
Elchanan	Elhanan	el-kha-NAN	אֶלְחָנָן
Eli	Eli	ay-LEE	עֵלִי
Eliav	Eliab	e-lee-AV	אֱלִיאָב
Elidad	Elidad	e-lee-DAD	אֱלִידָד
Eliezer	Eliezer	e-lee-E-zer	אֱלִיעֶזֶר
Elimelech	Elimelech	e-lee-ME-lekh	אֱלִימֶלֶךְ
Elisha	Elisha	e-lee-SHA	אֱלִישָׁע
Elishama	Elishama	e-lee-sha-MA	אֱלִישָׁמָע
Elisheva	Elisheba	e-lee-SHE-va	אֱלִישֶׁבַע

Hebrew Name	English Name	Pronunciation	Hebrew
Elitzafan	Eli-zaphan	e-lee-tza-FAN	אֱלִיצָפָן
Elitzur	Elizur	e-lee-TZUR	אֱלִיצוּר
Eliyahu	Elijah	ay-li-YA-hu	אֵלִיָּהוּ
Elkana	Elkanah	el-ka-NAH	אֶלְקָנָה
Elyasaf	Eliasaph	el-ya-SAF	אֶלְיָסָף
Elyashiv	Eliashib	el-ya-SHEEV	אֶלְיָשִׁיב
Enosh	Enosh	e-NOSH	אֱנוֹשׁ
Er	Er	ayr	עֵר
Eshtaol	Eshtaol	esh-ta-OL	אֶשְׁתָּאֹל
Esther	Esther	es-TAYR	אֶסְתֵּר
Eved Melech	Ebed-melech	E-ved ME-lekh	עֶבֶד־מֶלֶךְ
Even Ha-Ezer	Eben-Ezer	E-ven ha-E-zer	אֶבֶן הָעֵזֶר
Ever	Eber	AY-ver	עֵבֶר
Evyatar	Abiathar	ev-ya-TAR	אֶבְיָתָר
Ezra	Ezra	ez-RA	עֶזְרָא
Gad	Gad	gad	גָּד
Gadi	Gaddi	ga-DEE	גַּדִּי
Gadiel	Gaddiel	ga-dee-AYL	גַּדִּיאֵל
Gamliel	Gamaliel	gam-lee-AYL	גַּמְלִיאֵל
Gedalia	Gedaliah	g'-dal-YA (hu)	גְּדַלְיָהוּ
Gedera	Gederah	g'-day-RAH	גְּדֵרָה
Gershom	Gershom	gay-r'-SHOM	גֵּרְשֹׁם
Gershon	Gershon	gay-r'-SHON	גֵּרְשׁוֹן
Geshem	Geshem	GE-shem	גֶּשֶׁם
Geuel	Geuel	g'-u-AYL	גְּאוּאֵל
Gidon	Gideon	gid-ON	גִּדְעוֹן
Gilad	Gilead	gil-AD	גִּלְעָד
Gilgal	Gilgal	gil-GAL	גִּלְגָּל
Giva	Gibeah	giv-AH	גִּבְעָה
Givon	Gibeon	giv-ON	גִּבְעוֹן
Hadassa	Hadassah	ha-da-SAH	הֲדַסָּה
Har Eival	Mount Ebal	ay-VAL	הַר עֵיבָל
Har Gerizim	Mount Gerizim	g'-ri-ZEEM	הַר גְּרִזִים

Hebrew Name	English Name	Pronunciation	Hebrew
Har HaBayit	Temple Mount	har ha-BA-yit	הַר הַבַּיִת
Har HaZeitim	the Mount of Olives	har ha-zay-TEEM	הַר הַזֵּיתִים
Hashem	Lord/God		
Hayman	Heman	hay-MAN	הֵימָן
Hoshea	Hosea	ho-SHAY-a	הוֹשֵׁעַ
Ido	Iddo	i-DO	עִדּוֹ
Imanu-El	Immanuel	i-MA-nu ayl	עִמָּנוּ אֵל
Ish-boshet	Ish-bosheth	eesh BO-shet	אִישׁ־בֹּשֶׁת
Itamar	Ithamar	ee-ta-MAR	אִיתָמָר
Itiel	Ithiel	ee-tee-AYL	אִיתִיאֵל
Ivtzan	Ibzan	iv-TZAN	אִבְצָן
Iyov	Job	i-YOV	אִיּוֹב
Kadmiel	Kadmiel	kad-mee-AYL	קַדְמִיאֵל
Kalev	Caleb	ka-LAYV	כָּלֵב
Keesh	Kish	keesh	קִישׁ
Kehat	Kohath	k'-HAT	קְהָת
Keinan	Kenan	kay-NAN	קֵינָן
Kemuel	Kemuel	k'-mu-AYL	קְמוּאֵל
Keruvim	Cherubim	k'-ru-VEEM	כְּרוּבִים
Kilyon	Chilion	kil-YON	כִּלְיוֹן
Kiryat Arba	Kiriath-arba	keer-YAT AR-bah	קִרְיַת אַרְבַּע
Kiryat Sefer	Kiriath-sepher	keer-YAT SAY-fer	קִרְיַת־סֵפֶר
Kiryat Ye'arim	Kiriath-jearim	keer-YAT y'-a-REEM	קִרְיַת יְעָרִים
Kislev	Chislev	kis-LAYV	כִּסְלֵו
Kohanim	Priests	ko-ha-NEEM	כֹּהֲנִים
Kohelet	Koheleth	ko-HE-let	קֹהֶלֶת
Kohen	Priest	ko-HAYN	כֹּהֵן
Kohen Gadol	High Priest	ko-HAYN ga-DOL	כֹּהֵן גָּדוֹל
Korach	Korah	KO-rakh	קֹרַח
Kushi	Cushi	ku-SHEE	כּוּשִׁי
Lachish	Lachish	la-KHEESH	לָכִישׁ
Leah	Leah	lay-AH	לֵאָה
Lemech	Lamech	LE-mekh	לֶמֶךְ

Hebrew Name	English Name	Pronunciation	Hebrew
Lemuel	Lemuel	l'-mu-AYL	לְמוֹאֵל
Levi	Levi	lay-VEE	לֵוִי
Leviim	Levites	l'-vee-IM	לְוִים
Machla	Mahlah	makh-LAH	מַחְלָה
Machlon	Mahlon	makh-LON	מַחְלוֹן
Machseya	Mahseiah	makh-say-YAH	מַחְסֵיָה
Malachi	Malachi	mal-a-KHEE	מַלְאָכִי
Manoach	Manoah	ma-NO-akh	מָנוֹחַ
Mashiach	Messiah	ma-SHEE-akh	מָשִׁיחַ
Mefiboshet	Mephibosheth	m'-fee-VO-shet	מְפִיבֹשֶׁת
Mehalalel	Mahalalel	ma-ha-lal-AYL	מַהֲלַלְאֵל
Menachem	Menahem	m'-na-KHAYM	מְנַחֵם
Menashe	Menasseh	m'-na-SHEH	מְנַשֶּׁה
Menorah	Candlestick	m'-no-RAH	מְנֹרָה
Merari	Merari	m'-ra-REE	מְרָרִי
Metushelach	Methusaleh	m'-tu-SHE-lakh	מְתוּשָׁלַח
Micha	Micah	mee-KHAH	מִיכָה
Michael	Michael	mee-kha-AYL	מִיכָאֵל
Michaihu	Micaiah	mee-KHAI-hu	מִיכָיְהוּ
Michal	Michal	mee-KHAL	מִיכַל
Milka	Milcah	mil-KAH	מִלְכָּה
Miriam	Miriam	mir-YAM	מִרְיָם
Mishael	Mishael	mee-sha-AYL	מִישָׁאֵל
Mishkan	Tabernacle	mish-KAN	מִשְׁכַּן
Mitzpa	Mizpah	mitz-PAH	מִצְפָּה
Mizbayach	Altar	miz-BAY-akh	מִזְבֵּחַ
Mordechai	Mordecai	mor-d'-KHAI	מָרְדֳּכַי
Moriah	Moriah	mo-ri-YAH	מוֹרִיָּה
Moshe	Moses	mo-SHEH	מֹשֶׁה
Nachbi	Nahbi	nakh-BEE	נַחְבִּי
Nachor	Nahor	na-KHOR	נָחוֹר
Nachshon	Nahshon	nakh-SHON	נַחְשׁוֹן
Nachum	Nahum	na-KHUM	נַחוּם

Hebrew Name	English Name	Pronunciation	Hebrew
Nadav	Nadab	na-DAV	נָדָב
Naftali	Naphtali	naf-ta-LEE	נַפְתָּלִי
Naomi	Naomi	na-o-MEE	נָעֳמִי
Natan	Nathan	na-TAN	נָתָן
Naval	Nabal	na-VAL	נָבָל
Navi	Prophet	na-VEE	נָבִיא
Navot	Naboth	na-VAL	נָבָל
Nechemya	Nehemiah	n'-khem-YAH	נְחֶמְיָה
Negev	Negeb	NE-gev	נֶגֶב
Nerya	Neriah	nay-ri-YAH	נֵרִיָּה
Netanel	Nethanel	n'-tan-AYL	נְתַנְאֵל
Neviah	Prophetess	n'-vee-AH	נְבִיאָה
Neviim	Prophets	n'-vee-EEM	נְבִיאִים
Nisan	Nisan	nee-SAN	נִיסָן
Noa	Noah	no-AH	נֹעָה
Noach	Noah	NO-akh	נֹחַ
Nov	Nob	nov	נֹב
Nun	Nun	nun	נוּן
Oded	Oded	o-DAYD	עוֹדֵד
Ohola	Oholah	a-ho-LAH	אָהֳלָה
Oholiav	Oholiab	o-ha-lee-AV	אָהֳלִיאָב
Oholiva	Oholibah	a-ho-lee-VAH	אָהֳלִיבָה
Omri	Omri	om-REE	עָמְרִי
Onan	Onan	o-NAN	אוֹנָן
Otniel	Othniel	ot-nee-AYL	עָתְנִיאֵל
Ovadya	Obadiah	o-vad-YAH	עֹבַדְיָה
Oved	Obed	o-VAYD	עוֹבֵד
Oved Edom	Obed Edom	o-VAYD e-DOM	עוֹבֵד אֱדוֹם
Pagiel	Pagiel	pag-ee-AYL	פַּגְעִיאֵל
Palti	Palti	pal-TEE	פַּלְטִי
Paltiel	Paltiel	pal-tee-AYL	פַּלְטִיאֵל
Pekach	Pekah	PE-kakh	פֶּקַח
Pedael	Pedahel	p'-da-AYL	פְּדַהְאֵל

Hebrew Name	English Name	Pronunciation	Hebrew
Pekachya	Pekahiah	p'-kakh-YAH	פְּקַחְיָה
Peleg	Peleg	PE-leg	פֶּלֶג
Penina	Peninnah	p'-ni-NAH	פְּנִנָּה
Peretz	Perez	PE-retz	פֶּרֶץ
Petuel	Pethuel	p'-tu-AYL	פְּתוּאֵל
Pinchas	Phinehas	peen-KHAS	פִּינְחָס
Rachel	Rachel	ra-KHAYL	רָחֵל
Ram	Ram	ram	רָם
Rama	Ramah	ra-MAH	רָמָה
Re'u	Reu	r'-U	רְעוּ
Rechovam	Rehoboam	r'-khav-AM	רְחַבְעָם
Reuven	Reuben	r'-u-VAYN	רְאוּבֵן
Rivka	Rebecca	riv-KAH	רִבְקָה
Rut	Ruth	rut	רוּת
Salma	Salmon/Salmah	sal-MAH	שַׂלְמָה
Salmon	Salmon	sal-MON	שַׂלְמוֹן
Sara	Sarah	sa-RAH	שָׂרָה
Sarai	Sarai	sa-RAI	שָׂרַי
Selah	Selah	SE-lah	סֶלָה
Seraya	Seraiah	s'-ra-YAH	שְׂרָיָה
Serug	Serug	s'-RUG	שְׂרוּג
Setur	Sethur	s'-TUR	סְתוּר
Shaarayim	Shaaraim	sha-a-RA-yim	שַׁעֲרַיִם
Shabbat	Sabbath	sha-BAT	שַׁבַּת
Shabbatot	Sabbaths	sha-ba-TOT	שַׁבָּתוֹת
Shafan	Shaphan	sha-FAN	שָׁפָן
Shafat	Shaphat	sha-FAT	שָׁפָט
Shalem	Salem	sha-LAYM	שָׁלֵם
Shalum	Shallum	sha-LUM	שַׁלּוּם
Shamgar	Shamgar	sham-GAR	שַׁמְגַּר
Shamua	Shammua	sha-MU-a	שַׁמּוּעַ
Shaul	Saul	sha-UL	שָׁאוּל
Shealtiel	Shealtiel	sh'-al-tee-AYL	שְׁאַלְתִּיאֵל

Hebrew Name	English Name	Pronunciation	Hebrew
Shear Yashuv	Shear-Jashub	sh'-AR ya-SHUV	שְׁאָר יָשׁוּב
Shechanya	Shecaniah	sh'-khan-YAH	שְׁכַנְיָה
Shechem	Shechem	sh'-KHEM	שְׁכֶם
Sheila	Shelah	shay-LAH	שֵׁלָה
Shelach	Shelah	SHE-lakh	שֶׁלַח
Shelumiel	Shelumiel	sh'-lu-mee-AYL	שְׁלֻמִיאֵל
Shem	Shem	Shaym	שֵׁם
Shemaya	Shemaiah	sh'-ma-YAH	שְׁמַעְיָה
Sheshbatzar	Sheshbazzar	shaysh-ba-TZAR	שֵׁשְׁבַּצַּר
Shet	Seth	Shayt	שֵׁת
Shevat	Shebat	sh'-VAT	שְׁבָט
Shilo	Shiloh	shi-LOH	שִׁלֹה
Shim'i	Shimei	shim-EE	שִׁמְעִי
Shimon	Simeon	shim-ON	שִׁמְעוֹן
Shimshon	Samson	shim-SHON	שִׁמְשׁוֹן
Shlomo	Solomon	sh'-lo-MOH	שְׁלֹמֹה
Shmuel	Samuel	sh'-mu-AYL	שְׁמוּאֵל
Shofar	Horn	sho-FAR	שׁוֹפָר
Shofarot	Horns	sho-fa-ROT	שׁוֹפָרוֹת
Shomron	Samaria	sho-m'-RON	שֹׁמְרוֹן
Sivan	Sivan	see-VAN	סִיוָן
Tamar	Tamar	ta-MAR	תָּמָר
Tanakh	Hebrew Bible	ta-NAKH	תַּנַ"ךְ
Tapuach	Tappuah	ta-PU-akh	תַּפּוּחַ
Tavor	Tabor	ta-VOR	תָּבוֹר
Tekoa	Tekoa	t'-KO-a	תְּקוֹעָה
Terach	Terah	TE-rakh	תֶּרַח
Teveria	Tiberias	t'-ver-YAH	טְבֶרְיָה
Tevet	Tebeth	tay-VAYT	טֵבֵת
Tirtza	Tirzah	tir-TZAH	תִּרְצָה
Tola	Tola	to-LA	תּוֹלָע
Tzadok	Zadok	tza-DOK	צָדוֹק
Tzefanya	Zephaniah	tz'-fan-YAH	צְפַנְיָה

Hebrew Name	English Name	Pronunciation	Hebrew
Tzelofchad	Zelophehad	tz'-lo-f-KHAD	צְלָפְחָד
Tzeruya	Zeruiah	tz'-ru-YAH	צְרוּיָה
Tzfat	Safed	tz'-FAT	צְפַת
Tzidkiyahu	Zedekiah	tzid-ki-YA-hu	צִדְקִיָהוּ
Tziklag	Ziklag	tzi-k'-LAG	צִקְלָג
Tzion	Zion	tzi-YON	צִיּוֹן
Tzipora	Zipporah	tzi-po-RAH	צִפֹּרָה
Tzora	Zorah	tzor-AH	צָרְעָה
Tzuriel	Zuriel	tzu-ree-AYL	צוּרִיאֵל
Ukal	Ucal	u-KAL	אֻכָל
Uri	Uri	u-REE	אוּרִי
Uriya	Uriah	u-ri-YAH	אוּרִיָה
Utz	Uz	Utz	עוּץ
Uzziyahu	Uzziah	u-zi-YA-hu	עֻזִּיָהוּ
Yaakov	Jacob	ya-a-KOV	יַעֲקֹב
Yachaziel	Jahaziel	ya-kha-zee-AYL	יַחֲזִיאֵל
Yael	Jael	ya-AYL	יָעֵל
Yaffo	Joppa/Jaffa	ya-FO	יָפוֹ
Yair	Jair	ya-EER	יָאִיר
Yakeh	Jakeh	ya-KEH	יָקֶה
Yarden	Jordan	yar-DAYN	יַרְדֵן
Yarmut	Jarmuth	yar-MUT	יַרְמוּת
Yechezkel	Ezekiel	y'-khez-KAYL	יְחֶזְקֵאל
Yechiel	Jehiel	y'-khee-AYL	יְחִיאֵל
Yechonya	Jeconiah	y'-khon-YAH	יְכָנְיָה
Yedutun	Jeduthun	y'-du-TUN	יְדוּתוּן
Yehoachaz	Jehoahaz	y'-ho-a-KHAZ	יְהוֹאָחָז
Yehoash	Jehoash	y'-ho-ASH	יְהוֹאָשׁ
Yehochanan	Jehohanan	y'-ho-kha-NAN	יְהוֹחָנָן
Yehonatan	Jonathan	y'-ho-na-TAN	יְהוֹנָתָן
Yehoram	Jehoram	y'-ho-RAM	יְהוֹרָם
Yehoshafat	Jehoshaphat	y'-ho-sha-FAT	יְהוֹשָׁפָט
Yehoshavat	Jehoshabeath	y'-ho-shav-AT	יְהוֹשַׁבְעַת

Hebrew Name	English Name	Pronunciation	Hebrew
Yehosheva	Jehosheba	y-ho-SHE-va	יְהוֹשֶׁבַע
Yehoshua	Joshua	y'-ho-SHU-a	יְהוֹשֻׁעַ
Yehotzadak	Jehozadak	y'-ho-tza-DAK	יְהוֹצָדָק
Yehoyachin	Jehoiachin	y'-ho-ya-KHEEN	יְהוֹיָכִין
Yehoyada	Jehoiada	y'-ho-ya-DA	יְהוֹיָדָע
Yehoyakim	Jehoiakim	y'-ho-ya-KEEM	יְהוֹיָקִים
Yehu	Jehu	yay-HU	יֵהוּא
Yehuda	Judah	y'-hu-DAH	יְהוּדָה
Yehudi	Jew	y'-hu-DEE	יְהוּדִי
Yehudim	Jews	y'-hu-DEEM	יְהוּדִים
Yered	Jared	YE-red	יֶרֶד
Yericho	Jericho	y'-ree-KHO	יְרִיחוֹ
Yerovam	Jeroboam	ya-rov-AM	יָרָבְעָם
Yerubaal	Jerubbaal	y'-ru-BA-al	יְרֻבַּעַל
Yerushalayim	Jerusalem	y'-ru-sha-LA-yim	יְרוּשָׁלַיִם
Yeshayahu	Isaiah	y'-sha-YA-hu	יְשַׁעְיָהוּ
Yeshua	Jeshua	yay-SHU-a	יֵשׁוּעַ
Yiftach	Jephthah	yif-TAKH	יִפְתָּח
Yigal	Igal	yig-AL	יִגְאָל
Yirmiyahu	Jeremiah	yir-m'-YA-hu	יִרְמִיָהוּ
Yishai	Jesse	yi-SHAI	יִשַׁי
Yisrael	Israel	yis-ra-AYL	יִשְׂרָאֵל
Yissachar	Issachar	yi-sa-KHAR	יִשָּׂשׂכָר
Yitzchak	Issac	yitz-KHAK	יִצְחָק
Yizrael	Jezreel	yiz-r'-EL	יִזְרְעָאל
Yoash	Joash	yo-ASH	יוֹאָשׁ
Yoav	Joab	yo-AV	יוֹאָב
Yochanan	Johanan	yo-kha-NAN	יוֹחָנָן
Yocheved	Jochebed	yo-KHE-ved	יוֹכֶבֶד
Yoel	Joel	yo-AYL	יוֹאֵל
Yona	Jonah	yo-NAH	יוֹנָה
Yonadav	Jonadab	yo-na-DAV	יוֹנָדָב
Yonatan	Jonathan	yo-na-TAN	יוֹנָתָן

Hebrew Name	English Name	Pronunciation	Hebrew
Yoram	Joram	yo-RAM	יוֹרָם
Yosef	Joseph	yo-SAYF	יוֹסֵף
Yoshiyahu	Josiah	yo-shi-YA-hu	יֹאשִׁיָּהוּ
Yotam	Jotham	yo-TAM	יוֹתָם
Yotzadak	Jozadak	yo-tza-DAK	יוֹצָדָק
Yozavad	Jozabad	yo-za-VAD	יוֹזָבָד
Zanoach	Zanoah	za-NO-akh	זָנוֹחַ
Zecharya	Zechariah	z'-khar-YAH	זְכַרְיָה
Zerach	Zerah	ZE-rakh	זֶרַח
Zerubavel	Zerubbabel	z'-ru-ba-VEL	זְרֻבָּבֶל
Zevulun	Zebulun	z'-vu-LUN	זְבוּלֻן
Zilpa	Zilpah	zil-PAH	זִלְפָּה
Zimri	Zimri	zim-REE	זִמְרִי

Jewish Holidays

Chanukah	Hanukkah	kha-nu-KAH	חֲנוּכָּה
Pesach	Passover	PE-sakh	פֶּסַח
Purim	Purim	pu-REEM	פּוּרִים
Rosh Hashana	Jewish New Year	rosh ha-sha-NAH	רֹאשׁ הַשָּׁנָה
Shavuot	Feast of Weeks	sha-vu-OT	שָׁבוּעוֹת
Shemini Atzeret	Eight Day of Assembly	sh'-mee-NEE a-TZE-ret	שְׁמִינִי עֲצֶרֶת
Sukkot	Feast of Tabernacles	su-KOT	סֻכּוֹת
Yom Kippur	Day of Atonement	yom kee-PUR	יוֹם כִּיפּוּר

Biblical Measurements

Amah	Cubit	a-MAH	אַמָּה
Amot	Cubits	a-MOT	אַמּוֹת
Bat	Bath	bat	בַּת
Batim	Baths	ba-TEEM	בָּתִּים
Beka	half-shekel	BE-ka	בֶּקַע
Chomarim	Homers	kho-ma-REEM	חֳמָרִים
Chomer	Homer	KHO-mer	חֹמֶר
Efah	Ephah	ay-FAH	אֵיפָה
Geira	Gerah	gay-RAH	גֵּרָה

Hebrew Name	English Name	Pronunciation	Hebrew
Gomed	Gomed	GO- med	גֹּמֶד
Hin	Hin	heen	הִין
Kav	kab	kav	קַב
Kesita	kesitah	k'-see-TAH	קְשִׂיטָה
Kikar	talent	ki-KAR	כִּכָּר
Kikarim	talents	ki-ka-RIM	כִּכָּרִים
Kor	kor	kor	כֹּר
Letek	lethech	LE-tek	לֶתֶךְ
Log	Log	log	לֹג
Maneh	Mina	ma-NEH	מָנֶה
Manim	Minas	ma-NEEM	מָנִים
Omer	Omer	O-mer	עֹמֶר
Pim	Pim	peem	פִּים
Se'ah	Seah	say-AH	סְאָה
Se'eem	Seahs	s'-EEM	סְאִים
Shekalim	Shekels	sh'-ka-LEEM	שְׁקָלִים
Shekel	Shekel	SHE-kel	שֶׁקֶל
Tefach	Handbreadth	TE-fakh	טֶפַח
Zeret	Span	ZE-ret	זֶרֶת

Photo Credits

1:1 Protasov AN/Shutterstock.com, 2:7 Courtesy of Israel365, 3:1 MstudioG/Shutterstock.com, 4:1 RnDmS/Shutterstock.com, 5:6 Protasov AN/Shutterstock.com, 6:27 Courtesy of Israel365, 7:17 GotovyyStock/Shutterstock.com, 8:21 Dmitry Pistrov/Shutterstock.com, 10:18 Prostov AN/Shutterstock.com, 11:7 Liron-Afuta/Shutterstock.com, 12:22 Sergei25/Shutterstock.com, 14:7 John Theodor/Shutterstock.com, 15:4 mikhail/Shutterstock.com, 16:18 pioneerka888/Shutterstock.com, 18:20 Protasov AN/Shutterstock.com, 20:26 Avi Rozen/Shutterstock.com, 21:7 VanderWolf Images/Shutterstock.com, 22:3 Courtesy of Israel365, 23:8 Oleg Ivanov IL/Shutterstock.com, 25:2 MyStarHeimwerker/Shutterstock.com, 26:2 Shabtay/Shutterstock.com, 27:9 John Theodor/Shutterstock.com, 28:18 Sararwut Jaimassiri/Shutterstock.com, 29:5 Courtesy Israel365, 30:19 Konstantnin/Shutterstock.com, 31:40 Nancy Anderson/Shutterstock.com, 32:6 Inna Reznik/Shutterstock.com, 33:27 By איתי טיומקין – Own work, CC BY-SA 4.0, https://commons.wikimedia.org/w/index.php?curid=73401802, 34:2 Sergei25/Shutterstock.com, 35:10 Belt944/Shutterstock.com, 36:31 Protasov AN/Shutterstock.com, 38:4 Protasov AN/Shutterstock.com, 39:13 Avi Ohayon, Government Press Office (Israel), 40:8 By Andrew Shiva / Wikipedia, CC BY-SA 4.0, https://commons.wikimedia.org/w/index.php?curid=52363527, 41:11 Rob Swanson/Shutterstock.com, 42:8 Courtesy of Israel365

Map of Modern-Day Israel and its Neighbors

The following is a map of modern-day Israel and the surrounding countries

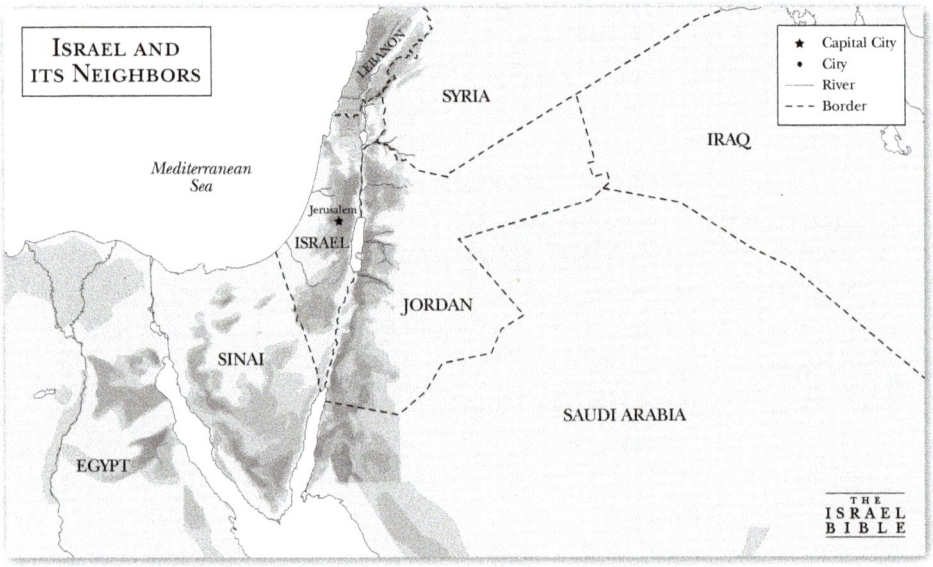

NOTES

NOTES

NOTES

NOTES

NOTES

For more inspiring commentary,
interactive maps, educational videos,
vivid photographs and more,
please visit our website

www.TheIsraelBible.com

THE
ISRAEL
BIBLE